THE AUTHOR

Edward Frederic Benson was born at Wellington College, Berkshire in 1867. He was one of an extraordinary family. His father Edward White Benson – first headmaster of Wellington – later became Chancellor of Lincoln Cathedral, Bishop of Truro, and Archbishop of Canterbury. His mother, Mary Sidgwick, was described by Gladstone as 'the cleverest woman in Europe'. Two children died young but the other four, bachelors all, achieved distinction: Arthur Christopher as Master of Magdalene College, Cambridge and a prolific author; Maggie as an amateur egyptologist; Robert Hugh as a Catholic priest and propagandist novelist; and Fred.

Like his brothers and sisters, Fred was a precocious scribbler. He was still a student at Cambridge when he published his first book, *Sketches from Marlborough*. His first novel *Dodo* was published in 1893 to great success. Thereafter Benson devoted himself to writing, ~~~~ing sports, watching birds, and gadding about. He ~~~~ ~~~~ith the best and brightest of his day: Marg~~~~ ~~~~rie Corelli, his mother's friend Ethel Smy~~~~ ~~~~tables found their eccentricities expo~~~~ ~~~~ious world of his fiction.

Around 1918, F~~~~ ~~~~ye, Sussex. He was inaugurated ma~~~~ ~~~~4. There in his garden room, the colli~~~~ ~~~~enson wrote many of his comical novels, hi~~~~ ~~~~tion, ghost stories, informal biographies, and re~~~~ ~~~~es like *As We Were* (1930) – almost one hundred bo~~~~ ~~~~ all. Ten days before his death on 29 February 1940, E. F. Benson delivered to his publisher a last autobiography, *Final Edition*.

The Hogarth Press also publishes *Mrs Ames, Paying Guests, Secret Lives* and *As We Are*.

AS WE WERE

A Victorian Peep-Show

E.F. Benson

New Introduction by
T.J. Binyon

THE HOGARTH PRESS

LONDON

Published in 1985 by
The Hogarth Press
30 Bedford Square, London WC1B 3SG

Third impression

First published in Great Britain by Longmans, Green & Co. 1930
Hogarth edition offset from original British edition
Copyright the Executors of the Estate of the Revd K. S. P. McDowall
Introduction copyright © T. J. Binyon 1985

British Library Cataloguing in Publication Data

Benson, E. F.
As we were: a Victorian peep-show.
1. England – Social life and customs – 19th century
I. Title
942.081′092′4   DA533

ISBN 0 7012 0588 1

Printed in Great Britain by
Cox & Wyman Ltd
Reading, Berkshire

INTRODUCTION

In *As We Were* E.F. Benson describes his parents' marriage in the terms of a realised Victorian idyll. The handsome young clergyman Edward White Benson plights his troth to his pretty twelve-year-old cousin Mary Sidgwick; she works hard to improve her mind and make herself worthy of him. Then, after the marriage, as he rises inexorably in the Church, she becomes a loving wife, an adored mother, an efficient house-keeper, a cherished friend and a gracious hostess. The reality was not quite like that.

It was inexcusable, of course, to place so heavy a respon-sibility on so young a girl, and to this burden were added feelings of guilt: Minnie knew that she was not, as she ought to be, in love with Edward. The honeymoon in Paris was an appalling disaster. Childbearing kept her occupied during the years at Wellington – Martin was born in 1860, Arthur in 1862, Nellie in 1863, Maggie in 1865, Edward Frederic (always known to the family as Fred) in 1867, and Hugh in 1871 – but the move to Lincoln was followed by a nervous breakdown and religious conversion. Real happiness came only later, when she formed an inseparable friendship with Lucy Tait, daughter of the former Archbishop of Canterbury, who, Fred records, 'slept with my mother in the vast Victorian bed where her six children had been born in Wellington days'.

Edward White Benson, though extraordinarily energetic, vigorous and enthusiastic, was also neurasthenic, suffering from occasional fits of black depression: a characteristic he bequeathed, to a greater or lesser degree, to all his children. His talent was for inspirational leadership, for breaking new ground. As first headmaster of Wellington he ruled with a rod of iron: not only pupils but also masters were forbidden to smoke, and boys were beaten mercilessly for minor infractions of school rules. In 1872 he accepted the invitation of the Bishop of Lincoln, Christopher Wordsworth, to become Chancellor of Lincoln Cathedral, where he immediately founded a theological college. The Wordsworths had been family friends for several years; indeed Elizabeth, one of the Bishop's daughters, later the first principal of Lady Margaret Hall, Oxford, seems to have felt far more than friendship for Benson. But the stay in Lincoln was short; he accepted the new diocese of Truro and, filled with missionary zeal, set out to revitalize the Church in pagan and remote Cornwall, and to build England's first new cathedral since St. Paul's. He could not complete the task, however: on the death of the Archishop of Canterbury in 1882 he was asked, although only fifty-two, to succeed him. He was not really suited to the post; the talents of a politician, a diplomat and an administrator were required; there was no room for the bold innovative vigour Benson had demonstrated elsewhere. But the combined entreaties of Queen Victoria and Gladstone were impossible to resist: the family moved to Lambeth and remained there until the Archbishop's death in 1896.

By this time Fred had already made a name for himself. In 1893 he had published his first novel, *Dodo*. The heroine is an infinitely fascinating society beauty, with an immeasurable capacity for talking charming nonsense. Unfortunately, she has no heart. She marries a stupid, but worthy nobleman; their child dies; her husband is killed in a hunting accident. Just as she is finally about to reward by marriage the long-suffering hero who earlier, to get over his love, had 'adopted the traditional English method of travelling, and shooting unoffending animals', she changes her mind and runs off with an Austrian prince, described variously as 'an unmitigated blackguard' and 'an unutterable cad'. The immense success of the book was hardly due to its literary qualities, even though Edmund Gosse described it as 'a novel of high moral beauty'. Its popularity came no doubt partly, as Fred remarks, from the fact that 'it was thought extremely piquant that a son of the Archbishop of Canterbury should have written a book so frankly unepiscopal'. But, beyond this, it had for its readers the fascination of the gossip column. It was believed to be a close and realistic portrait of high society, and the characters its thinly disguised celebrities. Dodo herself was immediately identified with Margot Tennant, shortly to become Asquith's second wife. She denied the similarity, saying that, although her sitting-room was exactly described in the novel, unlike Dodo she wasn't beautiful and didn't hunt in the summer. But the eccentric musician Edith Staines is obviously, trait for trait, the composer and feminist Ethel Smyth, a close friend of Fred's sister Nellie; while the saintly Mrs Vivian is Mrs Benson, Fred's mother.

The habit of putting into his books real people under fictitious names was an enduring one. In *Secret Lives* (1932) the novelist heroine, Susan Leg, who writes under the name of Rudolph da Vinci, is obviously closely modelled on Marie Corelli, and Arthur Armstrong, the critic who eats her dinners but reviles her books, on Arnold Bennett. Nearly all the Cambridge dons who are mentioned in chapter seven of *As We Were* appear without disguise, if under different names, in one or both of Fred's two Cambridge novels, *The Babe, B.A.* (1897) and *David of King's* (1924). Indeed, even some episodes recounted as real in *As We Were* turn up as fiction in the novels: Dr. Cunningham of Trinity's regrettable behaviour after Mr. Waldstein has kindly imitated the pose of the Discobolus to members of the Chit-chat Society, for example, is repeated almost word for word in *David of King's*. And it is tempting to see Frank Maddox, a character in the same novel, with his 'dark, full-blooded face', who, like Fred, is an undergraduate at King's, gets a first in the Classical Tripos, and stays on to read archaeology, as a portrait of the author himself.

Dodo was followed by an uninterrupted stream of books – almost a hundred by the time of his death in 1940. Like his brother Arthur, Master of Magdalene College, Cambridge, who left a four-million-word private diary, Fred had a compulsion to write. He wrote society novels of adultery or near-adultery (*Mammon & Co*, 1899, *Scarlet and Hyssop*, 1902); bloodthirsty and exciting historical novels about the Greek

War of Independence (*The Vintage*, 1898, *The Capsina*, 1899); macabre novels with a hint of the supernatural (*The Luck of the Vails*, 1901, *Colin*, 1923); comic novels set in a Ruritanian state carved out of the Albanian coast (*The Princess Sophia*, 1904) or – and these are undoubtedly his greatest achievement – in English towns such as Riseborough (*Mrs Ames*, 1912), Riseholme (*Queen Lucia*, 1920), Tilling (*Miss Mapp*, 1922) or Bolton Spa (*Paying Guests*, 1929). In addition, there are seven plays, fourteen collections of short stories, and thirty-two biographical, historical and miscellaneous works. This last category contains some surprises: *English Figure Skating* (1908), for example – Fred was the best English figure skater of his day. And with his friend Eustace Miles ('Amateur Champion of the World at Racquets and Tennis, Amateur Champion of America at Tennis, Racquets and Squash-Tennis', a vegetarian and dietary fanatic, who had been a fellow undergraduate at King's), he wrote *Daily Training* (1902), *A Book of Golf* (1903) and a manual on cricket.

However, when in the late 1920s he came to look back over his work, he was depressed by what he saw. 'Imperceptibly to myself, I had long ago reached the point at which, unless I could observe more keenly and feel more deeply, I had come to the end of anything worth saying,' he wrote. The easy success of *Dodo* had, in the end, not been a triumph, but a disaster for him creatively. He had failed in his intent to become a serious novelist. His only successes, he thought, were the comic novels, which were 'not faked or sentimental', together with a few books into which he had put 'emotional imagination': *Sheaves* (1907), *The Luck of the Vails*, *The Climber* (1908), and *David Blaize* (1916). For the present, he decided, he would leave fiction and turn to biography and memoirs. There, at least, one had to do some honest work before one began writing at all.

But even this necessity hardly slowed his rate of production. He brought out a biography of Drake in 1927, of Alcibiades in 1928, of Magellan in 1929, and of Charlotte Brontë in 1932. They're an odd, heterogeneous lot, and it's not easy to see why he should have chosen some of them as subjects for research.

There was, of course, a family connection with Charlotte Brontë, as he recounts in the third chapter of *As We Were*: she had been governess to the children of John Benson Sidgwick, and had used his house at Stonegappe as a model for Gateshead Hall in *Jane Eyre*.

Rye, where he was now living (in Lamb House, formerly inhabited by Henry James) had an important maritime history, which could have led him to thoughts of Drake and Magellan. And perhaps the fact that he was now virtually immobilized, with severe arthritis in both hips, made the prospect of vicarious circumnavigations attractive. Alcibiades, whom he describes as 'one of the most gifted and unprincipled men who ever lived', in his beauty, his charm, his ruthlessness and his amorality, resembles several characters in the novels – the eponymous hero of *Colin*, in particular. And there must have been a great sense of freedom and release in being able, for the first time, when writing about the manners of Athenian society, to discuss openly the theme which lurks so closely beneath the surface of so many of his books – that of homosexual love.

Although he speaks of turning to memoirs as though this were a new departure, he had in fact ventured into the genre earlier. In 1920 he had published *Our Family Affairs 1867-1896* and in 1925 *Mother*, completing a manuscript left unfinished by his brother Arthur on his death in that year.

Although all the Bensons took pleasure in writing about themselves and their family, Arthur was indefatigable, and the results were certainly his best works. Together with his sister Maggie he had compiled the official biography of his father; later, after Maggie's death in 1916, he was able to publish her life and to edit her letters; he wrote a memoir of the youngest Benson brother, Hugh, who became a Roman Catholic priest and died in 1914; and he brought out several volumes of reminiscences: *The Trefoil, The Leaves of the Tree* and *Memories and Friends*. One anecdote from this last book about Oscar Browning, the Fellow of King's who plays such a large part in Fred's stories of Cambridge, deserves to be quoted. Browning had left Cambridge in a huff, and retired to Bexhill, where he was converted to Christian Science ('such a convenient creed – it banishes the sense of sin') by the mayor. He took a dislike to the University, and would urge Benson to leave: 'You're wasted at Cambridge, old man. Go out into the world! Come to Bexhill.'

As We Were differs from the two earlier memoirs. It is not, as they are, limited to family history combined with personal reminiscence; nor is it, though it may occasionally seem to be, merely a string of anecdotes about Victorian personalities. Many are extremely good: the funniest, undoubtedly, is the story of Tennyson's braces; the wittiest, Whistler's letter to Watts-Dunton. But their purpose is not solely or even primarily comic. Gladstone's way with a sponge or the Duchess of Beaufort's remarks on viewing a portrait of her husband's mistress may be amusing in themselves, but they are also emblematic of the individual or the class. Minute description of family and personal life is set against a generalised treatment of public life and public figures to produce a social history of the second half of the Victorian and the beginning of the Edwardian era. *As We Were* may lack historical detail, and be confined to a narrow social class, but it undoubtedly succeeds in conveying the mood and temper of the period.

The book opens brilliantly with an almost microscopic examination of the crimson velvet pincushion, now vanished, which stood on the dressing-table of the best spare bedroom in the Master's Lodge at Wellington on the occasion of Queen Victoria's visit to the school in 1864: a symbol both for Victoria herself and for the Victorian age, into an impressionistic description of which the chapter gradually and naturally modulates. A history of the Benson family and an account of Fred's experiences at Cambridge and as an archaeologist in Athens are then subtly interwoven with chapters exemplifying aspects of Victorian life. We move slowly into the Edwardian era and finally, in a scene described as minutely as the opening – a summer's day on Capri at the end of June 1914 – hear the first ominous rumble of the storm that will bring the old order to a close.

At times Fred seems to be as great a snob as Oscar

Browning, and it is not always easy to sympathise with all his attitudes and prejudices. But he was an acute and sensitive observer who made excellent use of his privileged position; his comments are not profound – that was not his purpose – but they are far from shallow; and he writes, as always, with an easy and brilliant fluency. As the personal evocation of this epoch *As We Were* is only rivalled by Gwen Raverat's *Period Piece*. But while the latter is exclusively intimate and domestic, *As We Were* puts family life in the context of an age moving gradually towards its end.

T.J. Binyon, Oxford 1985

CONTENTS

NOTE

I HAVE to thank the Fellows of Trinity College, Cambridge, for their great courtesy in giving me the fullest possible access to the diary and private papers of my father which are the property of the College Library.

E. F. BENSON.

AS WE WERE

CHAPTER I

THE PINCUSHION

PERHAPS the pincushion will make as good a beginning as anything, that peerless object of the period, dated beyond dispute or discussion or suspicion, for which I have dived so sedulously and so fruitlessly into drawers full of Victorian relics, seeking it like a pearl in depths long undisturbed by any questing hand. But though I cannot find it, the search was richly rewarded in other respects, for it brought to light treasures long forgotten but instantly and intimately familiar when seen again : there was a dog-eared book of manuscript music, containing among other ditties the famous tear-compelling song 'Willy, we have missed you'; there was a pair of goblets incredible even when actually beheld and handled, chalice-shaped, of cloudy pink glass outlined in gilt ; there was a globular glass paper-weight, in which were embedded, like a layer of flies in amber, small gaudy objects, vastly magnified and resembling sections of jam roll and sea-anemones ; and there were oval cards with pictures of flowers on them, which once certainly belonged to the apparatus of the round game called 'Floral Lotto,' so justly popular in the seventies. But the pearl of great price, the pincushion, did not discover itself to my divings, and its disappearance is a matter of deep regret to me, for it must have been very rare and marvellous, even when it was quite new, and if it was in my possession to-day, I would confidently challenge the world to produce a similar specimen. But when I force myself to think dispassionately of it, I realize that it would be now sixty-six years old, so that even if I could put my hand on all of it that is mortal, I should but find there shreds of disintegrated red velvet and scattered beads, of which the thread had long perished. Yet, since it was (though not new when I first saw it) one of the earliest objects to which I gave my unstinted admiration, I can describe the sumptuous manner of it with a very minute fidelity, for it is one of those memories of early childhood, photographed on my mind in colours as bright as itself.

Picture then (with an effort) a domed and elliptical oblong, the sides of which, below the dome, were perpendicular. Its scale, shape and size were those of a blancmange for not less than eight people ; such was the pincushion. It was covered, dome and sides alike, with rich crimson velvet, and round the lower edge of the dome ran a floral pattern, worked in white glass beads, slightly opalescent. Down the perpendicular sides it was draped with many tassels of these, swinging free, and on the top of the dome was worked a Royal Crown, also of beads. So majestic and unusual an object, though strictly in the finest taste of the period, must have been made to order, or, at the very least, the Royal Crown must have been added to it, in order that the pincushion should worthily fill the very special part for which it was cast in the year 1864. Its one official appearance, the scene in which, behind closed doors, it stood on a certain dressing-table ready to perform the function which was the cause of its sumptuous existence, was only brief; indeed, we shall never know whether it actually ever functioned at all. But it was there, it was ready, it was worthy, and in order to make clear the full situation, it is necessary lightly to sketch the previous act of the drama in which it may have played (though I repeat that we shall never know whether it did) its dumb but distinguished rôle. For the moment the pincushion vanishes, waiting for the cue of its first appearance.

Wellington College, founded in memory of the Great Duke, was opened in 1859, and my father, not yet thirty years of age, was appointed first Head Master. It was intended to provide a good education on special terms for the sons of officers in the army whose widows were in needy circumstances, but other boys were to be admitted as well, and its charter was that of a Public School. The Prince Consort was Chairman of the Governing body and for the very short remainder of his life its welfare was a constant interest to him, and the subject of innumerable memoranda. At his desire, my father had spent the summer of 1858 in Germany and Prussia, in order to study the methods of education in the academies of the Fatherland: the Prince Consort hoped that he would pick up some useful hints as to the general lines on which Wellington College should be conducted. This hope was not realized, for he came back with a profound conviction that English methods were vastly superior to those which he had gone abroad to study, and that there were no hints whatever to be gained from Germany.

A few months after the school was opened, he married my mother, then just eighteen years of age, and they lived in a house that was part of the College building. The numbers were not large at first, and every evening after prayers, which the whole school attended, she shook hands with every individual boy and wished him good night; she was universally known as Mother Benjy, being, at the most, two or three years older than the senior boys.

The boys at first wore a uniform approved and partly designed by the Prince Consort, and it remarkably resembled that of the porters and ticket-collectors of the South Eastern railway on which Wellington College was situated. This gave rise to little confusions. Lord Derby, for instance, when paying a visit to the College on the annual Speech-day, presented the outward half of his return ticket to a boy who had come down to the station to meet his mother, and the boy was not as respectful as he should have been to a member of the Governing body, and permitted himself to say something unbecoming to a well-behaved ticket-collector. It was therefore better to modify the uniform than risk the recurrence of such incidents. The Prince Consort was still inclined to think that German academical methods were in many points more desirable than the freer and more self-governing notions of the English public school in which senior boys have a hand in discipline ; he did not approve of the fagging system, he did not like compulsory games, and he objected to masters (other than the head master) having the power to cane their pupils, for one master (so he pointed out) would almost certainly be stronger than another, and a more savage disciplinarian, and thus certain boys would suffer more than others for similar faults, which was obviously unfair. Then there was the question of the school chapel: he thought (with a great deal of reason) that contemporary English architecture was in a very poor way and proposed that the new chapel should be an exact model of the chapel at Eton, one-third of the size and built of brick. But with that sound wisdom which always characterized him, he very soon saw that the English were not as the Germans, and that German methods were incompatible with English ideas, and up to the time of his most lamentable death in 1861 he backed up the head master, who indeed was a very forcible man, with the utmost zeal and good-will, and Wellington developed on native lines.

Swiftly those lines shot out; the head master was personally astride of each of them, great and small they all were directly under his indefatigable eye. There were stone-masons at work on the capitals of the columns in the gateway to the chapel about to execute conventional volutes and sprays of a nameless foliage. He insisted that instead they should carve these images of the flora and fauna indigenous to the district. Squirrels must peer out of tassels of fir-leaves and pine-cones, and rabbits from fronds of hart's-tongue fern and heather and osmunda. There had been much ado about the chapel when the Eton design was turned down; at first the Governors would only vote £2500 for its building, and so he started a private subscription in order to raise a chapel worthy of the memory of the Great Duke and not merely 'a frightful and indestructible meeting-house.' He made his staff of masters feel that they were helping to construct a noble institution and that they must give their whole time and energies to its accomplishment.

Certainly he gave his own : one evening there arrived for him the printed agenda of the business to be put before the meeting of the Governors next day in London, and he felt that the facts of a case on which their votes would be taken had not been adequately presented to them. So down he went after dinner to the book-shop where printing could be done, and there wrote out a long exposition of what he thought it was needful they should know before making their decision. Page after page, as he wrote it, he handed to the printer to be put into type at once, and then all this had to be corrected and revised and fresh pulls must be made of it. It was finished and ready as morning broke, after an all-night sitting, and he sent off a number of the little pamphlets to the members of the Governing body so that all might read a clear, printed statement of his views before the business in hand came before them. . . . There was a hard frost one week in winter, continuing for several nights, and the whole school was eager to go skating and sliding on the lake. But no boy was permitted to set foot on the ice till the head master himself had traversed it and stamped upon it and assured himself that it was safe. But there was no skating for the school that day, for the ice gave way under him and he fell in. The college porter wrote a remarkable and sympathetic poem on this disaster.

Then he set to work to compile a hymn-book for use in his new chapel, and this must contain renderings, the best available, of the great Latin hymns. They would often, he knew, be of rather doggerel sort, but they would wake the boys' interest in such great songs as 'Vexilla Regis' and 'Aurora nunc.' He contributed several himself, and among them was ' O throned, O

crowned with all renown,' one of the stateliest poems in
the whole English hymnology. Then there must be a
book of tunes to which they should be sung, and the
compilation of this was indeed a feat of daring. Well-
known tunes, not in copyright, like ' Adeste Fideles '
and Haydn's ' Austrian anthem ' would be included, but
these would not supply sufficient melodies. So a lady
called Miss Moultrie, whom he held to have high musical
gifts, was called in, and by request she composed a
quantity of hymn tunes herself for this book, and when
her own invention failed, she took such airs as the
opening lines of one of Beethoven's Violin Sonatas, and
Spohr's ' How blessed are the departed,' and chiselled
them with ruthless carpentry into hymn tunes of the
required length and rhythm, cutting out a bar here and
a half-bar there and, where necessary, writing in extra
parts. It is pleasant to picture the meetings of this
musical committee, at which my father, who knew
nothing whatever about music of any sort, listened to
Miss Moultrie playing original or adapted airs on the
piano. If they were original and passed his audition,
they appeared in the hymn-book as Miss Moultrie's
own ; if she had utilized the ideas of other composers,
the fact was duly acknowledged, and they were ' from '
Beethoven or Spohr. My mother assisted, and, I think,
the chapel organist who kept a book-shop, but they were
not of much account. Miss Moultrie was the Muse and,
like Polyhymnia, her hymns were many. The Prince
Consort contributed a Chorale.

After the Prince Consort's death, Queen Victoria,
who had paid several visits to Wellington with him, did
not come down again (the pincushion moves nearer) till
1864, though in the interval she had sent for the head

master to come to see her at Windsor and tell her of the
welfare of the school in which her husband had taken so
keen an interest. She hoped it prospered; she would
always take an interest in it herself, and intended that her
son, Prince Arthur, now Duke of Connaught, who was
a godson of the Duke of Wellington, should do the same.
Before long she would come and see for herself how
it had developed; she had meant to do so before, but
she was overwhelmed with work and responsibilities.
' While the Prince Consort lived,' she said, ' he thought
for me, now I have to think for myself.' On the table
in the ante-room to the chamber where the interview
took place there were laid out his gloves and his
white wide-awake hat as on the day when he had last
used them.

The visit was arranged : the Queen still in the very
deepest mourning drove from Windsor, in a landau
with four horses and postilions, and was received by
the staff at the gate of the College. She walked about
the place full of sentiment and homeliness and dignity,
showing a shrewd interest in all that concerned domestic
arrangements for the boys. She wept a little over the
foundation stone of the chapel, which had been laid by
the Prince Consort and above which now rose a very
seemly building though not of the same design as Eton
College chapel : she insisted on visiting one of the
dormitories, where she found that the maids had not
yet finished their making of beds and emptying of slops,
and told them to carry on : she went into the class-rooms
of the fifth and sixth forms, shook hands with every boy
there, and asked him his name : she looked with doubtful
approval on the tuck-shop, and said that in her opinion
the young gentlemen would get on quite as well without

so many sweets, and then she came across to the newly-built Master's Lodge, where my mother, a mature matron now of twenty-three years of age, and dressed in the latest and most stupendous fashion of the day, was at the door to receive her. Then the Queen must see the nursery where she found two small boys, Martin and Arthur, aged four and two, and a baby girl not yet a year old. She kissed them and hoped they were good boys, and Martin, who had been regarding her with grave wide eyes, could stand it no longer, and with a burst of laughter told her that she had a very funny bonnet, which was most probably the case. After that my mother conducted her to the best spare bedroom to make herself tidy for lunch, and there were smart bows on the supports of the looking-glass, and a cascade of ornamental paper shavings in the grate, like the skirt of an elegant lady, whose body and head were up the chimney, and a can of hot water with a woolwork cosy over it, and on the mantelpiece the pink glass goblets and a malachite clock, and on the dressing-table that wondrous pincushion, then quite new, which I have not been able to find. There the Queen was left to make herself tidy for lunch, and, as I have said, we shall never know whether the pincushion was used or whether it had to be content to be beautiful. After lunch she planted a tree in the garden and asked for an extra week of summer holiday for the school ' if it is quite approved.' These were all great doings, but they seem to radiate like beams of light from that effulgent centre, the pincushion.

It was not till early in the next decade that I was in a position to take any definite personal notice of the world of Wellington, but then some very engaging film pictures begin to flicker and fix themselves on the square

of illumination.   There was a most agreeable clergyman
(though from his Norfolk jacket and knickerbockers
you could not have been expected to guess his sacred
calling) who used to come over from the neighbouring
parish of Eversley, where he was rector, to see his son
who was a boy in the school.   My parents were great
friends of his.   He smoked his pipe while he walked
with my father in the garden (and this was a very daring
thing to do, for tobacco was an abomination to him)
and he stammered in an attractive manner, because, so
I supposed, he preferred to talk like that, and he lay on
his face in the heather and peered about among the wiry
stems of it to observe beetles and caterpillars.   With
him came his wife, and her visits were very welcome,
for she never forgot her duties as godmother to myself,
and she gave me an enthralling book called ' The Water
Babies,' which her husband had written, and several of
Edward Lear's books of nonsense rhymes.   At the back
of my mind there is a belief, though it is dim and hazy,
that Edward Lear himself came over with her one day,
and I think he had a beard.   But I have no sort of real
recollection of him : his appearance and general habit
(if he came at all) must have been eclipsed by his distinction in knowing so many remarkable and amusing
people, for there was no sort of doubt that he numbered
among his actual friends the man on the Humber, who
dined on a cake of burnt umber, and the old person of
Looe who said ' What on earth shall I do ? ' and him who
made tea in his hat, and him in whose beard such an
embarrassing variety of birds habitually nested.   All
these were real people and Mr. Lear was fortunate
enough to know them and make pictures of them.   He
impressed himself on my memory less vividly than they,

for the man's friends were greater than he, and he realized that and very properly recorded them in immortal rhyme. That he himself was an exquisite artist in landscape was, of course, a piece of later knowledge : later also emerged the fact that he had taught drawing to Queen Victoria in the early years of her reign. One day, when she had finished her lesson, she asked him whether he would care to see her collection of miniatures, and they went into the room at Windsor Castle where were the cases containing that unique series. But Mr. Lear did not think very much of them ; perhaps miniatures seemed rather simpering and lifeless to one who was accustomed to render the faces of his friends in the grip of such various and powerful emotions. He sniffed and shook his head over them, he gave them only the cursory glances of indifference, and doubtfully asked the Queen where she had ' got ' them (as if she had picked them up at some second-hand dealer's). She very courteously replied, ' I inherited them, Mr. Lear.' So there was not very much more to be said about that.

Then there was Aunt Emmeline, my father's sister : she is a static and semi-recumbent figure in these moving pictures of mine because all that I knew of her was that she lay in bed, and had bronchitis (just as she might have had a dog or a canary). Quite unconnected in my mind with bronchitis was the fact that a kettle stood by her bedside over a spirit-lamp with steam puffing from a tube attached to the spout of it, and Aunt Emmeline amused herself by holding it near her mouth and inhaling it. This was an odd diversion, but not interesting for long, as it did not lead to anything. Far more vivid and highly enviable was Grandmamma Sidgwick, behind whom when she went to attend service in the school chapel, there walked a servant carrying her Bible, her prayer-book, her Wellington College hymn-book, and the book of tunes compiled and largely composed by Miss Moultrie. She herself carried a bead-bag containing her handkerchief and a vinaigrette, inside which was a tiny piece of sponge soaked in aromatic vinegar. All ladies of any refinement in those days were apt to feel faint in church, when they had to stand up without moving for so long a time : the less stout-hearted sat down, but the braver sort like Grandmamma continued standing with the refreshment of a tonic sniff at the pierced gold lid of their vinaigrettes if the psalms were lengthy. Crinolines, I regret to say, were dead before my memory was alive, and she wore a maize-coloured silk dress with many flounces of lace down the front of the skirt, from underneath which, as she walked, only the tips of her toes appeared. On her head was a bonnet with purple strings tied underneath her chin and according to the weather she wore a seal-skin jacket or an Indian shawl of many colours. Am I wrong in thinking that she held in her hand a chain with a hook or a clip at the end of it which prevented her skirt from trailing in the mud ?

In the evening she was more sumptuous still. I used to be privileged to see the final stages of her toilet when she dressed for dinner, and to this day I cannot help believing that her jewellery, kept in a large walnut-wood box with mother of pearls inlaid on the lid, was inexhaustible. Never could I complete the examination of these treasures down to the lowest tray. There was a necklace of garnets, consisting of delicate six-rayed stars, with earrings and brooch to match, a necklace of jet for sad anniversaries, a brooch of diamonds with a ruby in the centre, another representing a large bunch of white grapes, of which each several berry was a pearl, encompassed by gold vine-leaves, another of mosaic work in minute coloured tesserae showing a classical ruin, another a cameo of my father's head in profile set in solid sausages of gold. There was a bracelet, swarming like an ant-heap with small turquoises, a memorial bracelet, made entirely of the hair of some defunct relative with a clasp of emeralds and pearls, and one of broad gold with circular Wedgwood plaques let into it, and enamelled lockets also containing hair. By day and for evening toilet as well she, like every Christian lady of the time, wore a cross round her neck.

She had smooth brown hair on which mystic rites were performed and these perhaps were the most thrilling of all. First of all she let her hair down, and drew thick tresses of it (as much as she required) from the centre of her forehead in curving eaves over the tops of her ears, so that the lobes of them only remained visible, and holding these strands firmly in place, she applied to them a brown stick of adhesive cosmetic called ' bandoline,' till the hair which formed these eaves was glued together in one shining surface like a polished board : then the rest was twisted up at the back of her head in a chignon. Sometimes one of these boards cracked, and then more bandoline was applied till it again presented an unbroken area. Then she put on her evening cap, and her stiff satin dress with arms reaching to the elbow and trimmed with lace, and her maid buckled brooches all over it, and clasped the selected necklace round her neck, and proffered a choice of bracelets for her wrists. She would perhaps be occupying the best spare room, and on her dressing-table, where first I saw it, stood the famous pincushion and her ring-stand, a little china tree with bare branches on which she hung her rings, among which were always one or two which contained memorial hair. She besprinkled her handkerchief with *eau de Cologne* from a cut-glass bottle, and smeared a little on her forehead to refresh her after the labours of the toilet, and with fan and scent bottle and cashmere shawl and bead-bag and crochet and vinaigrette and that album of manuscript music containing ' Willy, we have missed you ' and little pieces for the piano, such as ' Yorkshire Bells,' and catches for concerted voices such as

> ' A boat, a boat unto the ferry,
> And we'll go over and be merry,
> And laugh and quaff and drink brown sherry.'

Grandmamma was ready on the stroke of seven to descend the pitch-pine staircase in the Master's Lodge, and spend a quiet evening with her daughter and son-in-law.

I pranced downstairs with her, feeling that this dainty and aged figure was somehow my handiwork by reason of the help I had given her in dressing, to say good night to my parents before they went in to dinner, my father giving his arm to my grandmother and my mother walking behind. Or, if Grandmamma got down a little ahead of time, she sat in a green velvet chair in my mother's sitting-room waiting for the gong to sound. On the table beside her stood two rose-wood work-boxes, hers and my mother's : the latter of these, to the best of my knowledge, was very seldom used for industrial purposes, but it contained white china elephants and amber beads and other agreeable toys. But Grandmamma was a worker, and now she took out her crochet from her bead-bag, or her sewing from her work-box, to make the most of these moments of waiting. If she wanted something from the table, which was out of her reach as she sat in her green velvet chair, she need not rise to get it, for she had been careful to put her 'lazy-tongs' close at hand. . . . How difficult it is to describe that anciently familiar weapon! There were two looped handles to it, like those of a pair of scissors, then a criss-cross of silver-plated bars, at the other end of which was a pair of metal claws. As you pressed the handles together with thumb and forefinger inserted, the criss-cross of bars elongated itself, the claws approached each other, fixed themselves on the desired object, picked it up, and brought it within reach. Sargent ought to have painted her when she was old, or made a drawing of her full of tender daintiness: as a young woman the elder Richmond made a delicious finished little sketch of her. . . . Then the gong boomed, and the three went in to dinner. On warm still nights of summer the table was laid in the garden on the gravel path outside the drawing-room windows which opened down to the ground, and leaning out of the nursery window upstairs I could see this romantic banquet in progress before I was taken away for bath and bed. There was a crib in the night-nursery now, and a small pink creature called Hugh slept there. At present he had no conversation.

These early memories are no doubt unwittingly supplemented with information learned afterwards, which has dripped into them, and it is not worth while, even if it were possible, to strain the two apart. Certainly I could never have witnessed a dinner-party in the early seventies, but I seem to know a great deal about it, partly from having been permitted by the butler to observe the magnificent preparations for it, partly from having personally watched through the bannisters of the gallery that overhung the hall the arrival of the guests, and partly from having been told later by my mother the manner of these Gargantuan feasts. But I can testify how immense was the perspective of the monstrous, round-backed mahogany chairs of the period that lined the elongated dining-room table. Upon it stood a pair of branched candlesticks and other lesser lights, and for centre-piece there was a wondrous silver epergne. Upon the ornamented base of it reclined a camel with a turbaned Arab driver : he leaned against the trunk of a tall palm-tree that soared upwards straight and bare for a full eighteen inches. At the top of this majestic stem there spread out all round the feathery fronds of its foliage, and resting on them (though in reality firmly screwed into the top of the palm-trunk) stood a bowl of cut glass filled with moist sand. In this was planted a bower of roses and of honeysuckle which trailed over the silver leaves of the palm-tree and completed the oasis for the Arab and his camel.

Against the long dining-room wall stood a great oak sideboard below a steel engraving of the 'Last Supper' by Leonardo da Vinci : beside this hung another steel engraving of the Prince Consort with his wide-awake in his hand. This sideboard had two fine panels from some sixteenth-century reredos let into the back, and the artificers of Wardour Street had built up the rest round them : it was considered very handsome. On it stood a row of decanters of port, sherry, and claret, and the dessert service made by Copeland late Spode. And now the tapestry curtains were drawn with a clash of rings over the windows, and the candles were lit, and I was haled away from this glittering cave of Aladdin and hurried upstairs on the first sound of the front-door bell, breathlessly to watch from the passage that ran round the hall, the arrival of the splendid guests. The men put down their hats and coats in the outer hall and then waited by the fireplace of the inner hall (of which through the bannisters, not over them, I commanded so admirable a view) for the emergence of their ladies from my mother's sitting-room where the work-boxes and lazy-tongs had been put away and pins and brushes and looking-glasses provided for their titivation. They had gone in mere chrysalides, swathed in shawls and plaids ; they emerged magnificent butterflies, all green and pink and purple. As each came floating forth, her husband offered her his arm and they went thus into the drawing-room. When all were assembled the gong boomed, and out they came again, having changed partners, and the galaxy passed into the glittering cave of Aladdin next door. Grace was said, and they sat down to the incredible banquet.

There was thick soup and clear soup (a nimble gourmand had been known to secure both). Clear soup in those days had a good deal of sherry in it. There was a great boiled turbot with his head lolling over one end of the dish, and his tail over the other : then came a short pause, while at the four corners of the table were placed the four *entrées*. Two were brown *entrées*, made of beef, mutton, or venison, two were white *entrées* made of chicken, brains, rabbit, or sweetbreads, and these were handed round in pairs ('Brown or White, Madam ? '). Then came a joint made of the brown meat which had not figured in the brown *entrées*, or if only

beef and mutton were in season, the joint might be a
boiled ham. My mother always carved this herself
instead of my father: this was rather daring, rather
modern, but she carved with swift artistic skill and he
did not, and she invariably refused the offer of her
neighbouring gentlemen to relieve her of her task.
Then came a dish of birds, duck or game, and a choice
followed between substantial puddings and more airy
confections covered with blobs of cream and jewels of
angelica and ornamental sugarings. A Stilton cheese
succeeded and then dessert. My mother collected the
ladies' eyes, and the ladies collected their fans and scent-
bottles and scarves, and left the gentlemen to their wine.
Smoking was not dreamed of at the after-dinner services
of this date: the smell would assuredly hang about the
dining-room, and no gentleman could possibly talk to
a lady in the drawing-room after he had thus befouled
himself. When he wished to smoke later on in the
evening, he always changed his dinner-coat lest it should
get infected ever so faintly with the odour so justly
abhorred by the other sex, and put on a smoking-jacket,
very smart, padded and braided and befrogged, while
for fear that his hair should be similarly tainted, he wore
a sort of embroidered forage-cap. Thus attired for his
secret and masculine orgy, he slipped from his bedroom
after the ladies had gone upstairs and with his flat candle
in hand joined his fellow conspirators, as in a charade,
in some remote pantry or gun-room, where his padded
coat would keep him fairly warm.

In these festive evenings of the seventies prolonged
drinking of port and claret had gone out, smoking had
not yet come in, and so when the decanters of port and
claret had gone round twice, and sherry had been offered

(it was called a white-wash), the host rang the bell for
coffee. The men then joined the ladies, and the ladies
who had been chattering together in a bunch, swiftly
broke up, like scattered globules of quicksilver, so that
next each of them should be a vacant chair, into which
a man inserted himself, prudently avoiding those who
had been his neighbours at dinner. A number of conversational duets then took place, but these did not last
long, for there was certain to be a lady present who sang
very sweetly, or had a lovely 'touch' on the piano
(indeed it was more probable that they all sang and
played delightfully), and now it was her hour, and her
hostess entreated her to play one of those beautiful
'Songs without Words' by Mr. Mendelssohn, who had
taught music to Queen Victoria, or sing a song with
words. She was not sure if she had brought her music,
but it always turned out that her husband had done so
and had left the portfolio with his hat and coat in the
outer hall. By the time he returned with the melodious
volume, another gentleman had escorted her to the piano
and had been granted the privilege of turning over for
her. She explained that she was terribly out of practice
as she put down on the candle-brackets of the piano her
gloves, and her fan, her handkerchief and, if she was
about to play, her rings and her bracelets also, and thus
stripped for the fray she cleared her throat, and ran her
fingers up and down the keys with the much-admired
'butterfly touch,' as a signal for the clatter of talk to
cease. The audience assumed expressions of regretful
melancholy if the music was sad, or of pensive gaiety
if it was lively, and fixed their eyes on various points
of the ceiling : the more musical instinctively beat time
with their fingers or their fans. A brilliant execution

was not considered very important, for music was an
' elegant' accomplishment : touch and expression were
more highly esteemed, a little tremolo in the voice was
most affecting, and these were also easier to acquire
than execution. Sentimentality was, in these little concerts, the quality most appreciated, and if a lady could
induce the female portion of her audience surreptitiously
to wipe a slight moisture from its eyes, and the males to
clear their throats before, at the end of the performance,
there rose the murmur of ' Oh, thank you, what a treat.
Please don't get up yet ! ' she was stamped as an artist,
the music as a masterpiece, and the audience as persons
of sensibility. Such songs as 'The Lost Chord'
(words by my cousin Adelaide Anne Procter, music by
Arthur Sullivan) were accepted as test-pieces for tears :
the singer tried her strength with them, as if they were
punching-machines at a fair which registered muscular
force. If there was not a dry eye in the room when she
had delivered her blow she was a champion. Men,
on these occasions, were not asked to sing, unless they
were notable comics : serious playing and singing were
purely feminine accomplishments.

Or if (rarely) there was no music, there might be a
game of some sort. Whist was unsociable and demanded
close attention ; besides, in those days young women,
it was well known, did not as a rule possess the sort of
brain that could grapple with its problems, and were liable
to trump their partner's best cards, or not trump their
worst. 'Floral Lotto' was far easier, both sexes could
play that, and it was very exciting to see your card covered
with pictures of the common flowers of the garden gradually filling up. But whatever the diversions, they were
all brief, for at 10 o'clock in came a hissing urn and the

tea-table was spread. The gentlemen handed the ladies cups of tea, and little hot cakes and buns ('Might I recommend you one of these with sugar on the top?'), and they nibbled and sipped and indulged in lively conversation, in order to restore themselves after the harrowing emotions caused by 'The Lost Chord' ('Beautifully sung, was it not? Such expression!') After tea, perhaps another lady sang, or she who had made them cry or clear their throats with 'The Lost Chord' was prevailed on just as the first carriage was announced, to give them 'The Summer Shower,' and this she did in so arch and playful a manner that everybody felt young and happy again instead of luxuriously miserable, and hummed the tune as they put on their wraps and rumbled away with smiles and compliments and firm incredulity at the lateness of the hour.

Now such an evening as this, designed and appreciated as an agreeable social dissipation, seems to us now more socially remote than the feasts of late Imperial Rome or the parties at the Pavilion at Brighton during the heyday of the Regent, and so no doubt it is. Though we may assume that human nature in the seventies was not *au fond* very different from human nature fifty years before or fifty years later, there was never surely a greater gulf than that which divides the gaieties of the middle period from those that went before and after. Many of the differences between their technique of amusement and ours are no doubt purely superficial. There is not much to choose between the ladies and gentlemen who, without knowing or caring anything about music, listened to 'The Lost Chord' and those who flock to operas which so unspeakably bore them. Music, then as now, was for the majority a fashionable stunt. Nor does it much signify whether you are offered two *entrées* during dinner or two cocktails before (probably the latter is the less deleterious in the long run), nor whether you play 'Floral Lotto' afterwards or Bridge. Again, the anecdotes and small salacities which men told each other then as they sat round the gun-room in their wadded and befrogged smoking-jackets did not probably differ very much in kind from those which they occasionally retail to each other now, and we may guess that women in their wrappers over their bedroom fires hold much the same conferences as did their mothers.

But a real gulf, vastly sundering, lies between the two periods in the matter of their ' company manners ' and in the conversation between the two sexes as they sat round the dinner-table and the subsequent tea-urn. Certain topics, like the weather, and the iniquities of the present Government be it Whig or Tory or Labour, must always have been, even as they are now, substantial standing dishes to be lightly pecked at.   They talked of archery and croquet then, whereas we talk of tennis and golf now; they talked of the wonders of invention, and the new Great Western Express, which ran its seventy-seven miles to Swindon without stop at the average speed of fifty-three miles an hour, corresponded to the aeroplane that winged its way across the Atlantic with its solitary voyager; they talked of books and plays, and these topics have only varied according to the progressive achievements of the age.   But when these were done, then yawns the gulf, for men and women now discuss together everything that they could only have spoken of before with the members of their own sex. They laugh together over the yarns of the smoking-room : a man recounts to his hostess the difficulties attending his wife's confinement, and she tells him the nature of the evidence in the late divorce proceedings, which caused the judge to clear the court.   Sappho and salvarsan, the culture of the lower colon and the nuptials of Pekinese dogs are subjects of unembarrassed conversation between the sexes, and with them they refresh their souls, much as they refresh their untrammelled bodies with sun-baths and mixed bathing.   Whether such frankness and freedom on topics of natural history and elimination and abnormality is desirable or not, is purely a matter of taste ;   nobody can pronounce about it, and nobody should desire to do so, for it is obviously proper that men and women should discuss whatever they think it proper to discuss.   And certainly, on general principles, there is a great deal to be said in favour of any besom that sweeps away the cobwebs of Victorian conventionalism, which harboured such dusty rubbish as the axiom that no nice girl knew anything about anything till she was married, and that if she remained a spinster she continued to believe that babies were found under the gooseberry bushes of the kitchen-gardens of married couples, or that the chance exposure of her calves to the lascivious gaze of men was a shock to her modesty which could only be correctly expressed by a timely swoon.   In those delicate days a certain lady more distinguished for wealth than correct spelling, wrote to the Chairman of the Peninsular and Oriental Company saying that she was going to India, and that she hoped he could manage to secure her a comfortable *birth*.   He replied that he would do his best, but that he could not guarantee her against *mal de mère*. This was considered witty but far from nice.   Rightly or wrongly the Victorian considered that there were certain subjects which

were not meet for inter-sexual discussion, just as they
held that certain processes of the feminine toilet like the
powdering of the nose and the application of lip-stick
to the mouth were (if done at all) better done in private.
These Victorian reticences and secrecies may also have
been profitable as well as prudish : for my part I only
wish to point out that the difference between the tone of
their topics and that of ours was a real and an essential
one, and not like the superficial difference between
smoking in the dining-room and smoking only in the
gun-room.   Queen Victoria once imprudently enquired
from a male person of her court, on which part of the
body were the rheumatic pains which had invalided one
of her maids of honour, and since she had asked, he was
obliged to tell her that they were in her legs.   She
replied, no doubt humorously, that when she came to
the throne young ladies (like the memorable Queen of
Spain) ' did not use to have legs.'   But before she quitted
the throne it had long leaked out that such was the
indelicate fact.   The seventies did not officially know it,
but the eighties strongly suspected it, and the nineties
considered it proved, though it was left to the young
ladies of the next century to demonstrate it.   In fact
long before the Victorian age was over, the flare of the
light-house which warned members of opposite sexes
off those rocks which must always be given a wide berth
in polite conversation flickered, burned low and finally
expired.

CHAPTER II

EARLY VICTORIAN

BUT what was the history of this smiling oasis of public respectability and sobriety into which the social caravans entered about the year 1840, and there so long and so decorously refreshed themselves? The reason of their entry was reaction : they fled to it from another and far less edifying encampment, where there glittered the amazing domes and pinnacles of the Royal Pavilion at Brighton, populous with houris and harpies. For close on ten years after the death of its presiding genius they had wandered rather aimlessly uncertain of their destination. Then Queen Victoria placed herself at their head and undeviatingly led them into this irreproachable environment. While it would be far too much to say that she caused this reaction, it is certain that she and the example set by her and the Prince Consort very strongly influenced it. Probably it would have come in any case, but without her it would scarcely have been so swift in its advance and of so overwhelming a momentum. The tide would have risen gradually instead of sweeping in with that toppling wave. She had had some rather dreadful uncles : George IV though credited, by reason of the inimitable grace of his bow and the dazzling quality of his waistcoats, with being the first gentleman in Europe was, more properly speaking, the first bounder in Europe, vain as a peacock, false to his friends and remorseless to those who had offended him, selfish, greedy, and quite devoid of decent principles. Of Hanoverian origin on her father's side, this daughter of the Duke of Kent and a princess of Saxe-Coburg had barely a drop of British blood in her veins. She married a German, she inherited the instincts of her race, but by virtue of her sense of duty and her shrewdness, she made herself the most English of sovereigns who had sat on the throne since the reign of Elizabeth, and became at once the most devoted servant of her people. These excellent gifts of hers were backed up with a will of iron, and though she may not have said ' They think I am a little girl but I will show them that I am Queen of England,' it was exactly that which she did, which is more to the point. England, though she was German, was her country, and the English were her people, and she knit the monarchy, which indeed was getting very much frayed and tattered, into a most durable piece. In order to understand just what it was that so completely crashed in the eighties and the nineties, it is necessary to form some idea of the character of the woman who to so substantial an extent founded the tradition of the earlier decades of her reign. She largely helped to make it, and she fashioned herself into the mirror which reflected it.

Queen Victoria was a woman of peerless common sense; her common sense, which is a rare gift at any time, amounted to genius. She had been brought up by her mother with the utmost simplicity, and she retained it to the end, and conducted her public and private life alike by that infallible guide. She had no imagination, no flight of fancy ever bore her away, she looked very steadily with her rather prominent blue eyes on every situation that presented itself, and made up her mind as to what was the level-headed and the sensible thing to do. But she had a sort of dual personality, which often supplies the key to the odd complexities and complications that she sometimes exhibited. One entity in her was that of Her Majesty the Queen of England, supreme (and determined to exercise her supremacy and to demand the due recognition of it) in all questions that concerned the welfare of her realm; the other entity was that of a very shrewd *bourgeoise*, and neither of these strains had much in common with aristocratic instincts and ideas. No human being of whom we have record, with the possible exception of Shakespeare, has possessed both imagination and common sense equally developed in a very high degree, for imagination gets dulled by common sense, and the bright mirror is clouded, while common sense gets dazzled by imagination. There was no such disturbing glitter in the Queen's mind : common sense poured out from her, grey and strong, like the waters of the Amazon.

Her intense admirer, Lord Beaconsfield, himself highly imaginative, once said that if he wanted to forecast the effect of some Parliamentary measure on the minds of the middle class, and distrusted his own judgment, he always consulted the Queen and always found he had been right in accepting her opinion. But it was not because she had imagination that she could foretell with such faultless precision what the middle class would feel. She was identical (in this piece of her personality) with the governing class of her subjects, which she saw, long before any of her Ministers perceived it, was no longer the aristocracy who then were the landlords of the greater part of English soil, but the middle class. She had that strain in herself : she needed no imagination in order to picture what they would feel, because she knew. Thus Lord Beaconsfield's dictum, which has been so often and so erroneously taken to mean that she was a woman of commonplace mind, had no such intention, but was in reality an expression of his highest admiration for her judgment. Her mind was not in the least commonplace, it was that of a genius of common sense who knew, as a Queen who was really a Queen should know, the mentality, political and social, of that class which would shortly be supreme in her realm.

Side by side in her mind with this invaluable instinct there functioned, with no less natural vigour, her sense of Queenship. She stood for Monarchy incarnate, just as she stood for the middle class, and all that protected and championed that sacred principle was to her sacred. Church and State were the buttresses that supported the throne, and the throne must support them, for otherwise they would all come clattering down together, and so, though officially she was of no political party, she was actually a Tory of the Tories. All legislation that threatened the solidity of these buttresses was intensely repugnant to her, and thus, though rigidly neutral officially with regard to the will of the people, she once told my father how exceedingly pleased she was, personally and privately, to think that the House of Lords would never pass Mr. Gladstone's Bill for the disestablishment of the Welsh Church, and that there was no constitutional means of removing their veto. Anything, however small, that threatened to diminish the property and privileges of these buttresses must be sternly resisted,

and she also strongly recommended my father, when
there was a question of Cuddesdon being given up as
the residence of the Bishop of Oxford, to oppose it.
'If you begin giving up,' she said, 'they will go on
grabbing till they get everything.' In precisely the same
spirit more than thirty years before, she had been unable
to see why the proposed new site for the National
Gallery should be ' exactly on the spot where Kensington
Palace stood, if not for the purpose of taking from the
Crown its last available set of apartments.'

There was, however, one point which deeply affected
the welfare of her realm, where her lack of imagination
led her into errors from which her common sense could
not save her.   She knew nothing whatever of the working classes, of the barbarous beggary, of the poverty and
suffering and squalor in which they lived, and when some
inarticulate protest from below seethed up into hoarse
murmurings and mutterings, she heard in them nothing
but the threats of rioters and revolutionaries who uttered
menaces against all which made for stability and ordered
government.   She was a firm believer in classes, but
she knew of only three : first came monarchy, then came
the upper and landed class which directly buttressed the
throne, thirdly there was the great middle class which
she saw was becoming the governing power.   Below
it there came no doubt a very large quantity of dim
human beings, but of these she neither saw nor heard
anything to any purpose.   There were, of course, crofters
round about Balmoral, and she took much interest in
their affairs, especially their funerals and their marriages,
and she records the visits she made in order to see how
the ' poor people ' lived.   To one she gave a warm
petticoat, and the old lady ' shook my hands and prayed

God to bless me : it was very touching.' Then there
was Kitty Kear who in her presence 'sat down and spun.'
She also received a warm petticoat, and Mrs. Grant 'who
is so tidy and clean' got a dress and a handkerchief.
But her knowledge of any class below the middle class
was limited to such as these ; of slums and overcrowding
and bestial existence she knew nothing whatever, and
being without imagination, she never formed any picture
of the condition of the millions of mournful workers
who never saw the sun, and certainly she never to the
end of her life conceived it possible that their votes
would put a Labour party in power at Westminster.
She would have regarded such a state of things as a
situation partaking of the horror of nightmare. If by
chance she had to drive through slums they were decorated with flags which looked very bright and gay,
or if on one of the surprise expeditions from Balmoral,
carefully organized by the Prince Consort, she found
herself in 'the dirtiest, poorest village in the whole
of the Highlands,' the sight of dismal, miserable
houses and people and 'a sad look of wretchedness
about it,' produced no more than a momentary and
entirely barren sense of ugliness with which she had
nothing to do. In her Irish tour, similarly, she only
records that 'you see more ragged and wretched people
here than I ever saw anywhere else. *En revanche* the
women are really handsome—*quite* in the lowest class.'
She had no imagination which could be kindled into
effective compassion for those whose needs were a disgrace to England. The warm petticoats were reserved
for the clean and tidy poor, the poorest villages in the
Highlands received none, and she got back to Balmoral
'safely at half past nine' full of gratitude to Albert for

having arranged ' such a delightful, successful expedition.'
The existence of a class who were milled into money
and starved and sweated did not penetrate into her; it
stained the surface for a moment and instantly passed
away, and to the end of her life she could not see ' why
people make such a fuss about the slums.' In this
immense endowment of common sense unlit by imagination she was the exact opposite of her grandson
William II of Germany, who had a prodigious imagination but no common sense which could be lit up by it ;
his imagination flared on to an empty void where he
beheld only the Brocken spectre of himself clad in shining
armour. But his imagination was largely responsible
for the war which brought disaster on his country, while
to Queen Victoria's common sense was largely due an
era of unrivalled prosperity for hers.

Though she was of almost unmixed German blood
and though—since her ancestor George I had come to
sit on the throne of the Stuarts and the Tudors without
a word of English to his tongue, but with the strongest
distaste in his mind for the country and the people over
which he ruled—there had entered into her veins not
a single drop of native blood, she was from the very
first completely English, and combined the instincts of a
Queen with those of the ruling class. She married a
German, she talked German in the bosom of her family,
she interlarded letters to her uncle with German words,
she married her eldest daughter to a German and was
on one occasion very properly and filially reminded
of the fact. Yet she could roundly declare that she
hated the Prussians, and though that was not literally
true (for she was very fond of them) what she meant by
it was exceedingly true: she hated Bismarck, whose

pro-Prussian schemes she rightly divined to be directed
against the prestige of England on the Continent, and
anything that threatened England made her see red.
Nobody, while she was Queen, should with impunity
attack the power and prestige of England nor the power
and prestige of the throne.   The Prince Consort, previous to his marriage, wanted to be made an English
peer : nothing could be firmer than her refusal to allow
it.   It would never do for the husband of the Sovereign
to have a seat in her Parliament, for political bias would
certainly be attributed to him, and political bias must
not be suspected of coming near the throne.   He should
be Royal Highness by all means, for he was her husband,
but just for that very reason he should not be of the
lowest grade of her peers.

Again, she at once determined that she would always
see her Ministers alone, for her business was with them,
and theirs with her, and when her mother, probably
with some German notion of chaperonage, suggested
that she should be present at Councils, she got a snub
from her daughter.   But with that unfailing common
sense of hers, she presently saw that her husband was
a man of very great sagacity ;   more and more she listened
to his advice and trusted the soundness of his judgment,
till at his death, she, who twenty years before said that
nobody should teach her what were the duties of the
Queen of England towards her people, wrote to her
uncle that now, less than ever, would she be guided by
the views of others.   She knew what Albert's views were,
and the principles she had learnt from him should be her
guides hereafter.   It has been somewhat the fashion to
judge the character of that eminently wise Prince by
the style of the decoration on the Albert Memorial : it

would be equally sensible to form an estimate of Dr.
Samuel Johnson from his monument in St. Paul's
Cathedral, where he appears with athletic limbs lightly
draped in a Roman toga, bare feet and curly ephebic
hair.

Queen Victoria did not regard art, letters or music
as in any way springing from national character : they
were something quite apart, elegant decorations resembling a scarf or a bracelet, and in no way expressive of the
soul of the country. But a pretty taste and competent
execution were part of the education of a young lady,
and as we have seen, she had her drawing lessons from
Mr. Lear, she learned to etch with considerable technical
skill, and Mendelssohn taught her singing. She was
very proud of this : once, when quite an old woman, she
suddenly made the portentous announcement to Alick
Yorke who was in waiting, that after lunch he and she
would sing duets. Someone sat down at the piano to
play the accompaniment, and the Queen propped up on
the table between the two vocalists, a copy of Gilbert
and Sullivan's opera ' Patience,' and found the place.
She said, ' Now, Mr. Yorke, you begin,' and Mr. Yorke
obediently sang to the Queen, ' Prithee, pretty maiden,
will you marry me ? ' He got through his verse fairly
well, and then the Queen in a very clear soft voice sang,
' Gentle Sir, although to marry I'm inclined.' She was
much pleased with herself, and stopped in the middle of
her verse to say, ' You know, Mr. Yorke, I was taught
singing by Mendelssohn.'

She perfectly reflected in matters of art the ordinary
educated ideas of her time, as held by those who had no
artistic perception. She liked landscape painters to
show her what she herself saw, and had a strong

preference for the scenes which Mr. Landseer so skilfully
painted : heather and bracken and stags and dogs with
sticks in their mouths, and brown Scots streams (so
like the ' originals '), and often on her exploring tours
from Balmoral, she wished she had his pencil and could
do justice to the lovely braes and glens. Mr. Turner's
imaginative landscapes on the other hand, particularly
those of his later period, meant nothing to her. She
thought them ' most extraordinary ' and there was the
end of that. A portrait, in the same way, was to be
estimated by its resemblance to the sitter, and if the sitter
was herself, it was highly important that the riband of
the Garter should be of the correct colour. If a disturbing light fell upon it, altering its tone, that made no
difference : she knew (no one better) what the colour
of the Garter riband was, and that was the colour she
wanted in her picture. Moonlight, sunlight, firelight
did not alter the colour, because the dye was excellent
and she told the artist so. Then when all such crucial
points of true fidelity had been settled, there was the face
and the expression of the sitter. About these there
should be nothing troubling : any suggestion of the
soul and its maladies, and of the history that the soul had
engraved on the eyes and the mouth, was very objectionable. It was like exposing a piece of her leg. You
did not want the artist to show what the sitter *was*, but
what she looked like : the spirit within was no concern
of the artist and it must be properly veiled, even as her
body must be properly dressed. So she much approved
the Prince Consort's happy idea of hanging the Rem-
brandts and the Van Dycks at Windsor higher on the
walls, for this enabled everybody to see the family
Winterhalters so much better.

Probably her artistic views were quite her own, the result of personal predilections, and they faithfully reflected the artistic feeling of the day, but certainly the Prince Consort confirmed and strengthened them, and in such matters she considered that his taste was quite flawless. It was he who converted the old Scottish Castle of Balmoral into the far more splendid German Schloss, who papered its walls with tartan, and himself designed the carpets of Balmoral tartan. 'All,' she wrote, 'is his own creation, own work, own building, and his great taste and the impress of his dear hand, have been stamped everywhere.' To all his views on 'scenery' she listened with reverence: when they saw Edinburgh together for the first time, he said of 'Arthur's Seat,' that he was sure the Acropolis could not be finer. That he had never seen the Acropolis did not matter: *ipse dixit*. In music similarly he was her infallible guide: he was quite a voluminous composer, and his 'Te Deum,' as I well remember, was performed in the Abbey at the Jubilee service in 1887, and his chorale 'Gotha' was incorporated into the anthem written by Sir Frederick Bridge, the Abbey organist, for the occasion. These compositions are technically quite correct, and if carefully played on the organ with a copious use of the swell, they seem, somehow, to cast a light on the Prince Consort's preference for the portraits of Winterhalter over those of Rembrandt. But it must be remembered that very few people, even among those who feel themselves to be well-equipped musical critics, could compose any sort of a 'Te Deum,' still less one that adhered to the strictest rules of harmony, and sounded, when performed, as it was meant to. It is not amateur work, but that of a trained though not

imaginative musician, who praised God very sincerely
in the key of C Major, without any passionate Hosannas
or difficult modulations.

Their life was conducted on the same straightforward
and wholesome principles as those on which his ' Te
Deum ' was composed. As Sovereign the Queen was
a slave to her duties, and no one ever worked harder or
more conscientiously at her job. This admirable devotion never left her, and up to the last years of her life,
when she suffered much from such fatiguing disabilities
as rheumatic joints and failing eyesight, she used often
to sit up till one or two o'clock in the morning, even
when on holiday at the Villa Palmieri or the Villa
Fabricotti at Florence, to get her work finished. Nothing
was ever allowed to interfere with her work, and in
those early years, when her royal tasks were fully done,
she found all her pleasure and relaxation in family life,
sketching with her children, playing round games,
escaping from her Queenship into the quiet of sheer
domesticity, with her husband for her constant and
adored companion. She cared nothing for state and
splendour in themselves, and though in the performance
of her royal functions she was of a superb and wholly
native dignity, thus showing that she was indeed Queen
of England and knew it, it was the sense of duty that
inspired her, and when her duty was done, she wanted
only to get back to the freedom of privacy. ' We leave
dear Claremont,' she wrote to her uncle, the King of the
Belgians, ' with the greatest regret. . . . Windsor is
beautiful and comfortable, but it is a palace, and God
knows how willingly I would always live with my
beloved Albert and our children in the quiet and retirement of private life.'

She was entirely sincere when she wrote that, but it was quite untrue, for she could no more have lived without her Queenship and remained alive in the very vivid sense in which she was alive, than she could have lived without her lungs : being Queen was part of the air she breathed. It was a great lark to pretend sometimes not to be the Queen, and to set forth on an expedition from Balmoral, christening the Prince Consort and herself Lord and Lady Churchill (Mr. and Mrs. Churchill would have been too great a violence), but the real lark lay in the fact that she was Queen all the time, and that when the guileless Highlanders guessed the majestic truth, they were ' ready to die of fright.' She was the Queen, and whatever her inclination, her will would never have allowed her to remain in retirement and see another than herself at ' comfortable Windsor.' But both as Queen and as housewife she conducted her life on broad simple principles, hating anything flamboyant or ' extraordinary,' quite uninterested in problems of human nature and in the dim mysterious yearnings which inspire art and music, simple and sincere in her religion, troubled neither by ecstasy nor by theological complexities, bringing up her children with affection and firmness in the fear of God and of herself. As such she both set a fashion and conformed to the type which she had been largely instrumental in making. Her private life was rational, respectable and unimaginative, and she made it public to her subjects in 'Leaves' and 'More Leaves from the Journal of a Life in the Highlands.' Then in 1861 came the death of the Prince Consort.

The whole fabric of her life was shattered, and as she wrote to her uncle, not only she ' but England, my

unhappy country, has lost *all* in losing him.' For many
years now she had trusted and leaned upon his judgment
in matters concerning the State, and not only the home
life of which he was the adored centre was broken,
but the prop on which she as Queen had leaned was
gone, and all that was left for her was to follow out
in every particular without interference from any, the
wisdom and policy that had been his. She was convinced she could not live long without him, and the only
thing that could make tolerable her waiting for the re-
union that would never be sundered, was to walk in his
steps. For many years she retired into a complete
seclusion, and made no public appearances of any sort.
Though for a time she would not even see her Ministers,
her devotion to her duty reasserted itself and she worked
as hard as ever, but her labours were as secret and
invisible as those of the queen-bee in the central darkness of the hive. Never had she had any taste for the
pageantry of the throne, now she said it was ' absolutely
impossible' to face it, and it was in vain that six years
after the Prince Consort's death, Lord Derby begged her
to receive the Sultan of Turkey, who was then in England.
He had been accorded an enthusiastic reception in France,
and it was really a matter of national importance that
the Queen should see him if only for a ten minutes'
interview at Windsor. But she still could not steel
herself to the ordeal of receiving a ruling monarch alone,
without the support of the Prince Consort. She was
not equal to it and again it was ' absolutely necessary '
that Lord Derby should see Dr. Jenner, who would no
doubt tell him of the ' real state of her nerves.' We
may presume that Lord Derby did see Dr. Jenner and
we can guess what his verdict was, for the interview duly

took place. Her subjects never saw her at all in any official capacity, for years she hardly set foot in London, and the effect of this neurasthenic seclusion was that she became very unpopular. Even staunch loyalists found it difficult to answer the question as to what was the use of a Sovereign whose existence was almost mythical.

But those twenty years of duty and domestic life had done their work, and though she ceased from 1861 onwards to exercise any direct social influence, the sixties and in part the seventies were still fed by the reaction from the days of the Brighton Pavilion and the revels of Carlton House. These waters were now diminishing in volume, the reaction, like a reservoir in the hills, was rapidly declining, and the stream-bed once bright with its water was getting overgrown with a tangle of vivid vegetation that was soon so to obscure it that it was only by diligent search that the pools could be found, stagnant and dwindled beneath the gaudy growth. During all this period the Queen remained socially cataleptic, and we can no longer refer to her as typical of what was going on. The decline and fall of Victorianism took place while she, busy and industrious as ever, was out of touch with everything. We may indeed compare her to the Sleeping Beauty, waiting the advent of the fairy Prince to hew his way through the thickets and overgrown avenues of Osborne.

CHAPTER III

MY father came of an exceedingly long line of ascertained persons, all entirely undistinguished. In the fourteenth century his forefathers were settled in the West Riding of Yorkshire, and were leaseholders of Fountains Abbey, first as tenant-farmers and subsequently acquiring by purchase acres of their own. By means of the Register of the Abbey and certain ancient wills, the whole pedigree from that time onwards happens to be known, both the names of these undistinguished people, of the places they lived in, and in most cases of their wives, and from then onwards for the space of five centuries my father was the first of that long line to attain any sort of eminence. There are a few collateral minor lights, such as a Chancellor of the Exchequer in the reign of Queen Anne, raised to the peerage as Lord Bingley, and a few of the women made interesting marriages, but in the direct male line there is no name at all, until my father's, which is even faintly notable. They prospered in a comfortable rural tranquillity, they lived on their freehold farms in small rather dignified manor-houses, they raised and educated large families, they went to York and Ripon for a little gaiety in the winter, and are only remarkable for having gone on so long and having done so little.

By the last half of the eighteenth century they were very substantial people, and, as always happens, sooner or later, had begun to drift from their country houses into York, where a couple of brothers, Christopher, and my great-great-grandfather, Edward Benson, owned considerable property. The fortune of the latter had been increased by the fact that a solitary old bachelor, named Francis White, left all his property in equal shares to three friends of his, of whom Edward Benson was one, who played whist with him once a week. . . . Then after these careful centuries of solid respectability there came the black sheep of this monotonous line, my great-grandfather, Captain White Benson. Perhaps black is too pronounced a hue for this mild monster who was in the main only a gay young spark with a reputation for wit and gallantry. He was in the 6th Foot (Royal Warwickshire Regiment), and a friend of Prince William, Duke of Gloucester, under whom he served in the Irish rebellion. He wrote and published a volume of Ballads, which are not very bad, and he had a great flirtation with the exquisite Lady Morgan, the much admired authoress of ' The Wild Irish Girl,' and ' Ida in Athens.' Some of his letters to her remain. They are full of modish sighs and aspirations. Beyond his facility in writing verse, his only real talent was that of getting through money with grace and rapidity, and having spent most of his own fortune he eloped with his first cousin, Eleanor Benson, then aged sixteen, who with her sister was joint heiress to what was then called ' a pretty little fortune,' and got through the greater part of that as well. Lady Morgan, who wrote a rather lively volume of memoirs, was in error over some points about her lover, for she recorded that he committed suicide in

1798. As a matter of family history, he married this young cousin of his in that year : perhaps that represented itself to Lady Morgan as the equivalent of suicide. He died from a fall off his horse eight years later, leaving one son with a much straitened fortune.

White Benson had a very remarkable sister, Anna Dorothea, younger than himself, who became by her second marriage the famous Mrs. Basil Montagu. She was first the wife of a York attorney, named Thomas Skepper, whose death in 1805 left her an extremely attractive widow of twenty-five years. She came up to London with her young daughter Anne to stay with friends who no doubt had held forth about her charms, for, as her friend Miss Frances Kemble tells, one evening ' soon after her arrival as she was sitting, partly concealed by one of the curtains in the drawing-room, Basil Montagu came rapidly into the room, exclaiming (evidently not perceiving her) " Come, where is your wonderful Mrs. Skepper ? I want to see her." ' He was already twice a widower, but the wonderful Mrs. Skepper was quite too much for him. Indeed she seems to have known that she had met her second fate, as he his third, ' for during the whole evening he engrossed her attention, and talked to her, and the next morning at breakfast she laughingly complained to her hosts that he had not been content with that, but had tormented her in dreams all night. " For," said she, " I dreamed that I was going to be married to him, and the day before the wedding he came to me with a couple of boxes, and said solemnly, ' My dear Anna, I want to confide these caskets to your keeping : in this one are contained the bones of my first dear wife, and in this those of my second dear wife. Do me the favour to take charge of them for me.' " ' And married they were as soon as the year of her widowhood was over.

Basil Montagu was the natural son of ' Jeremy Diddler,' Earl of Sandwich ; his mother was the actress Miss Reay, who was shot as she came out of the stage-door by an insane clergyman called Hackman. He was now a very successful Chancery barrister with high literary tastes, and his house in Bedford Square became under Anna Montagu's presidency the nearest approach to a salon that London has ever arrived at. Even Thomas Carlyle, eternally snapping and snarling at those who most befriended him, and finding Basil Montagu ' a bore by degrees and considerably a humbug if you probed too strictly,' confessed himself ' a thankful debtor to his wife, this noble lady, this high personage ' who was mistress there. He cannot find a flaw in her perfections, her tall figure, her penetrating face, her lips ' always gently shut, as if till the enquiry was complete and the time came for something of royal speech upon them. . . . You might have printed every word, so queen-like, gentle, soothing, measured, prettily royal towards subjects whom she wished to love her.' Indeed, the only satirical thing he could find to say about her was that her ' notable dress ' which so impressed him ' must have required daily the fastening of sixty or eighty pins.' About that dress Miss Kemble waxes dithyrambic. Mrs. Montagu was ' so superior in this point to her sex generally, that having found that which was undoubtedly her own individual costume, she never changed the fashion of it . . . it seemed the proper expression in clothes of her personality, and really a part of herself. It was a long open robe, over an underskirt of the same material and colour, always moonlight silver-grey, amethyst purple or black silk or satin of the richest quality, trimmed with broad velvet facings of the same colour, the sleeve plain and tight-fitting from shoulder to wrist, and the bosom covered with a fine lace half-body, which came like the wimple of old mediaeval portraits up round her throat, and seemed to belong in material and fashion to the clear chin-stay which followed the noble contour of her face, and the picturesque cap which covered without concealing her auburn hair and the beautiful proportions of her exquisite head.' A majestic figure surely with her queenly speech and her exquisite dress and manners. In a brusquer age, when manners are at a discount, we are apt to think that such a fineness of speech and of bearing denotes insincerity. But that is a hasty conclusion : there are those, and Mrs. Montagu was of them, who are as truly themselves in being well bred as others in being rude. The most finished politeness and reserve were natural to her : that was what she felt like. One day a friend came to her daughter and said, ' I am afraid your mother is ill : she has allowed herself to cough in my presence.' There, at 25 Bedford Square, she held this daily court of culture and politeness, and looked after her husband's two children by his previous marriage, and had a daughter by him who married Count William de Viry. Not the least remarkable of the inmates of Basil Montagu's household at one time had been a young tutor who taught the children of an earlier marriage ; his name was William Wordsworth and he had a great taste for poetry. Mrs. Montagu's cousin, Mrs. John Benson Sidgwick, had some years later an equally remarkable governess for her girls, whose name was Charlotte Brontë.

Anna Montagu's daughter by her first marriage

became the wife of the poet, Bryan Waller Procter, better known as ' Barry Cornwall ' : their daughter (here linking us up with the mid-Victorian age) was Adelaide Anne Procter, whose ' Lost Chord ' became the tear-test of the merits of ladies who found they had brought their music when they went out to dinner and sang afterwards. Mrs. Procter carried on her mother's tradition of salon and beautiful speech, but her tongue could have an exceedingly sharp edge to it, which earned her the sub-title of ' Our Lady of Bitterness.' Thackeray, Browning, and Kinglake were of her intimate circle, but Carlyle was ignominiously hounded from it, for that bilious temperament of his prompted him to attack her mother, whose ' thankful debtor he was,' and to write after her death in epilogue of his panegyric of her a scandalous and false statement to the effect that ' she had entered Basil Montagu's house under the name of " governess." Had succeeded well, and better and better for some time, perhaps for years in that ticklish capacity : whereupon at length offer of marriage which she had accepted.' The innuendo, more than hinted though less than stated, was absolutely untrue, and Mrs. Procter very properly printed and privately circulated some of Carlyle's letters to her mother, showing the kindly way in which he had been treated in that house, and labelled his statements as ' malignant lies ' : to which plain speaking there was no rejoinder.

The spendthrift Captain White Benson left one son, my grandfather, who had a genius for chemistry. He made two very valuable discoveries, the one a process for making cobalt, the other for the manufacture of white lead, out of which large fortunes were reaped, but not by him. He sold what his spendthrift father had

spared of the property in York, married Miss Harriet
Baker, sister of Sir Thomas Baker of Manchester, and
spent his days in the laboratory and in writing one
or two pious books : ' Meditation on the Works of
God ' was one of them.   He died at the age of forty-two,
leaving his wife to bring up a family of seven children
on an inconveniently small income.   My father was the
eldest and was then aged fourteen.

He spent much of his holidays with the numerous
aunts and uncles and cousins who bestrewed the West
Riding of Yorkshire, and his early diaries and letters give
the oddest glimpses into the sort of life which tranquil
well-to-do folk used to live then, but which now is
utterly extinct.   I draw upon these, for such first-hand
records are now few.   His grandfather's first cousin and
sister-in-law had married William Sidgwick, and she
lived, then a widow, in Skipton Castle, and he describes
in a letter to his mother that remote and delectable
existence.   ' My Aunt is not at all strict except that I am
obliged to eat bread and butter with a knife and fork,
not to set my feet on the chair staves, and not to tumble
off the Castle leads.'   She walked in the Castle grounds
every morning, she saw personally to the washing up
of the fine china, and did nothing else in particular.   She
was much horrified at the way in which people in this
year, 1844, gadded about.   One young lady who came
to stay with her was only going to stop for a fortnight
instead of her usual month, and meant to pay two more
visits before she went home (indignant marks of exclamation).   Another shocking thing was the extravagance in
living : people now wanted the most elaborate dinners.
' But give me,' she said, ' a trout from my own stream,
and a grouse from my own moor, and an apple tart from

my own orchard, and I ask nothing more.' That this
utterly delicious dinner implied the possession of a trout
stream, a moor and a garden did not seem to detract
from the spirit of Spartan simplicity which was content
with it. Every day Christopher and James, her two
unmarried sons, who were in the family business in
Skipton, used to pay a call on their mother, and when
they retired from business in the early prime of life, they
both came to live at the Castle with her. Christopher
spent his money in building a church at Skipton and the
Church Schools. He slept at the Castle, but went down
to attend service in the church he had built at seven
o'clock in the morning, after which he read church
history in his private library at the schools and ate a slice
of sponge cake which was brought in under a bell-glass
as the clock struck noon. He then continued his studies
till three in the afternoon, when he went back to the
Castle to dine, and spend the evening there. His
brother, James Sidgwick, led a less strenuous life, he
walked in the Castle grounds at eight in the morning
for half an hour, and passed the rest of the day indoors.
He was liable to catch cold and so he sat always in a
porter's chair with padded wicker sides and back, and
there read all day. His reading chiefly consisted of the
study of Bradshaw's railway guide, which, as railways
multiplied, became more voluminous and required
increasing industry: with its aid he worked out the
most elaborate cross-country journeys though he never
took any of them himself nor stirred out of Skipton
Castle. Every year, and on the same day of the year,
Messrs. Lincoln & Bennett sent him a new beaver hat
of precisely the same shape as its predecessor, for his
morning walks.

Then when the visit to Skipton was over, my father went to stay with the eldest of these brothers, John Benson Sidgwick, who lived at the fine house his father had built at Stonegappe. His greatest claim to fame is that Charlotte Brontë had been governess to his children and that he and his family appear in ' Shirley ' as the ' Yorkes.' Their intentions towards her seem to have been of the kindliest; if they thought she would like to take part in the family diversions out of lesson-hours, they invited her to do so ; if they thought she would like to be left to herself, they did not worry her. But these amiabilities sadly miscarried, for she bitterly satirized their treatment of her in letters to Mrs. Gaskell. For if she was asked to join the family, she complained that she was a mere slave, and that she was allowed no leisure at all, while if she was left to herself, she wrote that she only existed for her employers as a teacher of their children, and that when lessons were over she ceased to be.

There were odd stories, too, of superstition and magical beliefs still credited among educated people in those days, when the railway had not yet reached Skipton or come near Stonegappe : uncles and aunts and grandmother had creepy tales to tell on the long dark winter evenings. My father records how he heard of his father's upbringing : he was a delicate boy and not fit for school life and his education was entrusted to Dr. Sollitt of York, a great chemist, a notable astrologer and framer of horoscopes, and, apparently, a practiser of more dubious arts than these. He had drawn out the horoscope of Cousin Joanna Benson, who about the year 1800 was one of the beauties of the North country, and had found that the stars portended matrimony for her. This marriage, so Dr. Sollitt read in the heavens, would take place in March, and if anything came in the way of this March marriage of hers, she would never be married at all. Not long after the beautiful Joanna was very happily betrothed to one Colonel Shaw, and even as the stars had said (or perhaps in consequence of what the stars had said) the wedding was fixed for the month of March. It was to take place at her father's house in York, and the bridegroom that morning would ride in from his country house, breakfast with the family, and so to church. Breakfast was waiting, but still no bridegroom came, and the time went on, till at last a messenger on horseback was dispatched to see what had delayed him. The messenger returned with the news that Colonel Shaw had been thrown from his horse as he rode into York and had been instantly killed. His will, new-drawn, was in his pocket, and he left all he was possessed of to Joanna, but his will was still unsigned by him, and therefore invalid. Joanna fell into a deep melancholy, and having missed her March marriage, she died unwedded, even as Dr. Sollitt had predicted from the celestial signs.

Dr. Sollitt's education of my grandfather included the arts of astrology, and his pupil made some singular predictions which were duly fulfilled. The friendship continued after my grandfather married, and the two left York one day to pay a visit to one of his relatives and there Dr. Sollitt was cured of his darker studies. Alone in his room he locked the door and made ready the spell which would raise Satan. He marked out on the floor the circle in which he would himself stand, and he fenced it with signs of the cross and of the mystic pentagram, across which the powers of hell could not operate.

Then standing inside this circle he began his incantations and had got as far as the repetition of the Lord's Prayer said backwards, when he heard his name loudly called from somewhere in the house just outside his locked door, and he unbolted himself and ran out to see who called like that. There was no one on the landing nor on the stairs, but he ran down to see who this could be, and why he was wanted. But he had not yet reached the bottom step when he heard a tremendous crash from the room he had just quitted. Up he went again, and he found his bed overturned and his wardrobe lying on its face among splintered chairs and broken crockery. But the room was empty, and none could have entered it and gone again in so brief a space. At that, panic seized Dr. Sollitt; he saw how potent was the power he evoked, and he made a solemn bonfire of his magical books, and practised no more. My grandfather was of the same mind, and convinced that he too by means of astrology had acquired such knowledge as was not proper for men to attain to, burned his books likewise and devoted himself to more legitimate investigations into white lead instead of black magic.

Now such a tale as this, though written down by my father from the mouth of the narrator, is not interesting because of its intrinsic truth (for it is difficult to believe that Satan will manifest himself for the mishandling of the Paternoster) but because a hundred years ago there were shrewd and well-educated and sensible folk, living in remote places, where not so long before old women had been burned as witches, who did so believe. My father's grandmother (the eloping heiress of sixteen) was at this time not more than of middle age, and she too had a wonderful story-box for the long evenings.

A friend of hers, belonging to the Protestant religion, had been staying near the town of Waterford in Ireland, and his host was a Roman Catholic. One evening this host of his begged him to come to church with him, for it was expected that a great miracle would be performed, and the sight of it might turn his heretic heart into the way of salvation. He asked what this miracle would be, and was told that the Priest would show to the congregation certain souls who were now in Purgatory in visible form, for God would give them remittance for a little while, suffering them to appear before the eyes of those still on earth, thereby quickening their faith and encouraging them to have masses said on behalf of the departed for their speedier release.

Accordingly the two went to church, and they were bidden to kneel at the chancel rails in front of the altar, where they would get a very good view of the miracle. The church was not more than dimly lit, and presently as the prayers for the souls of the departed were being said, the Englishman saw that there were creeping out from under the altar small black, mysterious shapes which moved about on the floor of the chancel. The worshippers who knelt beside him showed great emotion at this sign of the souls from beneath the altar being thus made manifest and he himself was much perturbed, for this was indeed a miracle. But he took hold of himself, and observed more closely : there were several of these souls, and they seemed to be wrapped about in some black stuff like crape. Then one of them as it crawled slowly about, came very near to where he knelt, and a sudden impulse prompted him to catch hold of it and pick it up, and in the dim light, he did so unobserved. He was much comforted to find that it could be no

disembodied thing for it was of sensible weight, and he
put it away in the pocket of his great coat.   So all gave
thanks to God for the miracle, and when the service was
over, the two friends left the church, and when they
reached home, the Englishman said to his host :

' I've got a soul in my pocket and here it is.'

He took it out and laid it on the table.   It was, as
he had observed, thickly but loosely wrapped about with
crape, and he unwound it, layer after layer, not knowing
what he should find.   At length the last covering came
away, and there was a fine crab.   His host was much
troubled.

' Now you must away for your life,' he said, ' and
that's all about it.   The priest is sure to have counted
how many souls he put under the altar, and he'll find
that there's one missing.   You are known to be a heretic,
and you knelt by the altar rails, and they'll soon be after
you.   Take the first ship that leaves Waterford harbour,
for if you stay, you're a dead man.'

So with eyes round with pleasing terror, my father
would steal up to his bed at Stonegappe or Skipton
Castle, and when the holiday visits were over, returned
to his mother's house at Birmingham Heath, from which
every morning he walked to King Edward's school in
the town, where he was now a day pupil and one who
promised very well.   From the time when he was quite
a small boy, anything connected with the church and
priestly functions had been a passion with him : he had
always loved the forms of worship as well as the faith,
ritual and cathedrals and ceremonies, and in a letter of
his to one of his uncles, written when he was only just
ten years old, he asked him whether he thought there
was a chance that he might become a clergyman when he

grew up. He was of that way of thinking still, for his mother had given him a big empty room in her house, for his own purposes, and to use as he pleased, and he made an oratory of it. He draped a table for an altar, he got a faldstool to kneel at, he hung its walls with sacred prints and here, all by himself, every morning and evening he made his devotions. He had forbidden his sisters to enter it at all; it was his oratory, and nobody else should pray there. But now, when he was away at school all day, he suspected that the perfidious creatures trespassed there in spite of all their promises, and he set to work to ascertain that. So one morning before he set off for school, he put the door of his oratory enticingly ajar, and perched a crafty booby-trap on the top of it. And Emmeline, incautiously entering the precinct, loosed a clatter of books and other hard objects on her head, which cured her of her piety.

Throughout his school days this fire of ecclesiastical zeal burned ever higher, and in the holidays he corresponded with Lightfoot and Westcott, school-fellows then and lifelong friends ever after, and each in turn Bishop of Durham, about these matters. They carried on by letters the conversations they had held about Purgatory: they hurled at each other's heads Gregory the Great, the Council of Trent, Romans iii. 23, 24: they discussed the validity of lay-baptism, they kept (or intended to) Canonical Hours, they hatched a scheme for a Brotherhood of Holy Living, ' to bring the kingdom of God to the poor, to promote the spiritual unity of the Church and to practise the precepts of the Sermon on the Mount.' During another vacation Lightfoot entreated my father not to go to hear Newman preach, but he did, and came away, so he wrote to his friend, enormously struck by 'the sweet flowing unlaboured language, the frail emaciated appearance,' the thought that 'this timid-looking, little, weak-voiced man had so moved England. . . . Surely if there is a man whom God has raised up in this generation with more than common power to glorify His name, this man is he.' Lightfoot must have been perturbed at these high impressions, until he read ' But never turn Romanist if you are to have such a face as that : it was awful, the terrible lines deeply ploughed all over it, and the craft that sat upon his retreating forehead and sunken eyes ! ' But in all this correspondence, strange as it seems now in more tepid days, between boys of sixteen to nineteen, there is never the slightest touch of priggishness. They wrote with just such eagerness concerning baptism and canonical hours and heresies, as other boys might use when they wrote of cricket or golf. These were the subjects that interested them most.

His mother found that she could manage to send him to Cambridge, but to help the family finances he spent some weeks in the summer of 1848, before he went up to Trinity, as tutor to two boys whose father had taken Abergeldie Castle from the impoverished Gordons who owned it. The Queen came over to see Abergeldie while he was there, with a view to acquiring a lease of it, as she did not long after, and it became the Highland residence of the Prince of Wales, who with the Prince Consort accompanied her on this occasion. My father records this in a letter to his mother, and gives an odd account of the Highland games at Invercauld, which the Queen attended with her family; the Dukes of Atholl and Leeds, who were to receive her, were late. She was the most plainly dressed woman there, was his opinion ;

Prince Albert was 'horribly padded and belted,' the
Prince of Wales, ' a fair little lad, rather of slender make,'
the Princess Royal ' a plain child with a will and temper
of her own, I should think.' It would have surprised
them all to know that the rather shy, handsome young
tutor of nineteen from Abergeldie would in ten years
time be stoutly opposing Prince Albert's scheme for
the introduction of German methods of education
into England, that not thirty years later ' the most
plainly dressed woman there' would be ' ever his
affectionately,' and that ' the fair little lad of slender
make' would one day be hearing what this same tutor
thought about baccarat.

During his first year at Cambridge, his mother wrote
to him of a project which filled him with horror. She
was the owner of her husband's patent for the manufacture of cobalt, and she proposed with the utmost good
sense, as we should now think, to start a business for its
exploitation. The expenses of a growing family with
the eldest son at Cambridge were heavier than she had
anticipated, and being an exceedingly able woman, she
would very likely have made a success of it. But the
idea that his mother should embark in ' trade' was to
his notions too dreadful to contemplate. ' I do hope
and trust you will keep out of it,' he wrote. ' It will do
me so much harm here, and my sisters so much harm for
ever ! I trust that the scheme may be abandoned once
and for all.'

To-day it seems almost incredible that a boy should
have considered it an indelible disgrace that his mother
should supplement her income by running a business,
or that a mother should have given up her scheme
because of such fastidiousness in her son. But so

earnest was this supplication, that she abandoned her idea, and presently we find him taking pupils and sending her the half of what he earned. He was elected a sizar, and then a scholar of Trinity, and his sister wrote to him prophesying that if he went on like that he would soon be Archbishop of Canterbury. The great Dr. Sollitt, before he burned his books, could not have read the face of the heavens with surer skill.

Then there descended on this young family and their mother a tempest of woes. She invested a large portion of her not too abundant capital in some freshly floated railway company: railway companies were booming now, and also breaking, and she lost it all. Then two of her daughters fell ill with some virulent fever, subsequently declared to be typhus. She wrote to my father not to come back from Cambridge for fear of infection, and the next news he got was the death of his eldest sister Harriet. He instantly started to go home, but before he arrived a further tragedy had befallen.

His mother had refused to look again on the face of the dead, but that night, yearning to see it once more, she got up from her bed where another daughter was sleeping with her and told her she was going to the room where Harriet lay. Soon she came back, lay down and went quietly to sleep. When morning came she was lying very still and the child could not waken her. She got frightened and ran to fetch somebody, and then it was found that her mother had died as she slept at her side without a sigh or a movement. After the double funeral her money affairs were looked into, and it appeared that all she had left was the last payment but one of the annual sum for which she had sold the patent

which she had once thought of exploiting herself.
Beyond that there was nothing. She had given no hint
to any of her relations of the state of her finances.

The family of six children, the youngest of whom was
a boy of only eight years old, had to disperse, for it was
impossible to keep the home together. A grandmother
took two of them; the rest went to various cousins. An
uncle, Sir Thomas Baker, a wealthy business man and
a bachelor, offered to take the youngest brother, adopt
him, and make him his heir, but my father, just of age
and *in loco parentis*, absolutely refused to allow this, for
his uncle was a Unitarian, and whatever worldly pro-
spects the boy might thereby forfeit, all such considerations were dross compared with that pearl of great price,
the Christian faith which, so he held, would be imperilled
if Charlie was brought up in such guardianship. Nothing
was further from his uncle's intention than to attempt
to influence the child with regard to religion and my
father was solemnly assured of that, but he still saw
danger in committing his brother to a Unitarian household, and remained firm. A heated and painful correspondence took place between uncle and nephew, and
my father's final word on the subject, in which he undertook full responsibility for the boy's education and start
in life, is an extraordinary document, written as it was
by a young man of twenty-one. It burns with the
uncompromising faith out of which, in days of persecu-
tion, martyrs were made.

' My religious principle is not a thing of tender feelings, warm comforting notions, unproved prejudices,
but it consists of full and perfect conviction, absolute
belief, rules to regulate my life, and tests by which I
believe myself bound to try every question the greatest

and the least. . . . I shall constantly hereafter as a Priest in the English Church, if God will, several times in every service proclaim " Glory be to the Father and to the Son, and to the Holy Ghost " : I shall offer humble prayer on my own behalf and on behalf of the Church at large to my Redeemer—with what conscience or with what countenance if ever memory should suggest that in one person's case, and his the dearest that could be, I had robbed those Divine persons of the worship and the praise that should have proceeded from his heart, his mind, his lips, his whole life ? Whom could you more rightly brand as Hypocrite than him whose professions should be so loud, whose actions so discrepant ?

' This is a very serious matter, and I hope you will not think bitterly either of the young man's presumption, or the young churchman's bigotry. Bigot, thus far, a conscientious Christian must be.'

In addition to these relations there came forward a man who had no connexion with the family, but who instantly begged to be allowed to take upon himself the whole of my father's expenses at Cambridge, and all future maintenance till he was earning an adequate income for himself and for the support of his brothers and sisters. This was a middle-aged bachelor don and bursar of Trinity College, Mr. Francis Martin, who had a romantic and devoted affection for him : had Francis Martin been a poet we should surely have had some sonnets. He furnished new rooms for my father in college, cheques were ready for all his reasonable needs and small luxuries, he took him on tours and expeditions in the vacations, and reading parties in the Lakes, he nursed him if he was ill, humorously lamenting that he was not worse and would need more ministrations, he

treated him with a half lover-like, half paternal adoration,
assuring him that it was a privilege of which he felt
himself unworthy, to be allowed to do anything for him.
Not content with these present personal services he put
by £500 for each of his sisters as a dowry for their
marriages, or to be used in any way that seemed useful.
All he wanted in return was the boy's companionship
and confidence. And indeed that companionship must
have been to such a man a very delightful thing, for the
boy who could write so uncompromising a letter to his
uncle, was one of gay and sky-scraping spirits, exceedingly handsome, loving long walks and bathes in high
tarns, and study of noble books, and silly jokes and all
the beauty of the visible world, crazy with the joy of life
on a summer morning, and with a mind alert and sensitive. One day he had twisted an ankle jumping down
from the top of a coach and his ' misery-leg ' only allowed
him to hobble down to the ledge of Grasmere, where at
sunset he watched the herons coming in to roost in the
fir-trees, and so he scribbled a little poem about them for
his friend :

> One floating o'er the gorge, and one
> > Down dropping o'er the scar,
> And one, wide-oaring o'er the wood
> > The Herons come from far,
> From lonely glens where they had plied
> > All day their feasts and war.
>
> Ah, goodly lords of a goodly land,
> > How calm they fold the wing :
> How lordly beak on bosom couch'd,
> > To their pine-hung eyrie swing,
> And stand to see the sun go down
> > Each like a lonely king.

He read it to him that evening and Mr. Martin stroked
his hair, and said he was a poet ; then they had a great
discussion as to whether it was ever justifiable to kill
a moth that fluttered about the lamp and on to your
book when you wanted to work, and then they talked of
the future. My father said he would marry when he
was thirty, the other told him it must be much sooner
than that.

After two more years at Cambridge with this fine
friend always constant, my father took a brilliant degree
and won the Classical blue riband of the year, the
Chancellor's gold medal, given by the Prince Consort.
In his holidays now he often spent weeks with his
widowed cousin, Mrs. William Sidgwick, sister-in-law
to James and Christopher of Skipton Castle, and it was
to her house at Clifton that Mr. Martin came flying down
from Cambridge to carry the magnificent news of the
Chancellor's medal. Mrs. Sidgwick was the mother of
William, Henry and Arthur Sidgwick, and of one
daughter. The daughter Mary was my mother and
this is what my father wrote in his diary about her in the
year 1852, he being now twenty-three years of age, an
earnest, young Victorian wooer.

Mrs. Sidgwick's little daughter, Mary, is this year eleven
years old. From a very young child great parts and peculiarly
strong affection have been discernible in her, with a great
delicacy of feeling. She is remarkably persevering and though
(naturally) lacking the taste for dry sorts of knowledge, which
her brother Henry, whom she most resembles, had from an
infant, she has much fondness for histories, above all the
ancient, and a most striking love for poetry, and taste in fine
poetry, and has a wonderful deal of it committed (always of
her own inclination) to memory. As I have always been very
fond of her and she of me with the love of a little sister, and

as I have heard of her fondness for me commented on by many persons, and have been told that I was the only person at whose departure she ever cried, as a child, and how diligent she has always been in reading books which I have mentioned to her, and in learning pieces of poetry which I have admired, it is not strange that I, who from the circumstances of my family am not likely to marry for many years to come, and who find in myself a growing distaste for forming friendships (fit to be so called) among new acquaintances and who am fond indeed (if not too fond) of little endearments, and who also know my weakness for falling suddenly in love, in the common sense of the word, and have already gone too far more than once in these things and have therefore reason to fear that I might on some sudden occasion be led . . . [here the manuscript takes refuge in cipher] it is not strange that I should have thought first of the possibility that some day dear little Minnie might become my wife.

Now we must remember that this very able and masterful young man, who here perhaps rather chills us by the painstaking quality of his emotions, had lately, as we shall see, been reading Tennyson's ' Princess ' with Minnie, and his communings with his diary are clearly inspired by certain very elevated and properly expressed passages in that typically Victorian poem, and in especial by the homily which the Prince there reads his young lady on the nature of love. He could not endure to ' keep his wing'd affections clipt with crime ': he reminds her that the nature of a woman has to grow in sweetness and strength,

> Till at the last she set herself to man,
> Like perfect music unto noble words.

That sounds remote enough from modern notions of mating : not one girl out of a hundred but would have a fit at the thought of fitting herself like music to the

noble words of her suitor, but that was emphatically the
Victorian ideal of marriage ; man was the superior and
supreme sex, and the more thoroughly that women
recognized that fact, the happier would marriage be.
And if this passage from his diary sounds a little too
enumerative of Minnie's promising points, it must also
be remembered that she was only eleven years old, and
that he was not in the least in love with her, nor professed to be, but only confiding to his diary in very
proper language what he thought might someday happen.
But immediately after this there follows a passage that
makes us suspect that there was some pleasing agitation
already at work below the correctness.   The edifying
discourse of Tennyson's ' Princess ' did not cover the
whole ground.   He goes on :

Whether such an idea ever struck the guileless little thing
herself I cannot tell.   I should think it most unlikely.   Yet
I could not help being surprised one night when she was half
lying on the sofa on which I sat, by the following conversation :
MINNIE : Edward, how long will it be before I am as tall
as if I was standing on that stool ?
EDWARD : I don't know very well, Minnie, five years
perhaps. . . .
MINNIE : When I am twenty I shall be taller than that ?
EDWARD : Yes.
MINNIE : When I am twenty, how old shall you be ?
EDWARD : Thirty-two.
MINNIE : Thirty-two ! Edward, I shan't look so little
compared to you, shall I, when I'm twenty and you're thirty-
two, as I do now that I'm eleven and you're twenty-three ?
EDWARD : No, no, you won't, Minnie.
This unexpected close made me blush indeed, and the
palms of my hands grew very hot.

Somehow one feels that Minnie has got in behind
the edifying sentiments recorded in the diary, though

after this surprise he tries, not quite successfully, to entrench himself in them again.

'The Princess' we read through, and she introduced me to 'The Lord of the Isles,' who was a mighty favourite with her. I had on many occasions reason to be struck with the keenness and depth of her thought : how her eye would flash at a fine expression, and the really striking voice and gestures with which she would read through a fine passage. Whatever she grows up to be, she is a fine and beautiful bud now. Whatever she may be in countenance hereafter, I think that the fineness of her expression in these cases will remain. She is remarkable for great beauty and changefulness of expression : one of the sweetest things I ever saw is her look of affection or of tenderness.

Though still holding on to the Tennyson ideal, he could not keep the growing perturbation to himself, and one night talking to her mother he told her that 'if Minnie grew up the same sweet clever girl she was, she would make such a wife as I had often said I should most pray for myself.' Mrs. Sidgwick not unnaturally was a good deal startled at this sort of option which he claimed on a child of eleven, and with much tact told him that no doubt he would constantly come across maturer incarnations of what Minnie might become : he mustn't attempt to make up his mind yet, and Minnie, he must remember, had not yet got a mind at all in these matters. But this good sense and prudence did not serve to stop his feeling, and the very next year he persuaded her mother to allow him to speak to Minnie on 'The Subject.'

In our rides [he records], those charming rides, many little things occurred which made me believe that she saw something of my thoughts, and so at last the day came and

I spoke to her.   Let me try to recall each circumstance : the
arm-chair in which I sat, how she sat as usual on my knee,
a little fair girl of twelve with her earnest look, and how I said
that I wanted to speak to her of something serious, and then
got quietly to the thing, and asked her if she thought it would
ever come to pass that we should be married.   Instantly,
without a word, a rush of tears fell down her cheeks, and I
really for the moment was afraid.   I told her that it was often
in my thoughts, and that I believed that I should never love
anyone so much as I should love her if she grew up as it seemed
likely.   But that I thought her too young to make any promise,
only I wished to say so much to her, and if she felt the same,
she might promise years hence, but not now.   She made no
attempt to promise, and said nothing silly or childish, but
affected me very much by quietly laying the ends of my handkerchief together and tying them in a knot, and quietly putting
them into my hand.   I asked her whether the thought had
never struck her when she read ' The Princess ' to me so constantly.   ' Never,' she said.   She would then turn the pages
backward and forward and say again she wondered she had
never thought of it, and again she would exclaim she never
understood this passage and that till to-day.   She could say
it almost by heart : she repeated the words ' Love, children,
happiness.'   ' Two of those are mine now,' she said.

This same year my father was elected a Fellow of
Trinity, Cambridge, and became a master at Rugby
School.   Mrs. Sidgwick had now gone to live there,
for her boys were being educated at the school, and my
father became part of the family and made his home with
her.   And then this little authentic Victorian love
story, so precise and fabulous with its readings out of
Tennyson's ' Princess ' and its adorable heroine of twelve
years old, tenderly and exquisitely plighting herself, and
striving to ' set herself to man,' without as yet the
slightest notion what it all meant, becomes a very real
affair (though indeed it was that already but somehow

disguised to our thinking by its mode) full of hesitations and misgivings. My mother wrote down soon after her marriage a little inner history of those years, and it is a unique revelation of the mind of a child, sensitive and affectionate, and filled with the notion of the responsibility she has undertaken. From the moment that she had pledged herself with that true lover's knot which she had placed in his hand, she regarded herself as his : her destiny was sealed and signed, and she must fit herself for it. She must certainly grow taller, she must get to be as high as when she stood on that footstool, and she must cultivate her mind and be much more diligent at the reading and the lessons which he now daily set her, as lover but as tutor also, so as to be worthy of him. She must study architecture because he was so fond of churches, and be able to recognize without any mistake whether this arch was Perpendicular and that window Early English. And she must be more painstaking with her arithmetic, for before long she would be keeping house for him and adding up the weekly bills. She was 'more volatile,' so her mother wrote of her, than her brilliant brothers, and that volatility must be sobered (*laus Deo*, it never was) and she must become more serious, or else Edward, who in this wondrous way had chosen her and to whom she now utterly dedicated herself, would be disappointed with her. She admired him, she revered him, she was not ever the least afraid of him, as many others were, but was she at all in love with him ? She was happiest, she confessed, when she knew he was happy, but not necessarily when she was with him. She confessed too, that though her mother had forbidden any private endearments, she had allowed him to kiss her in the garden and that weighed heavy on her, for it must somehow have been her fault. And his ways were different from hers : if people had done wrong, he was stern with them. No doubt that was quite right, for he was anxious for their sakes that they should not err again, and if they were well scolded, that would help them to keep straight. But her plan was otherwise : if any one was suffering even for his own fault, her instinct was first of all to make him happy again at once, and after that it was time to see about being good. 'And though he was right,' she wrote, ' I was right too,' and to the end of her life she continued to be right, and to be that well-spring of comfort and love and humour to all who dipped therein.

And so a few years slipped by ; my father was providing now out of his own purse for that big family of brothers and sisters, for this he considered was the first charge on him, and his income did not yet warrant a wife and family of his own. Then, when my mother was just seventeen, there came his appointment to be first head master of Wellington College, and it was settled that as soon as he was established there his marriage should take place, and so the little girl whom he had chosen at the age of eleven, and who had plighted her troth to him at the age of twelve, was his. From that time onwards she was the staff on which he leaned, and the wings that gave him flight.

CHAPTER IV

LINCOLN AND TRURO

EARLY impressions are like glimpses seen through the window by night when lightning is about. The flash leaps out without visible cause or warning, and the blackness lifts for a second revealing the scene, the criss-cross of the rods of rain, the trees shining with moisture, the colours in the flower beds, and then darkness like a lid snapped down hides all, till the next flash flickers. So it is with memory; my early blinks are exceedingly vivid, but they are sundered, and though the passage of time does not dim them, as it dims the more fading impressions of later life, they do not form part of a continuous picture. Grandmamma and her bandoline, the table laid for a dinner party, my mother playing croquet and with poised mallet sending her opponent's ball on to the gravel path, my father's figure in rustling silk gown, the gardener killing an adder with a pair of shears, Charles Kingsley lighting his pipe, the agitating but interesting moment when on biting a piece of toffee something gave way inside my mouth, and I found a front tooth embedded in the sweetmeat, and must detach it before consuming the rest; the mystical and remunerative visits at Christmas and on birthdays of the fairy Abracadabra, during which, for some reason gradually conjectured, my mother was always invisible : all these are blinks, each separate. By degrees the blank spaces of darkness between such flashes grew shorter, until they became more like a film of moving pictures, still misty in places and jerkily exhibited, but fairly continuous and connected.

My father, who had hewn Wellington out of the heather, left it in 1873 a full and prosperous public school. The pioneer work was over : he had launched this ship, he had steered it safely past innumerable shoals, he had coaxed it along through contrary cross-currents of the Prince Consort, and now it was sailing brave and free on the high seas. His boyish devotion to the Church, its organization and its place in the life of England, was still a passion with him, but his exclusive view of the benefits of prayer, as shown in his oratory with the booby-trap on the door to catch trespassers, had given place to the widest catholicism, and the schedule of devotional activities for the day of rest at Wellington, not forbidden to boys but compulsory on them, was really prodigious. There was chapel at nine in the morning, after which Bible verses were learned by heart and repeated to formmasters at ten. There was chapel again at a quarter to twelve, and after dinner, at half-past one, there was more Bible-study, followed by a Bible-class in school at half-past three. A third chapel service was held at half-past six, and there were prayers in the dormitories at nine. No secular books could be taken out of school library that day, but a special section of it, furnished with devotional and religious volumes, was open for those who wanted them. It was not indeed to be wondered at that the Prince Consort had asked my father to consider ' Whether there may not be too much excessive employment in Religious Exercise in the present system of the College.' But he did not think so : a day spent like that was festival to him.

But now his work at Wellington was done, and with the desire to devote himself more directly to the service of the English Church, he accepted a Canonry and the Chancellorship of Lincoln, and swept everyone along with him in his ecclesiastical fervour. He instantly established a Theological College for young men studying for Orders, where he lectured twice a week, he opened night-schools for working men and boys and taught there regularly, and he and my mother blew like a spring wind through the calm autumnal Close. For her part, she started, under the auspices of John Farmer, organist at Harrow, a musical society which met weekly not only to sing the consecrated Victorian glees like ' Oh, who will o'er the down with me ? ' and ' Since first I saw your face,' but Chorales of Bach with interspersed gavottes and sarabands on the piano. She sang alto, and firmly beat a rigid time with a paper-knife. This, for mid-Victorian ladies and local musical societies, was distinctly advanced. She was also very daring (for a clergyman's wife) in her open advocacy of George Eliot's novels, in spite of all that was known about her life. She read ' The Mill on the Floss ' aloud to her children and she thrust ' Adam Bede,' which had some very shocking passages in it, into the hands of Canons' wives and told them not to mind. I think indeed that she must have read ' Adam Bede ' to us as well, for an acquaintanceship with Mrs. Poyser seems to date from then, and she would certainly have been ready with some adroit answer if any inquisitive creature had asked why Hetty and Arthur Donnithorne should not meet and talk in the wood. And she was equally up to the mark when one of her children publicly demanded to know the difference between a bull and an ox, for she at once said that the bull was the father and the ox the uncle.

At Riseholme three miles from the city lived Bishop Christopher Wordsworth, who was recognized to be kind at heart, but was felt to be formidable. At the same time he was enviable, because he could skate on one foot, holding the other completely off the ice. Riseholme was an earthly Paradise : it had a scagliola hall, a house-keeper with ringlets and an inexhaustible mine of Osborne biscuits. Then there were two lakes of infinite depth and acreage which held monstrous pike of which Arthur caught one, a prodigious thing of over two pounds, and we had it for nursery tea, since which day I have never cared much for pike at table. Upon these waters were swans as befitted the home of the successor of St. Hugh of Lincoln, and I was presented with one of their eggs. I essayed to blow it for my collection, but it was addled, and since that day I have left the blow-ing of swans' eggs to those who do not mind the risk —such are the simplifications of life which experience teaches. Bishop Wordsworth (to descend to lesser matters) was the nephew of the late Laureate, and he talked about Uncle William, whose poetical aptitude he had inherited, for he wrote a complete hymn book entirely out of his own head, called ' The Holy Year,' and in my father's oratory at the Chancery (unguarded by booby-traps and open to all) we often sang those hymns at family prayers, accompanied by my mother on a minute harmonium with a tremolo stop, which occasionally collapsed with a polyphonic groan and pinched her feet as they plied the bellows. Some of these hymns were fine poetry : ' Hark the sound of holy voices ' was among them, and ' Gracious Spirit, Holy Ghost,' but Bishop Wordsworth also inherited his uncle's tendency to lapse into meaner strains. One hymn, for instance, contained a stanza which few could call felicitous—

> ' What the Holy Prophets meant
> In the Ancient Testament,
> Thou revealest to our view,
> Lord, for ever, in the New.'

Emotional appeal is somehow lacking in such a lyric : there seems no particular reason why it should be sung, and presently there was a very particular reason why some of these hymns should not be sung at family prayers in the Chancery. One of them for instance, an ode in honour of the day of St. Philip and St. James, was better avoided. It began—

> ' Let us emulate the names
> Of St. Philip and St. James,'

and it became known that some of the children had composed a somewhat similar opening for another apostolic feast, and were heard chanting—

> ' Let us try and be as good
> As St. Simon and St. Jude.'

It was wiser therefore to sing something else on the feast of St. Philip and St. James, for fear of giving rise to deplorable levity.

But the Lincoln days were brief ; hardly had my father got his Theological School working, when Lord Salisbury privately inquired of him whether he would accept the Bishopric of Calcutta if he was offered it.

He declined that : there was a young family of six
children ranging from the age of sixteen to five, who
would have to spend the formative years in England
without their parents, and also his heart was in the
Church at home. But it was certain that episcopacy
somewhere was imminent for him, and next year Lord
Beaconsfield, at the suggestion of the Queen and with
her expressed wish that he should accept it, offered him
the newly created See of Truro. That was a very
different matter ; there was pioneer work to be done
there as at Wellington, and after an interview with the
Prime Minister he accepted it. Lord Beaconsfield's
comment was ' Well, we *have* got a Bishop ! '

He had hardly set foot in Cornwall when he began
raising funds for the building of a Cathedral, the first
that had been erected in England since the Reformation.
There was a church situated in the centre of Truro,
mostly empty, for the place was a stronghold of
Methodism, and just as, forty years before, he turned
the empty room in his mother's house into an oratory,
so he made this empty church into the nucleus of his
cathedral. £100,000, he estimated, would be needed for
the completion of this new oratory, and Cornwall, with
the decline of its tin-mining industry, was a very poor
county, but he never had a moment's doubt that this
big sum would be raised. Old Lady Rolle of Bicton,
daughter of a Cornish clergyman, and born in 1793,
instantly lost her heart to him ; she called him ' my
bishop ' and supported her claim to him by sending a
cheque of £40,000 for the purposes of the See. She was
an ancient and picturesque figure, she drove out in a
chariot with four horses and postilions, she ruled her
local kingdom with a rod of iron, and was herself

terribly afraid of being left alone for a moment either by day or night. There must always be someone in the room with her to scare away the thought of the journey she must soon take without companion. She had been present as a peeress at the homage following on Queen Victoria's coronation, and her husband, Lord Rolle, vastly older than herself and very infirm, had tripped in his robes as he ascended the steps of the dais where the young Queen sat, and had *rolled* down to the bottom of them as if he was acting a dumb-crambo. So the Queen rose and went down the steps herself to receive his salutation there : perhaps she whispered in his ear that she had guessed. . . .

As at Wellington, there was nothing concerning the new See which my father found too great to be tackled, nothing too small to claim his absorbed attention. The first meeting of the Committee for the building of the Cathedral produced £15,000 raised in the room, the work began within a year, and he lived to see the dedication and opening of his last oratory, though not its completion. He appointed a Chapter for the Cathedral not yet built (they could do without a Dean at present, and also without any income, since there were no available funds); he made his friend, A. J. Mason, whom he subsequently appointed to a Canonry at Canterbury, chief missioner of the diocese to war against Methodism and that ' confusion of sensual excitement with religious passion,' so characteristic of ' revivals '; he selected figures of Cornish saints, Petroc and Piran and Probus and Austell and Neot and the rest to fill the windows (when there should be any) of his Cathedral : he applied to the Heralds' College for a design of the arms of the See quartered with his own, and, when they sent him a sketch, he pointed out the errors of the blazonry, and sent a friend a message to be conveyed to the Heralds that he would not accept such stuff and that ' he would sooner have

THIS IS
THE SEAL OF
E. W.
BISHOP
OF TRURO

than submit for an instant to the rubbish which Heralds' College called a " Design." It is not fit for the sign of a public house.' He was up at six in the morning for his hour of private devotion before work began, and with a couple of hours out-of-doors on horseback, or on foot, was at his tasks again till two of the next morning, thriving on labours that would have driven most men into a rest-cure.

Railway communication was non-existent, except just down the spine of the county from Saltash to Penzance, and he drove over the whole of his diocese to visit and confirm, dictating letters to his chaplain on the way, and receiving from the warm-hearted folk such a welcome as was rarely accorded to 'a foreigner from England.' There was not a parish in the remotest coasts and fastnesses of the county which he did not periodically visit. Perhaps the church was in such disorder of repair that the sky showed through its gaping roof and the ivy penetrated through the walls of its aisles, and then he gave squires and landowners no peace till they had taken the necessary restoration in hand. There were queer pastors in many of these isolated hamlets ; he arrived one morning, for instance, to preach and celebrate the Sacrament at one of these, and while he was talking to the Vicar before church-time, the parlour-maid came in to ask for the cellar-key that she might take a bottle of wine to the vestry for the Communion. 'We'll have a bottle of white wine to-day,' said the Vicar, 'just for a change.' . . . Another incumbent candidly acknowledged that he had little time for visiting his flock as his garden gave him so much pleasant occupation; but the most remarkable of all was a Vicar who never set foot in his church at all, far less held any kind of service there. Occasionally some neighbouring parson came over to minister to his unshepherded parishioners, but their rightful parson would not even then consent to attend church as a member of his own congregation. It was quite in vain that the patron of his living pleaded with him. 'I don't ask you to do anything,' he said, 'but for the sake of example couldn't you just go to church yourself sometimes?' But it was no use: he preferred to stroll to the garden-gate of the vicarage which adjoined the church clad in a flowered dressing-gown and smoking a hookah, and when his parishioners came out he chatted with them very amiably. There he was, living in the vicarage, a beneficed priest performing no duties of any sort, and there was no ecclesiastical process by which he could possibly be deprived of his house and his income.

Many of the livings were miserably endowed, and their occupants had a hard struggle against poverty and Dissent. From one of these my father rented his vicarage for a month, so that the incumbent might get a holiday, and took the duty himself by way of enjoying his own. The Vicar's wife there played the organ, so my father deputed one of his sons to take her place in her absence. On a certain Sunday morning it was announced that the offertory would be devoted to the ' organist and choir fund,' and that son still labours under the sense of injustice that was his, when he found that not one penny of the congregation's subscriptions was allotted to him. . . . Then one winter's day my father had a nasty accident when riding, straining his knee very badly, but next day there was a confirmation to be held ten miles away, so, strapped and bandaged, he was hoisted into his landau, and on arrival lifted on to a sofa and wheeled into church, where he took the service. There had been a fall of snow the night before : this had half melted during the morning, but in the afternoon a great frost such as had not been known for years in Cornwall set in, and turned the roads to ice. The Bishop's carriage came slewing and skidding down the steep street into Truro with him perfectly helpless inside, looking out of the window straight down the road, and wondering in what fashion he would arrive at the bottom.

On these diocesan travels church people and Wesleyan ministers alike gave him the warmest welcome. They found him personally irresistible, so intensely jolly, so full of enjoyment and keenness and humour, and even when they considered that he was frankly an enemy, that he had the bitterest hostility to Methodism and was come to blow the trumpets of the Church of England till (as he hoped) the walls of their conventicles would fall flat down like those of Jericho, they quite appreciated that he was doing his duty. And when he went back to his Cathedral town they did their duty too, and made the most violent attacks on him and his work, exhorting their congregations to stand firm against the intruder. He knew all about that, and he loved his enemies, vowing that of all mankind the Cornish were the most God-fearing and the best-hearted. The walls of his Cathedral were now rising apace, and that would be a fort in the enemies' country whose guns would carry far. For relaxation he worked at the 'Life of Cyprian,' which once, in those days of comparative leisure at Wellington, he had promised his patient publishers should be ready in six months for certain, but which was to occupy him for twenty-two more years instead, and still lacked at his death its final revision. It was no wonder that he wrote this impressionistic comment to a friend : ' You have no idea what life is becoming to me, a humming top is the only thing that resembles it : perpetual motion, very dizzy, hollow within, keeping up a continuous angry buzz.' But Christmas was approaching, and, buzzing or not, he must send a card of greeting to all his enormous family of godchildren, not with a word just scribbled on the back, but with a letter to show that the spinning top, in spite of its dizziness, was not so hollow within, but was really thinking about them with a strangely wistful tenderness. This is one of those Christmas letters accompanying a picture of a river with an empty boat drawn up on its bank.

Decr. 24, 1881.

MY DEAR LITTLE BOY,—I wish you and your Papa and Mamma and everyone you love a very happy Christmas, and may the love of Jesus Christ make it happy.

The picture of the river which I send you is very like the river near to us. And that is why I liked to choose it for you. I hope it will be like your life. It is all covered with bright reflections of earth and heaven.

And I should like you and life to reflect calmly the beautiful things that are in heaven and that are in earth, and not to be soiled and not to be rough.

Do you understand that? You will if you think a little. Again, there is the boat waiting with her masts ready, but no sails set. That is the boys', waiting till they go to school.

I wish you a happy voyage whenever it begins.

I thought your first letter was very well written, and I hope the sums and the Bible lessons and all else going on are well. I suppose you are thinking about Latin too.

God bless you and keep you. Give my love to your papa and mamma.

Your affectionate friend,
E. W. Truron.

But there fell over his life at Truro, within a year of his appointment there, a shadow out of which he never wholly emerged. It was the one event, in a life of ceaseless work and success, of keen and vivid interests and energies and of unquestioning faith in the decrees of God, which remained enigma to him and stood apart, just a little apart, from all other experience. This was the death of my eldest brother Martin, so called after that friend of Cambridge days, at the age of seventeen. Mentally he was a boy of extraordinary brilliance. He had a gay passion for sheer learning which made its acquisition more of a pastime than a task: in a few weeks, for instance, merely for amusement, he taught himself enough Italian to be able to read it with perfect ease. The bent of his mind, its character and attitude, was wholly that of my father's, intensely serious, intensely religious and without the smallest touch of priggishness. In him my father saw one who would carry on the work of the Church militant here on earth. He would be a great scholar refuting the sceptical conclusions of the higher criticism by a more exalted learning: perhaps he would heal the breach now rapidly widening between the revelations of science and those of religion : perhaps, apart from the world, he would live in that mediaeval air of saintliness and scholarship which sometimes seemed to my father the highest call of all, and indeed, the boy's mind from its intellectual grip and from that gay holiness of his, seemed capable of a unique maturity. Then one morning there came from Winchester, where he was at school, a telegram that took my father there without delay. Martin, without any warning of approaching illness, had been stricken with aphasia. But in a day or two that passed off : it went as causelessly as it had come, and though he was weak, he appeared to be perfectly well again. Had it not been for the length of the journey he would have gone home, so instead, the head master, Dr. Ridding, suggested that he should come to stay in his house for his convalescence. Martin was very fond of him, but whimsically alarmed at the prospect. ' It would be dreadful afterwards,' he said, ' to break down in scholarship. A false quantity would seem like a breach in hospitality.' My father went back to Truro, for all cause for anxiety seemed over. The seizure of speechlessness had been alarming and its origin mysterious, but it had completely passed, and Martin was quite cheerful and normal. Then, after three days, he had a relapse, he lost all power of speech again, and it was evident that there was grave mischief somewhere. My father and mother were sent for, and his diary written fifty-two years ago records the rest.

' He looked from one to the other, and took our hands for a moment, then dropped them again, and folded his own together and placed one of mine against the other that I might pray.

'Soon after we began thus to pray I worked into my prayer the clauses from the Communion service that the Body

and Blood of Christ given and shed for us might preserve his
soul unto Everlasting Life, and placed my fingers upon his
lips, saying " you receive this in the spirit."

'But he would not let me then proceed, but looked very
anxious and imploring and rather tearful. He was restless,
and moved his hands and his fingers until at last I saw, and said
to the nurse " he wants to speak on his fingers." Then he
quickly formed the letter B, and I said "Bread and wine,"
and he was happy again instantly. A little bread was brought,
and we all received when I had consecrated it, and wine in a
glass. The matron put a little wine in a spoon for me to give
him, but he would not take it so, and most reverently grasped the
glass, and he received the Lord's Blood with the happiest look.

'His breathing was loud and difficult, and his mother
began to say gently in his ear " When I survey the wondrous
Cross," and his very soul went with it. But when she came
to the second verse—

> " " See from His head, His hands, His feet
> Sorrow and love flow mingling down "—

he with a sudden momentary look of enquiry, which instantly
changed into an expression of both awe and pleasure, the most
perfect look I ever beheld of satisfied adoration, gazed at
something, Someone ; tried with his eyes to make me look
at the same, and then pointed to it with his fingers.

'Presently I went on, " Thou who art in the midst of the
throne amid Thy angels and Thy holy ones," and at that I
wish it were possible to describe the gentle and strong and
distinct sweep with which, stretching out his left arm, he gently
waved it along a quarter circle from a point just above him.

'He beheld ἄρρητα—things which it is not lawful for
men to utter, and perhaps it was for this that he was silenced,
that he might see such things and not utter them. So passed
on silent hours, yet so much faster than we imagined. Every
now and then at shorter and shorter intervals a flush passed
over his face, and his breathing changed. There was a sigh
like weariness, and again the heavy breathing.

'A few minutes before ten the heavy breathing quite passed

away to become quite soft. His lips gathered themselves nearly together : it looked like a baby's mouth, so soft and sweet and small. The nurse placed her hand gently across his eyes. He breathed in soft little gentle sobs and these ceased to come, and our Martin was gone to God.

'My dearest wife understood it all more quickly, better, more sweetly than I. At once she knew that she had never cared for anything but his happiness and that it was come.

'On that Saturday night we were indeed broken. But his dear mother was even then Christ's, and felt Christ to be God. The moment after he had gone, her exclamation was "Oh, my Martin, how happy you are now, my darling."

'His mother's bearing of all seems to me as perfect as anything can be. A few hours after she knelt in our room and prayed aloud "It is Thy will only that we will. He is Thine, Thou hast a right to him." I cannot reach to this.

'To him, we know, going is gain, pure gain, and I am learning from my wife to subdue the longing for his sweetness back again. She has never faltered.'

The work in Cornwall went on in a stream of ceaseless activities, and now the stream was spreading outside the diocese. He had rooms in the Lollards Tower of Lambeth Palace, he preached as Chaplain to the Queen at Windsor, he preached also in Westminster Abbey on three not very auspicious occasions, for he recorded that :

(i) The first time I preached in the Abbey I lost my voice, so nobody could hear me.

(ii) The second time there were six inches of slush and violent rain after snow so there *was* nobody to hear me.

(iii) The third time, to-morrow, owing to the fog I believe there will be no light in the sky, and so there will be no one to see me.

In London he had interviews with General Booth about the work of the Salvation Army : these were of an ambassadorial nature, and altogether it looked as if some force was beginning to exert its pull from somewhere outside the orbit of his Cornish activities. Archbishop Tait of Canterbury came to stay with him at Truro, and in the autumn of 1882 he was sent for to Addington, where the Archbishop, then in his last illness, spoke directly to him, expressing the hope that he would succeed him at Canterbury. On Archbishop Tait's death, just before the end of the year, Gladstone, who was Prime Minister at the time, went to see the Queen about the new appointment, and this was one of the not very common occasions on which he and the Sovereign were entirely of one mind. They agreed that Bishop Harold Brown of Winchester was too old for the post, and that there was only one man, and he among the junior Bishops at present without a seat in the House of Lords, who could adequately fill it. Gladstone instantly wrote to my father, offering him the Archbishopric in these terms :

Downing Street,
Dec. 16, 1882.

MY DEAR BISHOP OF TRURO,—I have to propose to your lordship with the sanction of Her Majesty that you should accept the succession to the Archbishopric of Canterbury now vacant through the lamented death of Archbishop Tait.

This proposal is a grave one. But it is, I can assure you, made with a sense of its gravity, and in some degree proportioned to it, and it comes to you, not as an offer of personal advancement but as a request that, whereas you have heretofore been employing your talents in the service of the Church and Realm, you will hereafter employ them with the same devotion in the same good and great cause.

I have the honour to be,
my dear Lord Bishop,
with cordial respect,
Sincerely yours,
W. E. GLADSTONE.

The same day there came a telegram from the Queen saying that she was writing. Her letter arrived just before Christmas. She spoke of the high esteem in which she and the Prince Consort had always held my father during his years at Wellington College, and expressed the earnest hope, both on ecclesiastical and personal grounds, that he would accept the appointment.

A week had already elapsed since the Prime Minister had offered him the Archbishopric and he had not yet made up his mind whether to accept it or not, for he knew himself that his gifts lay in personal, pioneering work, such as had been his in the creation of Wellington College and in the new diocese of Cornwall, and the Primacy was mainly an administrative post, much concerned with political legislation, and, though large in scope, fettered by tradition. All his life, supremely sincere in purpose, and of a masterful will and energy that carried all before it, he had occupied positions where, having made up his mind, he got his own way. But now, though entrusted with a far larger responsibility, he knew that his freedom would be far more curtailed. As a small boy he had informed his mother that he intended to be Archbishop of Canterbury, and his sister had chaffingly told him that, even at Cambridge, the fulfilment of his ambition was growing appreciably nearer. And now it was given him. But he saw that there would be no more of that militant liberty through which he had driven to accomplishment his own policy on his own responsibility : whatever he did now as head, under the Sovereign, of the Church, was a matter of State. His measures would be bills for which the Government of the day must find a place on their programme, and of which Parliament must approve. But

now with the personal appeal from the Queen, he
hesitated no longer, and he wrote to Mr. Gladstone
accepting the Primacy.

God give grace. God give all that I only can know to
be so fearfully wanting. I will give all that He gives to the
service of the Queen and people and Church.

That Her Majesty herself approves it, knowing almost
better than anyone my earlier work, is a thought full of
strength.

CHAPTER V

TWO SISTERS

THE reticences and reserves which were practised in the intercourse between men and women in the seventies seem now to our minds as remote and outlandish as whiskers or crinolines and there is nothing easier than to make fun of them, for the habits of one generation are always a legitimate source of amusement to the next. But they were founded on a tradition that was wholly worthy of respect, the principle of which was that when the two sexes met together for social enjoyment they should preserve a certain outward form of dignity and politeness. Of course there was as much scandal then as now, women had their lovers and men their mistresses ; but there was not general gabble on these and kindred subjects. To many of the women of that time this dignity and reserve were perfectly natural, and, just then, that tradition prevailed and governed the speech of mixed intercourse. Men did what they thought good, and saw what they chose, and said what they liked to each other, but women according to the same code only saw what it was fit for them to see, and however vividly a domestic scandal or outrage was thrust in front of their eyes, the traditions of a certain class enjoined on them to assume in public a bland blindness to it ; fine breeding demanded that a woman

should be unconscious of it.   Any public recognition
of it was unthinkable, and even more unthinkable was
it that she should talk about it, or seek to protect herself
against a domestic situation even if it threatened to ruin
her life or render it intolerable.   It was correct to be
blind and dumb, and to see or speak was an offence
against the laws that governed the behaviour of her class.
Tragic could be the consequences, if she took steps to
defend herself.   The life of one of the finest women I
have ever known was thus temporarily wrecked, but out
of the wreck her courage constructed an ark for others.
The story is full of typical figures, of which the central
one, though grimly Victorian by upbringing and marriage,
was at heart the most amazing mixture of modernity,
saintliness, humour, and humanity.   She was also one
of the pioneers who have won for their sex liberty and
the right to work.

To realize the different strains of character which
determined the situation in which this very noble woman
was entangled and from which she triumphantly extricated herself, it is necessary to begin rather far back.
Her grandfather on her mother's side was a certain
Mr. Pattle, merchant in Indian tradings, who had made
a very considerable fortune.   He married the daughter
of one of Marie Antoinette's pages of honour, and that
strain of French blood was destined to play a part in
a wholly English drama.   Mr. Pattle was the father of
five extremely attractive and handsome daughters, and
was himself remarkable for his reputation of being the
greatest liar in India; somehow we feel inclined at the
outset to like Mr. Pattle, though we shall see nothing of
him except that which was not meant to be seen.   But
to have such a reputation is endearing; it connotes a

garrulous and clubbable fellow. He died out in India, and since he had expressed his wish to be buried in England, his widow procured a large barrel into which the deceased was folded, and the barrel was then filled up to the top with some reliable preservative, rum or Pondicherry liquor, something with body in it, in two senses of the word. The widow then travelled back to England, where her daughters awaited her, on the ship which conveyed the remains. Steam in those days was unknown as a propulsion, the shorter route through the Suez Canal not yet made, and off the Cape of Good Hope the vessel encountered so violent a buffeting from a storm that Mr. Pattle's barrel broke loose from its moorings and rolled about with a very dreadful liveliness. Before it could be bridled again, a violent collision with the ship's side broached it, smashing off the top and spilling such contents as were liquid : what was solid peered starkly over the battered staves. There was not enough liquor on the ship nor a large enough barrel to make possible any further homing of the contents, and after the widow had formally identified them, they were buried at sea. Before the ship reached England Mr. Pattle's widow also died and his large fortune descended to his daughters.

The youngest and far the most beautiful of them all was Miss Virginia. From her mother she inherited an exquisite patrician charm and a strong strain of melodrama. In 1850 she married Lord Eastnor, eldest son and heir of Earl Somers, to whose title and estate he presently succeeded. Two years after her marriage was born a daughter Isabel, and later another daughter Adeline, but there the family stayed. The two were brought up by their mother according to the strictest

Victorian standards as set up by the Prince Consort for
the education of the Royal children, with this difference
that she did not give much personal supervision to it.
Backboards and scales on the piano, French exercises
and the use of the globes, lodgings at the sea-side for
the sake of its healthful and tonic airs, rugs for the knees
and scarves for the neck, prohibition to read anything
amusing, particularly novels, charitable expeditions to
the village with jellies and knitted articles for the de-
serving poor, restricted pocket money and cloistered
ignorance of all that was likely to be met with in later
life, were the principles of it and a governess the administrator, while their exquisite mother entranced the
fashionable and artistic world of London and made
romantic journeys to Italy, constantly writing to her two
girls the most affectionate letters, but not really seeing
very much of them until they were of ripe years to be
shewn to men and under her deft guiding hand to make
brilliant marriages. The system of their education, in
fact, had a strong French flavouring mixed with its
English mode.

The first to appear was, of course, Isabel, and it
looked as if almost immediately a very suitable man,
with a dukedom waiting for him, would carry off
this lively heiress to Eastnor Castle and a very ample
property. But another mother had her eye on the
Marquis of Lorne, who shortly became the husband of
Princess Louise, and Lady Somers must look elsewhere.
The sooner Isabel was suitably married the better, for
her mother had ideas already for the younger Adeline,
and the correct use was that the elder of the two daughters
must be married first: anything else was irregular.
Then Lord Henry Somerset came on the scene ; he was

not quite as good, for he had an elder brother, unmarried
at present, who stood between him and the Dukedom
of Beaufort, but the Somersets were a very great family
and he would do. He was a very attractive man, of
artistic tastes, he composed songs which made the
Victorians dissolve into copious tears, and Isabel would
be reigning daughter-in-law at magnificent Badminton.
So the marriage took place, and quickly she captured
the hearts of her father- and mother-in-law. She had
not got Lady Somers's beauty, but this girl of twenty
must have been an enchanting creature, deliciously pretty,
auburn-haired, and full of grace and gaiety and wit.

She told me once of a scene that took place at Badminton shortly after her marriage, which admirably
illustrates the high-bred reserve of great Victorian dames.
The Duke of Beaufort was away, but there was a party
in the house, and one day the butler told the Duchess
as they went in to lunch that a case had arrived for
His Grace, which he had unpacked: it contained a
picture, and he wanted to know where he was to hang
it. So the whole party went into the corridor, when
lunch was over, to see the picture, and there they found
the portrait of a very pretty young lady whom everybody
knew to be the Duke's mistress. Was that an awkward
situation? Not in the least. The Duchess with complete self-possession looked admiringly at it, and said,
' Is it not charming? A fancy portrait, I suppose,' and
without a grin or a wink or a whisper, they all looked at
the fancy portrait, and liked it immensely. It would
do very well, thought the Duchess, just where it was,
hung on the wall there. Then as they moved quietly
on, she changed her mind. ' His Grace might like it
in his own room perhaps,' she said to her butler. ' You

had better hang it there.' That was all. Reticence and dignity had perfectly solved the method of dealing with this awkwardness, and when the Duke came home there was the fancy portrait hanging in his room as a pleasant surprise for him.

But there was an unpleasant surprise for him not long afterwards, for the lady determined to transfer her charms to another admirer, and wrote to tell him so. Victorian reserve was not binding on men, and with tears he bewailed to his sons and daughter-in-law his cruel fate. Being a thoroughly religious man, he sought spiritual consolation in his trial, so the order went forth that next Sunday every groom and coachman and helper in the Badminton stables should attend church and receive the Sacrament with their master. This was quite characteristic of the time : a man could be a sincere and devout Christian and yet be keeping a mistress : besides his mistress had left him, so he no longer had one. In just the same manner, a certain notable Oxford professor of strict tractarian views who kept a mistress in the town learned casually from her that she had never been confirmed. He was very much upset by this, and persuaded her to receive instruction and repair this shocking omission. That made him quite happy, and their relationship was renewed with no cloud to mar its brightness . . . Lady Henry Somerset, devoted to her father-in-law, full of humour and intensely comprehending, shook with kindly laughter that must not betray itself, and delighted in him.

Then tragedy developed. Lady Henry became aware of things in her husband's life that made it impossible for her to go on living with him. For a long while she bore them in silence and then could bear them no more, and said she must be separated from him. Possibly the affair might have been managed without public scandal, but at the moment when careful thought and wisdom were most demanded, Lady Somers descended on the situation, in a whirlwind of French horror and dramatic tableau, and persuaded her daughter not to spend another night in her husband's house, but to take refuge with her baby at Eastnor. A more unwise handling of the situation cannot be conceived, for instantly it flamed into a public scandal of the most atrocious kind. Lady Somers had not in the least understood what would be the result of that French flamboyant gesture, and it was perhaps lucky for her sense of maternal duty that she had already married her second daughter to the next holder of the Dukedom of Bedford.

Lady Henry sought for and obtained her separation, stating her grounds. She did not ask for a divorce because her religious principles forbade that, for she believed that marriage was an indissoluble tie : God had joined together and no sundering was possible. Nor indeed could she have obtained the divorce for which she never sought, for there had been neither desertion nor technical cruelty. But by making public the reason for her separation, she had outraged the sacred principle of womanly reticence, and dire was the wrath of the silent ones. The code of Victorian 'Reticence for Women' had been violated, and it showed, when defied, of what savagery it was capable. For it was not, as it now proved itself, a mere matter of convenient blindness that affected not to see what was disagreeable, nor a matter of acquiescing dumbness, which considered it just a piece of good taste not to talk about subjects which were better passed over in silence, but a rooted and sacred principle that a woman in Their class, must, whatever her domestic trouble, hold her tongue. They would have nothing more to do with the offender, and ' Society ' cut her.

So fire and brimstone rained down on Lady Henry, and she retired from the world of her upbringing and marriage, which would no longer receive her. She had delighted in its glitter and splendour, she had revelled in its gaiety, its operas, its jewels, but she never, in the middle-class manner of Byron, shook off the dust of it from her feet, nor pretended to think that the world in which she had lived was all dross and malice and corruption ; it remained, though she was no longer of it, a most delightful place, full of agreeable and congenial and amusing people. She lived for a while at the Priory, Reigate, a beautiful house belonging to her father, and at his death she established herself at the Norman Castle (rather late Norman, since it was built at the end of the eighteenth century) at Eastnor, where she had been brought up. Her mother, half French by blood, and wholly French by instinct, retired to Aix-les-Bains where, still a marvel of distinguished charm and beauty, she made a centre for the more notable sections of the shifting population who came there for cures. For that particular sort of supremacy she had a real genius and, taking the house of Dr. Brachet, a leading physician there, she exercised a gracious and queen-like and slightly theatrical hospitality.

Lady Henry at her father's death was only thirty-three years old, of rich and radium-like energy, for which there seemed no outlet. She could not marry again, she was cut off from the world which she knew, and there seemed nothing for it but just to live at Eastnor unoccupied and chiefly alone, and that, to one overflowing with life and with the strongest need for bringing herself into human relationships, was absolutely impossible. She looked after her estates, she visited her tenants, and from that developed her work among women, which she continued to the end of her life. She interested herself especially with those who had come to ruin through drink. Drunkenness she never thought of as sinful, it was just a consoling habit, leading to wretched results, which was the natural effect of living in beastly houses and in sordid and depressing conditions. So she began rebuilding, regardless of expense, the insanitary cottages on her estate, in order to give women of intemperate habits a chance of regaining the self-respect which would break the curse, and she exhorted them, of course, to take the pledge of total abstinence, instead of messing about with compromises of the harmlessness of an occasional indulgence. Then it seemed to her humorous and candid mind that it really was not fair to expect others to practise an abstinence which she did not observe, and most regretfully she decided that she must become a teetotaller herself. She wanted to make this ceremony impressive, and arranged to take the pledge publicly at Eastnor (was there a touch of her mother's dramatic quality in that ?) among her assembled tenants and dependents, so that all should see that her practice was as thorough as her preaching. The rite was to take place in the hall in the Castle on her return from London, but on the way back she had to change trains at Worcester, and she recounted with peals of the most delicious laughter that ever came from human mouth what happened at Worcester. ' I hurried to the refreshment room and had two glasses of rich fruity port.   Just that one more drink ! '

It was thus that she began the rebuilding of a life that seemed so utterly wrecked. Instead of having nothing to do, she was overwhelmed with the work she had taken up. She was a born orator, humorous, incisive, convincing, she had a voice of gold and she travelled not only over England, but made tours to America, speaking in the cause of temperance. There was no nonsense about her : she did not say that alcohol was evil in itself, or that the Last Supper was celebrated, as the fanatical affirmed, with an unfermented juice of the grape. Alcohol, according to her, was as good a gift of God as roast chicken, and only dangerous to the vulnerable. Religion and rescue-work were the motives of her life, no saint ever devoted himself more unreservedly to the practice of his faith, and yet saintliness was the very last quality that could be associated with her, so wholly secular was her sense of humour, and so abhorrent to her was anything like asceticism or ecstasy. She attended, for instance, a Salvation Army meeting, and (though she hated doing it) she felt herself obliged to stand forth and kneel at the ' penitence form,' a thing that surely required a good deal of courage and sincerity. But she could not see herself in the regulation poke bonnet, though, as she told me, a pathetic appeal had been made to her by an aged leader of the movement. ' Oh, Lady Somerset,' she had said, ' How I pray God that before I die, I may see you in a saved 'at ! ' Or again, when about to stay with her at Eastnor, I was astonished to receive a telegram from her reading, ' Please bring a bottle of whisky.' I obeyed, and she explained this curious request to me on my arrival with her irresistible merriment. Her principles, she said, forbade her to supply me with alcohol in her house, but her sense of hospitality revolted at the thought of my finding myself forced to be an abstainer. ' So I had to send you that telegram,' she said, ' though I know that now I'm completely in your power. You've only got to tell everyone that though I preach teetotalism and affirm that I practise it, I get my friends to bring me drink on the sly. My telegram proves it.' Later, she gave up Eastnor, for she wanted all the money she could possibly get hold of to support her settlement at Duxhurst which she had opened to reclaim drunken and criminal women. She took them from their squalid surroundings and established them in bright cheerful little abodes, she gave them outdoor work to do, she established a further colony of children whose presence satisfied their womanly instincts.

She went entirely on the admirable lines that women take to drink in order to put colour and a sense of enjoyment into drab and dreary lives, and at Duxhurst she established herself as matron, and apart from rare holidays spent the rest of her life there. She wore a uniform of a nunnish nursish sort, and one day, having gone down from London to visit her, I was astonished to see her abstaining from cigarettes. In answer to my question whether there was a crusade against smoking also, there came that laughter which was surely the most infectious expression of amusement ever heard : no one could help laughing when she laughed. ' I had to give it up,' she said ; ' I saw in the train the other day a stout elderly woman like me in a nurse's dress smoking a cigarette. An awful sight ; I couldn't bear the idea that I looked like that.'

While Lady Henry was still at Badminton, Lady
Somers had had the happiness of seeing her second
daughter Adeline married to Lord Tavistock, the eldest
son of the Duke of Bedford, and installed as daughter-
in-law at Woburn Abbey in the midst of such high
traditions of antique aristocracy as are now scarcely
credible. Her father-in-law had just such an outlook
on life as David attributed to Jehovah : ' all the beasts
of the forest are mine, and so are the cattle upon a
thousand hills.' He was prodigiously wealthy—how
should he not be, being Duke of Bedford ?—and had an
immense property in London, for all the streets and
squares of Bedford and Russell and Woburn and Ends-
leigh and Tavistock were his. ' If one hadn't a few
acres in London in these times of agricultural depression,'
he said, ' I don't know what one would do.' So as he
had a nice acreage there, he did nothing. Covent
Garden with its filthy slums belonged to him, and it
was a disgrace to any civilized town, but where was
the use of being a landlord if you had to expend vast
sums on your property? Indeed it required full-page
cartoons in *Punch*, in which he appeared in his coronet
holding up his Garter-robes for fear they should trail
in the stinking puddles of Mud-Salad Market, before
he could be induced to remedy its monstrous dirt
and squalor. As well as his wealth, he inherited the
brains of one of the cleverest families in Europe, and
he devoted their keenest edge to the nirvanic enjoyment of being what he was. It was better, too, that
his eldest son should leave the House of Commons,
for he in turn would be Duke of Bedford, and that
gave anybody enough to think about. It was time
also that he should marry, for it was a proper thing

that a future Duke of Bedford should have a wife, even if her whole duty was confined to looking graceful and reserved and well-bred. But it was not fit that the future Duchess, when at Woburn, should drive about in an open carriage where anybody on the roads could stare at her, and his wishes were conveyed to her, that when she went out into the country roads round Woburn, where neither she nor her equipage could be *incognita*, a brougham would be more suitable. As regards her unfortunate sister she was not forbidden to see her, but neither the Duchess nor he would meet her.

Duchess Adeline (as she duly became) had neither the irrepressible vitality of her sister nor her unfailing sense of humour, and while the lack of the former made her suffer less under this stifling tyranny and emptiness, the lack of the latter prevented her from seeing the ludicrous side of these rich pomposities. Lady Henry would have found in this arid existence bright spots of the ridiculous, but though Duchess Adeline found none, she had inherited from her mother (which her sister had not) a perception that after all it was something to be a Duchess ; it supplied a palliative to the aching joylessness. Like Lady Henry she had a strong devotional and religious sense, and on the appointment of my father to the Archbishopric, she formed the two closest friendships of her life with him and my mother. She was often at Lambeth and Addington, she went abroad with us on Swiss High-Alp holidays, where, with a Parisian sense derived from her mother of what was suitable, she walked about on the paths through the meadows with an elegant stick fitted with a chamois-horn as a handle, and a spike on its ferule. From then onwards she kept up a most intimate and constant correspondence with them both, and there was nothing in her own life which she did not confide to one or other of them. My father delighted to consult her on points connected with Church policy and organization : if he had to write a charge to his clergy, he talked to her about it, taking long straying strolls with her, deep in discussion. It was a very shrewd and intelligent sympathy from outside that Duchess Adeline gave him, he wanted to know just what she could tell him, namely the ' lay view ' of movements in the Church. On his side he brought to her whole regions of interests outside herself.

This bond between the three of them, which grew ever stronger as the years went by, was first really woven when in the early days of their friendship she, while still Lady Tavistock, asked if she might bring to Lambeth a deputation of personal friends of hers who wanted his help and counsel in a matter which they all had very much at heart. He consented to receive them, and among them were the Duchess of Leeds, Marchionesses Tavistock, Bristol, Ailsa, Countesses Aberdeen, Zetland, Haddington, Stanhope, Ladies Mount-Temple, Muncaster, Harriet Ashley, Welby-Gregory, Mrs. Lowther (the late Speaker's mother) and Mrs. Reginald Talbot. They were, in fact, very fairly representative of the influential and serious women of the day, and the deputation was significant in two ways ; it was concerned with the break-down of the conventional proprieties of the seventies, and with that of the Victorian tradition that the first duty of women was to be blind and dumb. Women like these, ten years before, could never have taken part in a concerted movement of which the object was to disclose scandalous matter. But the ice of convention, which before had frozen them in, was now swiftly melting, and they broke through it. The whole story of the deputation, not a word of which ever became public, now violates no reasonable discretion, but to place it in its right setting a few words of explanation are necessary.

The Queen, it may be remembered, had completely retired after the Prince Consort's death ; almost her only public appearance had been when she attended the service of thanksgiving for the recovery of the Prince of Wales from typhoid ; she attended no State functions, and her influence on the social life of the upper classes was non-existent. She saw her Ministers, she visited her crofters, but she was otherwise invisible, and socially she was represented by the Prince of Wales. But while she remained thus utterly withdrawn, she kept in her own hands every atom of the more solid functions of the Crown, and neither consulted the Prince of Wales on affairs of State or diplomatic relations with foreign countries, nor paid the smallest attention to his views. Twenty-three years ago she had declared to her uncle, the King of the Belgians, that nobody, now that the Prince Consort was no longer there with his help and counsel, should be her adviser ; she knew precisely what his views were on every matter that concerned the realm, and she would undeviatingly follow them and not allow anybody to come between her and her people. She still adhered to that disastrous resolution, and instead of consulting her singularly intelligent son, and committing to him those diplomacies and administrations, which he, vividly in touch with the times, was so competent to conduct, and which he so sagaciously conducted as soon as he had the chance of doing so, she withheld from him everything of the kind. She refused

to let him be Governor-General of Canada or Viceroy
of Ireland, and to open a few docks and bazaars and lay
a few foundation-stones was not employment for a
mentally energetic man, now in the very prime of life,
who would have been of inestimable service in imperial
concerns ; she even saw in his visit to Ireland reasons
for regret that it coincided with the Punchestown
races.   It was therefore not only natural but laudable
that, denied the work to which he longed to devote
himself, he used his energies in enjoying himself, for
which also he had a very enviable aptitude.   He was
handsome, he was popular, he had tearing spirits, and
if he was not allowed to fill the proper office of a Prince
of Wales whose mother was in complete retirement,
but was shut out of all the State business of the country
he would someday rule, he must occupy himself by
making the most of a Prince's pleasures.   He had had
a most repressed and depressing youth, saddled and
bridled with tutors, and cut off by the well-meaning
unwisdom of his father from any free intercourse with
his contemporaries : he had been to no public school,
and at Oxford and at Cambridge, to both of which
Universities he went up as an undergraduate, he had
been made to live with his tutor in a private house,
instead of having rooms in college like everybody else.
It had been a regime to which no young man could
adapt himself without asserting his own rights to youth.
No doubt it was intended to rouse in him a due sense of
the responsibilities that would one day be his, but now,
when he was grown up and eminently capable of assuming some of them, he was denied all exercise of them,
and being debarred from being *bon ouvrier*, there was
really nothing for him to do except to be *bon vivant*.   To

him more than to anyone was due the break-up of the mid-Victorian social tradition of frozen pompous dignity, and all its repressions and reticences. He toppled over that futile forbidding old idol, he broke down the staid hedges that surrounded society, and beckoned in a quantity of lively and gay young persons with whom, as he was forbidden to work, he could play, and just as, towards the close of the fifteenth century, Columbus discovered America, so now Columbia discovered England, and came over in fleets of Mayflowers to receive the welcome of genial John Bull. And though into those exclusive coteries of New York no Jew was ever allowed to penetrate, Columbia found that she must not be so particular in England, for Jews were always among the closest of the Prince's friends.

And now for the business of this deputation of ladies for which these reactions were responsible. With the best and highest of motives they had come to ask my father if he could do nothing to stop the moral rot which, they affirmed, was ruining London. Girls newly ' come out,' they said, of high tone and upright intentions, were speedily corrupted by it, and what they had been brought up to regard as evil they soon regarded as natural and inevitable ; young married women had no standard of morality at all, and the centre of the mischief was the Marlborough House set. They wanted my father to start a sort of moral mission for women of their class and to hold devotional meetings for them at Lambeth, thus creating a powerful and influential nucleus of those who aimed at high ideals and would not tolerate the looseness of life which was becoming general. They thought it would give a great impetus to the movement if the Princess of Wales would come to these meetings : it was no use trying to get the sympathy of the Queen, for that would have no effect as ' she was not smart enough.' Finally they all agreed that my father should talk to the Prince about the harm that was going on ' for he would listen to no one else.'

It was a situation which required thinking about before he could make up his mind exactly what to do. Many of these ladies were friends of his, and he had nothing but the warmest sympathy with the object of their deputation—namely, the setting of a higher moral tone in society. He was quite at their service there, and since their desire was that he should hold devotional meetings at Lambeth he at once instituted them, and from that year, the first of his Archiepiscopate, he annually held a series of these, till the time of his death. There was a short service followed by an address, and the attendance filled Lambeth Chapel to overflowing. But as regards telling the Prince of Wales that he and his friends were setting a bad example, that was a very different affair. He was a friend of the Prince's, all he had heard was of the nature of vague gossip, and to go to the Prince of Wales and tell him he must mend his ways, seemed to him an unwarrantable intrusion into his private affairs, though when a few years later a certain scandal became public, he had not the smallest hesitation in telling the Prince what he thought about it. Besides, this was not, to his mind, the right way to set about raising the tone of London life, and he suggested a better one at the first of these meetings which took place within a week or two. He addressed his ladies on the subject of sincerity, and the pith of his advice, as recorded in his diary, was ' Don't meddle, or try to improve any-one, but lead your own life well yourself.'

Then there was the question of whether the Princess of Wales would attend these meetings, and she was asked if she would. Before she could give an answer to this, she felt she must consult the Queen, for devotional meetings were outside the general routine of royal engagements. The Queen did not like the idea, for in spite of her own firm religious convictions and the faith of which she was the Defender, religion was not a thing to be mixed up with life, nor could she, by any possible elasticity of terms, be called devotional. To go to church or chapel on Sunday mornings with unfailing regularity, to ask God's blessing on launched ships, docks, regimental colours and foundation-stones, to attend all family christenings, marriages, funerals and anniversary services, comprised the sum of public religious observances. She indicated her attitude to one in whom she much confided with some vexation. ' I can't understand,' she said, ' why princesses should want to go to Lambeth meetings. It's all sacerdotal. I can't think what it's all about.' She was impatient of such notions. Of course she went to church on Sunday morning, but to want to go on a week-day to Lambeth Chapel for purposes of prayer and devotion was ' most extraordinary.' We may guess that she regarded my father as the leader in some sacerdotal conspiracy, and for quite a long period she ceased to write to him in the second person, and sign herself, ' ever yours affectionately,' but became ' The Queen.' Or had she somehow got to know that the conspiring ladies did not think her smart enough to be of any use ?

CHAPTER VI

THREE MONUMENTAL FIGURES

THE experience of going back to a house familiar in childhood but not seen since, and finding it strangely dwindled in size, is a common one, but one that is easily accounted for. It took more steps for a child to traverse a passage, the door handle was on a level with the face, the bed of seeding asparagus in the garden was a thicket in which it was possible to be completely hidden, a table draped in a dust-sheet was a cave of ample proportions for the domestic comfort of several brigands. All is a question of relativity : these things were proportionately bigger to a child than they are to an adult. And when it comes to mental impressions made on youth or early manhood by eminent folk, there may be some similar reason to account for their appearing to the memory (since we cannot actually revisit those years as we can a house of childhood) of greater psychical stature than the corresponding eminent folk of the day. But the illusion, if it is one, is absolutely convincing, and nothing can make me believe that a person like Mr. Gladstone was not of some higher voltage of power than more recent Prime Ministers.

I once attended some political meeting addressed by him, and saw there, so I believe, a greater demonstration of sheer force than can be equalled to-day by any politician. He was being heckled by one of his audience as to the views he was then expressing which seemed (as indeed they were) to be flatly contradictory of those which he had propounded with no less emphasis and authority a year or two before. He could not get on with his speech : the interrupter was surrounded by his friends, he was persistent, he had a loud voice, he was sitting close to the platform, and he was ready with chapter and verse to support his contention. Mr. Gladstone bore it for a little, but suddenly he had enough of him. He pointed at him, thrusting out his arm as if stabbing him, with furious face and fierce imperious gesture. Three times there shot out that menacing hand, and the heckler could not stand against it. He sat down and thereafter was dumb. Then Mr. Gladstone, in a voice quivering with indignant energy, said ' It would be tedious to compare what I may have happened to say a year ago, or perhaps two, with what I have the honour to be saying to you now.' He made no explanation nor attempted to prove with that incomparable ingenuity of his, that though a year ago (or perhaps two) he had seemed to say precisely the opposite, he had quite clearly meant precisely the same, for it was not worth while. It would be tedious ; and so he went on with his speech without any further interruption. He was the stronger : instead of arguing he knocked the man out by pointing a finger charged with irresistible force. Indeed one might say that the rash fellow had touched that awful dynamo and his mind was instantly electrocuted.

All that Mr. Gladstone did was charged with that terrific voltage. I went more than once to Hawarden when, after taking my degree at Cambridge, I was

archaeologically employed in examining the north wall
of the city of Chester, into which had been built a quantity
of tombstones from a Roman cemetery.   There I had
the good fortune to discover some inscribed monuments
to men who had served in the Tenth Legion, ' Valeria
Victrix,' of which no record in Britain had hitherto come
to light, and I took over to Hawarden, to show to Mr.
Gladstone, blotting-paper ' squeezes ' of some of them.
(The method of making these squeezes is to spread a
sheet of damp blotting-paper over the inscription of
which you desire a facsimile and then to tap it gently
with a clothes-brush, until the blotting-paper has
moulded itself into the lettering : when dry, it thus
becomes a portable cast of the stone.)   Mr. Gladstone
was enormously interested in the discovery of this legion
having been in England, though it was only the minutest
contribution to the details of the Roman occupation
seventeen hundred years ago, and he got down some
books of military inscriptions for reference.   But equally
fiery was his advice about making squeezes. The
blotting-paper, he said, ought certainly to be laid down
dry on the face of the inscription, and then be sprinkled :
otherwise it was liable to tear.   For the same reason it
should be left on the stone till it was dry again : otherwise damp fragments might stick to it, and the squeeze
be spoilt.   I felt that Mr. Gladstone had devoted his
whole life to making squeezes and that he occupied
his leisure only in conducting the affairs of the nation.
Though Mrs. Gladstone had come to remind him that
lunch was ready, he would not go till he had conjectured
about a few missing letters in one of these inscriptions :
the thing might have been a dispatch from Downing
Street which must be deciphered and dealt with at once :

otherwise some hideous European imbroglio would
follow. And there was the table at which his political
work was done, and close by the ' Homer-table ' where
he found coolness and refreshment when hot with
polemics.

At lunch there was a discussion about the dismal task
of packing a bag, when one was leaving by an early train
in the morning ; the sponge was wet from the traveller's
ablutions and it always oozed dampness into neighbouring linen. Then came the oracle : ' You none of you
know how to pack your sponge. The only way of
packing a sponge is first to wrap it up in your bath towel,
and then to stamp upon it.' Surely he had never done
anything all his life but pack sponges in bags for early
morning travel ! On another occasion he had retired
after some such oracle into remote regions of his own
again, while the table-talk went on. Clever women was
the subject now, and it was generally agreed that my
mother was the cleverest woman in England. Out he
came again from his meditations. ' No, you're wrong,'
he said, ' she's the cleverest woman in Europe.' Everything that he was engaged in for the moment was of
supreme importance : it was the same with his back-
gammon, with which he relaxed himself in the evening.
But relaxed ? He rattled and threw the dice, as if he
was playing with the devil for his own immortal soul,
and was temporarily engaged in a war with the powers
of darkness. One afternoon he drove me to St. Deiniol's,
the library of his own books which he was arranging
with the purpose of bequeathing them to the clergy of
the Church of Wales, which he hoped to disestablish.
That was exceedingly like him : his conscience told
him that the Church should be disendowed, and in

anticipation of that he began to endow it personally with
a magnificent library, for the clergy must have access to
sources of learning. A pony-carriage came round, and
I was aware that he was going to drive himself. Before
getting in he went round to the pony's head and peered
at him. ' He's a beast,' he said, ' I must get a heavier
whip.' Out he came again with this more formidable
weapon, and off we went, he the intrepid charioteer of
something over eighty years. He whacked the pony
over the rump, and talked about the manner in which
men who had retired from active work in their profession should employ themselves. He wanted to know
what I thought my father would do if ever he retired
from the See of Canterbury, and chuckled when I told
him he would certainly apply for the post of librarian
at St. Deiniol's.

Always there was this huge concentration of force ;
purpose at white heat roared like a furnace in every
action of his life. When once he had convinced himself
on any subject, it ceased to be his opinion, and became
a cosmic truth, which it was the duty of every right-
minded person to uphold. Just as the only method of
packing up a damp sponge was to begin by stamping on
it (he being merely the exponent of this dazzling truth
to an ignorant world), so he was convinced, and said so,
that the will of the English people was set on giving
Home Rule to Ireland, and that he was the appointed
instrument to accomplish their will for them : God
gave him his health and vitality for that. Thus his conscience was invariably clear of personal ambition : he
was working not for his own idea but for some great
cause external to him. Never, so Mrs. Gladstone told
my mother, did the estrangements and execrations of

those who had been his friends cause him to say ' I wish I had never done it ! ' He might regret the bitterness he had aroused, but he never regretted those measures which had caused it.

This remorseless inflexibility was one of the reasons why in his official relation with the Queen he so often irritated her. He always paid her the most profound respect, but his deference to her person did not include the slightest deference to her statecraft and nothing she said influenced him in the least when his mind was made up, for he knew he was right, whereas she, on those many occasions when their views differed, was equally certain that he was wrong. Though she maintained an impeccable impartiality in politics and would never attempt to resist the will of her people, she was a thorough Tory at heart, and regarded him as an enemy to Church and State, and thus an enemy to the throne, for he had disestablished the Irish Church and now he wanted to give Home Rule to Ireland. It was therefore with the most unfeigned pleasure that she saw the fall of his last ministry in 1894, and she commented on it privately to my father with remarkable frankness : this was perfectly correct on her part for he officially had no politics any more than she. ' Mr. Gladstone has gone out, disappeared all in a moment,' she gleefully observed, ' his last two ministries have been failures, indeed his last three. Mr. Gladstone takes up one or two things, and then nothing else interests him. He cares nothing for foreign affairs which are always essential to England, knows nothing of foreign affairs, and is exceedingly distrusted on the Continent. They have thought he might abandon Egypt at any moment. He will not attend to any suggestion but his own mind's. He does not care

what you say, does not attend.   I have told him two or
three facts of which he was quite ignorant of foreign
tone and temper.   It makes no difference.   He only says
" Is that so ?   Really ! " '   Indeed it must have been
most irritating, for the Queen had an unfailing fund of
first-rate common sense, and her very long experience
of foreign affairs made her a far more dispassionate
observer than Gladstone on the war-path for an idea.
Besides, she happened to be Queen of England, and it was
surely reasonable that she should expect to be listened to.

There was another reason why she disliked him, and
when that was made known to him his reception of it
was characteristic of the real greatness of the man and
his uprightness.   There had been from time to time
odious and unfounded gossip of the falsest sort, arising
from his interest in the deplorable women on the streets.
He used to talk to them when he walked back at
night, as he so often did, from the House, trying to
persuade them to go home.   He even brought one, with
Mrs. Gladstone's full knowledge and approval, into his
house for a night's shelter.   Very possibly he behaved
imprudently, but such imprudence was due to his own
consciousness of his high motive, and no one who knew
him could fail to be aware of his absolute moral rectitude.
The gossip had somehow reached the Queen's ears, and
she hinted at what she had heard to Lord Beaconsfield,
who, at the least, did not tell her that there could be no
truth in it, but, for whatever reason, let her continue to
suspect ugly things of him.   Mr. Gladstone was speaking one day about the Queen's coldness and unfriendli-
ness towards him to the late Lord Stanmore who was an
old and valued friend of his, and Lord Stanmore thought
he had better tell him that the Queen suspected him

of immoral behaviour with common women. And Mr. Gladstone's answer was one that could only have been made by a man of truly great nature. ' If the Queen thinks that of me,' he said, ' she is quite right to treat me as she does.'

That was his scale : he was like that all through. He had in his late years to undergo an operation on his eyes, which was performed by the oculist Mr. Nettleship, and after it was over the light had to be kept from him for a few days. During this time Mr. Nettleship examined his eyes to see whether the result of the operation was all he hoped, and was not quite satisfied. He said nothing to Mr. Gladstone, but went to his daughter, Mrs. Drew, and told her that he was afraid the operation had not been as successful as he had hoped. They settled that Mr. Gladstone had better know, and she undertook to tell him. So she went into the room where he sat in the dark, and broke it to him. At once he replied ' How dreadful for Mr. Nettleship ! '

Whatever entered his mind (and what did not ?) was subjected to his fiery scrutiny, and came out molten with the heat of it. Dining one night at Lambeth, he discussed ' George Eliot's Life,' lately published, with my mother, and passionately exclaimed ' It is not a Life at all. It is a Reticence, in three volumes.' Presently it was time for the ladies to move, but for a while she could not stir, for Mr. Gladstone was denouncing some view of a problem as presented in this Reticence. Eventually she was obliged to get up, and he sprang to his feet with her and summed it all up. ' It is disgusting,' he proclaimed, ' and repulsive, and revolting.' The more tepidly minded man of to-day would have been content to say ' horrid ' and leave it at that, but such

undocumented disapproval would not do for him.
Besides, each of his epithets was deliberate; ' It is disgusting, because such a notion nauseates you ; it is
repulsive, because you instinctively recoil from it : it is
revolting, because——' I forget why it was revolting,
but the reason, I am sure, was logical.   Whatever came
within the wide circle of his interest was to be taken
seriously, he pounced on it, he pronounced upon it.
He even took ' Robert Elsmere ' seriously, and devoted
to its discussion a solid article in the *Nineteenth Century*,
in which he examined it as if it had been a heretical
document of the Early Church.   It was believed that
Mr. James Knowles, the editor of the magazine, paid
him £250 for this article ; that seemed in those days an
almost incredibly large sum for even a Prime Minister
to receive for a magazine article, though to subsequent
politicians who, deprived of political leadership, have
devoted their talents to writing, it would seem a very
paltry remuneration.

In that tremendous mind there was not much room
for lightnesses.   Jocular conversation perished in his
presence, it was like the prattle of a brook which the
torrent of molten lava streaming out from the mountain
side silenced and turned into a whiff of steam before
it really touched it.   But occasionally there was a lull.
One night, for instance, my father and mother were
engaged to dine with the Gladstones, and Mrs. Gladstone had written the invitation on paper stamped
with the die of ' Dollis Hill ' (a house belonging
to Lord Aberdeen, some five miles out of London,
which he frequently lent to Mr. Gladstone), forgetting
that before the date of the dinner they would have
moved up to their house in Carlton House Terrace.

The evening happened to be that of Derby Day, and naturally assuming that, as the invitation came from Dollis Hill, the dinner was to be there, my father and mother drove out there on this hot June evening, much enjoying the air. But on arrival they found that the house was in the hands of a caretaker and that the Gladstones had gone up to London the day before. There was nothing to be done but to get back into the carriage for another pleasant drive of three-quarters of an hour (those were the days before motors existed) and go to Carlton House Terrace. Meantime the rest of the dinner-party had assembled, and had waited and had waited, but still they came not. Mrs. Gladstone was sure (quite sure, for sometimes she was a little vague about such things) that she had invited them and that they had accepted. Mr. Gladstone got rather fussed, and after a full half-hour had elapsed, they settled that they must go in to dinner without them. And as Mr. Gladstone gave his arm to his lady, he turned to the room in general. 'We must not forget that it is Derby Day,' he said. 'His Grace has evidently been delayed by the congested traffic on his way back from Epsom.'

In spite of their strong antagonisms on matters connected with the Church, he and my father had the greatest respect and liking for each other. Though Mr. Gladstone had disestablished the Irish Church, was hoping to do the same with the Welsh Church, and would have liked to see the English Church disestablished also, he was a devout churchman, and had its welfare most keenly at heart, thinking that these drastic operations were for its good. On all such subjects as the appointment of bishops he invariably consulted my father, and adopted his nominee ; a further bond between them was

the study of the classics.   It was to Hawarden that my
father and mother came on the last evening of his life ;
he had been making a tour in Ireland, on a pastoral visit
to the churches which Mr. Gladstone had disestablished
there, and the two sat up late together on that Saturday
night, deep in classical and ecclesiastical topics.   My
mother had got to bed when my father came up, and as
he undressed he came in and out between his dressing-
room and the bedroom, full of the delightful talk he had
had with his host.   Then a curious thing happened.
A woman, in a room not far away, heard loud sounds of
knocking from my father's room ; it vaguely occurred
to her that perhaps he had lost the key of some despatch
box which he wanted to open, and was hammering at it.
After a little the knocking ceased, and she thought no
more of it.   Simultaneously a servant had heard exactly
the same thing, also localizing the noise as coming from
my father's room.   He started to tell my father's valet,
thinking that he might be wanted, but did not rouse
him, as the knocking ceased.   The matter was alluded
to at breakfast next morning, but neither my father nor
mother had heard anything whatever.   An hour or so
later, they walked across to church, he apparently in
excellent health and spirits.   He stood up for the
exhortation, knelt for the confession, and during it sank
back and died.

   The next day the rest of us arrived, and I went in to
see Mr. Gladstone in his study.   He spoke of my father
warmly and weightily, and soon he said, ' I remember
when you were here once before, you brought me some
very interesting squeezes of tombstones of soldiers in the
Tenth Legion.'   That was over four years before, and yet
that colossal memory had it all docketed and available.

During these years of the eighties and early nineties, when so many of the stereotyped values were altering, and so much of the old coinage of social laws and customs was being called in and put back into the melting pot to be minted anew and to receive the stamp of fresh images and superscriptions, three great figures seem to stand out. They were like rocks of granite which the surge and stress of the new tides were powerless to batter or undermine. Gladstone was the first of these, the other two were Queen Victoria and Tennyson, and all three seemed antique and imperishable. Tennyson had been Laureate since 1850; he was a peak much shrouded in mist, and the clouds were thick round that Parnassus. In spite of Mr. Swinburne, who had written some biting criticisms about his ' Idylls of the King,' he was still, in the opinion of a large and intelligent majority, the only authentic incarnation of English poetry, and it was generally considered that when Mr. Gladstone recommended the Queen to crown his laurels with a coronet, the House of Lords was more honoured by his entering it than he. He was recluse, he did not appear much in London, but a somewhat famous occasion of the sort was when he attended a garden party at Marlborough House. He was there seen by Mr. Oscar Browning, a Fellow of King's College, Cambridge, who had an amiable and insatiable passion for intercourse with the eminent. So he went up and shook hands with him, and as the poet seemed not to have the slightest idea who he was, he introduced himself by saying, ' I am Browning.' Tennyson must have thought that he was impersonating Robert Browning, so he merely replied, ' No, you're not,' and seemed disinclined to listen to any explanations.

This brusqueness was rather a way of his; at another function of the kind near his country house at Aldworth, there was a young lady of the neighbourhood the dream of whose romantic soul was to be introduced to him. Her heart's desire was granted her, and they sat down side by side on a garden seat. Dead silence fell: she was far too rapt and reverent and overpowered to speak, and he had nothing to say. Suddenly he found something to say, and he pronounced these appalling words, ' Your stays creak.'

Nearly swooning with horror and deeply hurt at this absolutely unfounded accusation, she fled from him without a word, and recovered her composure as best she might by converse with less alarming folk. Presently she observed that he was stalking her; she tripped from one gay group to another, and always the poet followed her, like a bloodhound on her trail. The dream of her soul had turned into a nightmare: certainly he was after her, and who could tell what he would say next? She dodged and she doubled, she hid behind trees, but she could not shake him off. Then she made a dreadful tactical error, for she scurried up a long path in the kitchen-garden hoping to distance him beyond pursuit, only to find that she had entered a *cul-de-sac* bordered by cabbages and asparagus and closed at the far end by the potting-shed. She fumbled at the latch, intending to hide herself from the dreadful presence, but it was locked, and now he closed in on her. ' I beg your pardon,' he said, ' it was my braces.'

Again, a certain Doctor of Music had set one of his poems as a Cantata, and went down to see the author in order to play him some melodious morsels. Tennyson had no taste for music, but there was nothing he more enjoyed than reading aloud, with deep emotion in a hoarse rumble, his own verse, and so it came about that instead of the composer playing his music to the author, the author read his own poem to the composer. That was very pleasant, though it was not quite what the composer had in view. But he was very appreciative, and at a pause in the reading, he said, ' That's an awfully jolly stanza.' Tennyson eyed him. ' Don't say " awfully," ' he said. ' What shall I say, then ? ' asked the composer. ' Say " bloody," ' said Tennyson.

This disconcerting brusqueness, so unlike the smooth sweetness of his work, was coupled with a theatrical avoidance of the hordes of inquisitive worshippers who, he felt sure, were for ever scheming to catch a glimpse of him, but possibly he did not really dislike the pilgrimages of the devout. For if, when walking on the cliffs at Freshwater, he observed some stranger approaching, he would pull his hat over his eyes, and cast his cloak about his mouth, but it was noticed that if the pilgrim (he was sure it was a pilgrim) paid no attention whatever to him, and went whistling on his way, instead of being rooted to the spot and reverently saluting, Tennyson seemed very little gratified at the success of his shrouding of himself, and would make some rather acid comment about great men not being recognized. Like Queen Victoria, he liked being flattered, if it was done to his taste, and just as Lord Beaconsfield called her the Fairy, so Mr. Alfred Austin, who succeeded Tennyson in the Laureateship, used always to address him, so he told me himself, as ' Bard ' or ' Immortal Bard.' He once gave me a great discourse about his visits to Tennyson, but his memories of them entirely consisted in what he had

said to Immortal Bard, and though that was rich and
precious, I should have liked to have heard a little more
of what Immortal Bard said to him.   Perhaps he said
nothing: he was able to say nothing for long periods
together.

A pleasant link between the author of so much noble
verse and the lover of less exalted rhymes was his affection
for the form known as the 'Limerick.'   He liked its terse-
ness, he also, it is idle to deny, took a sort of school-boy
pleasure in the hectic situations which it sometimes
disclosed.   Little tales of the same sort pleased him: he
could tell them himself with considerable gusto.   In this
connection I cannot forbear to recount a story which,
though I will not vouch for its authenticity, I give on the
authority of Sir Edmund Gosse.   He and my father were
talking about Tennyson: they were contrasting him
with Dickens; Dickens, they agreed, was not very
markedly Puritanical in his life, whereas Tennyson was
Galahad.   But Dickens abhorred any sort of coarseness
in conversation, whereas Tennyson had no great objection to it.   Then said my father:

'Yes, that's quite true.   I went out for a walk with
him the last time I ever saw him, and he suddenly said to
me, " Shall I tell you a bawdy story ? "   Of course I said,
" No, certainly not." '

Their talk went on for a little, till there came a pause.
Gosse broke it with a touch of that impish humour of his.

'I feel sure Your Grace heard that story ! ' he said.

My father was a little off his guard.

'Well, it wasn't so very bad after all,' he replied.

Swinburne shared Tennyson's taste, but his friend,
Mr. Watts-Dunton, must be consulted first.   'Shall
I tell our visitor about the man of Peru ? ' he once asked

Mr. Watts-Dunton. But no. ' I think that goes a little too far, Algernon,' was the reply, and so the doings of the man of Peru remained shrouded in a discreet mystery.

Throughout his life Tennyson was abnormally short-sighted, and the genesis of that sonorous line in ' Locksley Hall,' ' Let the great world spin for ever down the ringing grooves of change ' is an odd instance of his deficiency. In the very early days of railways he came across, for the first time, one of the newly laid lines of rails, and did not perceive that they were metals laid upon the earth, on which the wheels of the trains ran, but thought that they were parallel lines of grooves cut in it. The mistaken image sank into his mind, and he used it in his poem. But what did that matter ? A fine line of poetry was worth more than the truth about the railway line.

The third of those imperishable peaks, round which was wrapped an even denser mist than round Tennyson's Parnassus, was Queen Victoria. Her long seclusion, as we have seen, had at one time been extremely un-popular, but, as the years went on, another effect of this invisibility asserted itself. Though so seldom seen, and never in the pomp and splendour of Monarchy, she became something august and mysterious. She began to get a hold first on the imagination and then on the hearts of her people, and it was with a sense of deep reverence and affection that the Empire awaited the year of her Jubilee in 1887, when the whole of her subjects, with delegates from the far-flung lands, would give thanks to God for the fifty years of her glorious reign, and she would once more inspire the nation with that thrill of

romantic loyalty which had been hers when half a century
ago the slim girl received its homage.   She was growing
old now, she was stout, she was lame, and vain were the
efforts to induce her to put on robes of State : the last
emissary to attempt it was the Princess of Wales, who
came out from her mother-in-law's presence with a
humiliated mien, saying that she had never had such a
snub in her life.   My father submitted to her the order
of the proposed service ; she 'admired' the prayers,
and thought that a '*short*' portion of Scripture should
be read, or a Psalm chanted.   But the whole thing must
not be too long, 'for the weather will probably be hot,
and the Queen feels faint if it is hot.'

I had come up from school for this day, and drove to
the Abbey with my father.   He had forgotten to give
his coachman the carriage-pass, which would admit him
within the cordon of police and troops through which,
coming from Lambeth, he had to pass, and a polite but
quite firm inspector refused to let his carriage proceed :
nobody without a carriage-pass was allowed to penetrate.
On which, with an engaging smile, he leaned out, and
said, ' They can't begin till I get there,' so all was well.
The Abbey was already packed, and the tiers of seats
that rose high in the transepts were crammed to the top.
Then from outside came the sound of the saluting guns
and a murmur that rose to a roar, as the Queen drew
near with the princes on horseback for her retinue.
The whole Abbey rose and up the nave came the kings
and the queens and the princes and princesses, and went
to their seats on this side and on that of the throne.
And after the jewels and the robes and the uniforms
had flashed by, there moved up one solitary little
figure in a black satin dress with a white front and a white

bonnet with a band of black velvet.   How right she had been to come like that, and not listen to those who would have her in robes of State.   She was Queen of England and Empress of India, and she was mother and mother-in-law and grand-mother of that regal company, and there she was, a little old lady coming to church to thank God for the long years in which she had ruled her people. She listened once more to her husband's ' Te Deum,' and the hand that held her book trembled, for she remembered how he had played it to her on the organ he had built at Windsor.   Then when the service was over, her family and the kings and queens, her brothers and sisters in Royalty, came to make their obeisance to her and kiss her hand, and as they rose she kissed them on the cheek.   Long and affectionately did she cling to her eldest daughter, the Crown Princess Frederick of Germany, for she and her husband, the noblest figure in the Abbey, had come to England not only to attend this celebration, but to seek medical advice for a persistent hoarseness in his throat, and a fear, undefined as yet, lurked in the shadow of his imminent throne.   The first anniversary of this day had not come round before he had become Emperor of Germany, and his son had succeeded him.

The Queen had looked forward to that day as a frightful ordeal, and had a fit of weeping before she could nerve herself to set out on that triumphant drive to the Abbey, but having faced it, she never went back again into an unbroken seclusion.   She opened the Imperial Institute ; the little black figure rose in her box, she addressed the vast assembly in that clear quiet voice which penetrated into every corner like a ray of light, and, when she had done, she made three low curtsies to her people.   She opened the Tower Bridge, and the miles of streets through which she drove were a roar of welcome to her.   My mother, I remember, attended the function, rather pleased with herself and her smart landau with its pair of black horses and her coachman in a wig.   But that little bubble of pride was soon pricked for her, and she was very properly put in her place by a ribald voice in the crowd which shouted, ' 'Ullo ! 'Ere comes the Queen's cook ! ' . . . And the Queen enjoyed these appearances very much herself, recording with a delightful touch of regal vanity that ' Bertie and Alix ' never evoked half the enthusiasm that she did.   She had kindled the imagination of her people, as no other English monarch perhaps had ever done, and the throne had never been held in such love and reverence.

CHAPTER VII

CAMBRIDGE

IN this year of the Queen's first Jubilee the horizons of school broadened out for me into those of Cambridge. I followed my elder brother to King's College which, not many years before, had been exclusively a college of Etonians : boys from the Foundation at Eton became, without competition from outside, scholars of King's, and in due course Fellows, as long as they remained unmarried, for life. Indeed from the age of twelve or thereabouts, they lived on the bounty of the pious Founder, King Henry VI, in quiet scholastic competence, most of them without duties, to the end of their days. They had their rooms provided for them, their Commons and their dinner, and a salary of several hundred pounds a year, because they got a scholarship at Eton in their early teens. The system gave them the leisure of the lilies of the field, freed them from any care concerning the necessities and moderate luxuries of life, and while they could thus devote their whole time to scholarly research, they could equally well devote it to the gentle art of doing nothing at all. If we look at the lists of the men whom King Henry's bounty enabled for centuries to give themselves up to scholarship, it must be confessed that the vast sums thus expended had not yielded any very notable dividends. Tutors who

continued to hand on the torch of learning to generations
of undergraduates received extra emoluments for their
work, but for the rest there was no need to work at all.
Young men came up yearly from Eton, and in time grew
into old men in these celibate surroundings, and it was
not to be wondered at that there were some very queer
old men among them, not Victorian at all, but belonging
to some far earlier epoch, strange mastodons and plesio-
sauri, learned lizards in human form, with caps and
gowns.   One of these, for instance, not so long before
my time, had lived since his earliest manhood in a set
of Fellows' rooms from which he never emerged except
in the evening gloaming.   He then shuffled out on to
the big lawn, with a stick in his hand, and he prodded
with it at the worms in the grass, muttering to himself,
' Ah, damn ye : ye haven't got me yet.'   He said with
Dr. Faustus, ' This feeds my soul,' and after this
psychical refreshment, he returned to his rooms till the
same hour next day.

The throwing open of King's to other schools and
the abolition of these life-fellowships caused a dwindling
in the number of such, until they finally perished.   It is
impossible not to regret their complete extinction, but
the modernizing of the College implied that there was
no longer any place for them.   Their extinction was
brought about gradually : those who held life-fellowships under the old Order were not deprived of them,
and some odd persons still lingered, not quite like anything else ever seen, degenerate as mastodons, but bearing some of the marks of type.   One of these, till the
young gentlemen of the College set to work to modernize
him, according to the standards of 1887, was certainly
of an older civilization.   Though he had no truck, as

far as was known, with worms, he, too, seldom appeared
in the open blaze of day, but at precisely three minutes
to five of the afternoon he came out from his rooms
which none entered save his bed-maker, and crossed the
same grass as the worm-poker to attend chapel. It
happened that two of these young devils were looking
out from the screen of their window-boxes at this
moment, and one of them began, quite casually, to
whistle. Instantly Mr. Mozely stopped, but on the
cessation of the whistle started off again. Then rather
less casually and observing his movements the whistler
whistled more piercingly, and again Mr. Mozely stopped.
A definite suspicion concerning cause and effect now
entered the brains of the watchers, and they continued
to whistle. Mr. Mozely could face the music no longer,
and instead of going to chapel went back to his
rooms.

The two proceeded to verify their theory that the
sound of whistling prevented his going to chapel, and
it was soon proved beyond all possible doubt that if one
whistled he went home. Any student of human nature
(and where is a nobler calling?) must want to know
more of so rare a type, and they left their cards in his
letter-box. Mr. Mozely duly returned their formal visit,
and the ice being thus broken, they asked him to tea.
Other young devils happened to drop in while he was
there, and they were all introduced to him. Not long
afterwards they all received invitations to go to tea with
Mr. Mozely, but only one of them could manage to go.
He found a table with a white linen cloth, laid for eight
persons, with knives and forks for each : at one end
there were teapot and milk-jug and sugar-basin and
eight cups and saucers, at the other was a cold leg of

mutton and a pile of plates. As nobody else appeared,
Mr. Mozely suggested that we should sit down : he
poured out tea, and I cut the cold mutton. As we
talked, it was discovered that he played the violin, and
there was just time for a tune before evening chapel.
Thereafter there came to him an extraordinary blossom-
ing : his stem shot up like that of the flowering aloe.
There were more tea-parties, there was more playing
of the violin, and before long he played a solo at a
College smoking concert. Then the madness of
modernity got hold of him, and though well advanced
in life he married a girl who played in the band of the
Salvation Army and went to live in Guernsey, because
there was no bother about vaccination laws in that
island.

Then there was Mr. J. E. Nixon : though he was of
the earlier day and held a life-fellowship, he was no
recluse but wildly sociable. He had realized that the
old order was changing and had enthusiastically gone
out to meet the new. He was Dean of the College, he
was lecturer in Latin, and for sheer experimentalism he
was farther ahead in the van of progress than the most
extravagant of modern pioneers, and had more new
notions every day than most people have in a lifetime.
He held glee-meetings once a week after Hall, at which
he sang Victorian catches and madrigals arranged for
male voices. Dr. Ford, the present Dean of York, sat
by his elbow, and with him sang the tenor part, while
Nixon beat time (like my mother at Lincoln) with a
paper-knife. Faster and faster under the intoxication
of the music rang out our melodies, until the paper-
knife flew from his hand, like Excalibur, and crashed
into the fender. Between the songs he handed round

hot buttered buns, anchovy toast, Borneo cigars, and Tintara wine.

In person he was small: a short honey-coloured beard framed his chin, he had one glass eye, and only one hand: in place of the other he had a tight black kid glove (I think pneumatic, for it sometimes seemed to be deflated) which was attached to his wrist, and protruded from the sleeve of his tail-coat. But these physical deficiencies were no handicap to his activity: rather, they seemed to stimulate it, as if he was gallantly bent on showing how much could be done with how little. He rode a tricycle intrepidly about the traffic-crowded streets of Cambridge, he played lawn tennis on fine summer afternoons in the Fellows' Gardens, taking down there a small black bag containing tennis-balls and sealing-wax and pieces of string (for there was no telling whether some emergency would not arise when string or sealing-wax would be urgently required) and Borneo cigars. When he served he lodged a ball in the crook of his arm, and by some unique jerk of his body, tossed it into the air, and gave it a savage underhand blow. Everything he did was performed at top speed, and he generally dropped something. His mind whirled incessantly in a maelstrom of new dodges for counting the attendance of the undergraduates in chapel, for registering votes at Fellows' meetings, for ensuring regular supplies of toilet paper in such places as the dons needed them, or for ascertaining the speed of the train in which he was travelling. He was also (God knows how or why) a Gresham lecturer in London, and I once went up from Cambridge in order to attend one of these discourses. The subject was either 'Poetry in Rhetoric' or 'Rhetoric in Poetry'; but the course of the lecture

did not make it clear which it was, and there has been
complete confusion in my mind about it ever since.

On Sunday in May week at Cambridge, there was
always an immense crush to get into King's Chapel for
afternoon service, and in preparation for this Nixon
printed a small leaflet ' On the Management of Large
Crowds,' which he distributed to the vergers, so that they
should know what to do.   The crowd this year was more
unwieldy than ever, and Nixon popped out of the organ-
loft where he had been observing the management of it,
and cried in a lamentable voice, ' If there is any more
shoving, there will be no Divine Service at all.'   As a
teacher of Latin prose he was chiefly remarkable for
correcting the exercises shown up to him, partly in red
and partly in purple ink.   Red ink indicated grammatical errors, purple ink errors of construction or something of the sort.   But he was not very clear about it
himself, and he could not always read what he had
written, and sometimes he had evidently dipped his pen
first in red ink and then in purple so that there was no
clue to the nature of the correction, for it was of a rich
lake tone, and denoted neither grammar nor construction. . . . I do not pretend to reproduce these details
with literal accuracy, but I will vouch for their impressionistic truth.   The world to Mr. Nixon consisted of
Latin prose, lawn tennis, and glee-singing, and contained
besides numbers of problems to which he sought solution : how to turn envelopes inside out and use them
again, how to cut pencils without blackening the forefinger, how to stop a draught from an ill-fitting window
sash.   Each of these was as bright as a new pin, and he
never succeeded in picking any of them up.

But the really outstanding figure of that time, not

among the dons of King's only, but of the whole of Cambridge, was Oscar Browning : he would have been notorious and absurd and remarkable anywhere, and if he had ever succeeded in getting into Parliament he must have made a mark of some unusual kind there, as surely as he had made it everywhere else. He was a tragic instance of such stupid jokes as Nature plays when, after she has formed by means of cosmic pressures and secular incandescences some noble gem, she proceeds with a silly giggle, to plant a fatal flaw in the very heart of it. He was a genius flawed by abysmal fatuity. No one had finer gifts than he : he could think on big lines, he could strike out great ideas, he had wit, he had the power of planning largely and constructively, he had courage and a high scorn of ridicule, it was impossible to come into contact with him without being conscious of great intellectual force. But it was impossible not to be aware that he was a buffoon. As an Eton master, before he came to take up his fellowship again and reside at King's, he had been the first to grasp the fact that boys had minds, and that public-school education should not merely consist of loading those minds with irrelevant knowledge about Greek particles, but of opening them to the reception of ideas, and of teaching them how to think. His colleagues of that day looked with traditional suspicion on such crazy notions, and instantly the flaw began to manifest itself, for he always took any opposition to his ideas as a personal attack, and instead of defending them, defended himself. He was immensely liked by his house and his pupils, he treated them with the warmest friendliness, he had Sunday concerts for them, he had social gatherings in which, without the least encouragement to priggishness, he interested them in topics of history and politics. But with a fatal silliness he made pets of those who were handsome and attractive, and the head master, Dr. Hornby, who looked with the darkest suspicion on everything he did, took advantage of a technical breach which he had committed in the school rules concerning the number of boys in his house, and dismissed him.

He then took up residence at King's as a life-fellow, and became a unique institution. He was appointed a lecturer in history : probably there was no epoch on which he was not prepared to discourse without any preparation. He was very inaccurate, for he never was a scholar, nor took the trouble to learn anything thoroughly, but he had the superlative gift as a teacher of being interesting. Then, just as at Eton he had made social gatherings for his boys, so at Cambridge he opened his rooms every Sunday evening, to anybody who cared to come. The idea was excellent, for there poured into King's, still rather a close corporation, dons and undergraduates and general intelligentsia from other colleges. There were members of that mystic and elevated society called the Apostles who were supposed in their lighter moments to chat about Determinism ; there were sporting gents from the Athenaeum, which, in spite of its name, had nothing whatever to do with learning ; there were lights from the University Musical Society. For these there was special provision, for O.B. had four instruments of the nature of harmoniums, popularly known as Obeophones, possessed of a pleasant buzzing tone, remotely resembling that of stringed instruments, and vividly that of combs wrapped in toilet paper. They were of different compasses, one had the compass of a 'cello, another of a viola, two others, one of an inconceivable shrillness, did duty for violins, and the quartettes of Mozart and Beethoven rent the air. But then that fatuous egotism came in : O.B. found the slow movement rather tedious, and said ' Ha, ha, isn't it awfully jolly ? Let's stop.' So instead he went to the piano and bellowed ' Funicula, funicula ' or collected a group round him and gave them a curious pink liqueur tasting of furniture polish, and told them about the Empress of Austria's visit to Maloja, when, dressed like a Roman Emperor, and attended by four youthful lictors, he went out to welcome her, and made her a speech in Latin. His snobbishness was of a really remarkable order : it was impossible not to respect a quality of such fire and purity, for, although already waddling with obesity, he took to playing hockey simply for the pleasure of being wiped over the shins by H.R.H. Prince Edward of Wales when he was an undergraduate at Trinity.

Whatever he did was a matter that aroused attention and comment : that was because he was a great man. But whatever he did also aroused opposition and ridicule, and that was because he was such a silly ass. His facility and his exuberance of ideas made him indolent : he could not bother to work any of them out, because it was so much easier to think of fresh ones ; besides, there were so many small grudges which he cherished against those who had belittled him, and they must be dealt with before anything else was done. He must speak to the Provost about the conduct of the Classical Tutor, and when he had spoken he would certainly have to complain to some one else about the lack of sympathy the Provost had shown him. Then there were many diversions : it was a cold winter afternoon, and he would go after lunch to the Coffee Club in the college, always sociable, but always wanting to shine, and there one day he imprudently asked Jim Stephen what was the derivation of the word ' microbe.' Jim instantly replied : ' It's derived from the Greek word, μικρός, meaning small, and O.B. meaning you. It's a little O.B.' After that it would be pleasant to have a Turkish bath, and he tried to persuade some member of the Coffee Club to come with him. ' Awfully jolly : you can't be healthy unless you sweat every day as the Greeks did. Hesiod says that " Sweat is the threshold of many virtues." ' So he went off to the small hot closet which represented a Turkish bath, and after sitting copiously on the threshold of many virtues, he reclined in a small cool closet, wrapped in towels, and ate quantities of hot buttered toast. Or if it was summer he found it pleasant to have a bathe at the University sheds, on the upper river ; some sort of Charley or Bobby would row him up there, and tie his shoe-laces for him when he had dressed again. Then came the end of term, and he went up to London for a month, taking lodgings as nearly as possible opposite Marlborough House.

As he grew old he became impossible to work with : he quarrelled with every one who was associated with him on board or committee, accusing them of plagiarizing his ideas and organizing them. He left Cambridge and went to live at Bexhill, where he played golf in cap, coat and gloves of bright red, and became a Christian Scientist. After that he settled in Rome, where with incredible fluency he occupied himself in writing a history of the world. He calculated that he wrote about a million words every year, and wondered that he could not get them all published, suspecting conspiracy : in the intervals of composition he learned Polish. Never was there a man of so much originality of mind who did less with it, or one of so much genuine kindliness which was so curdled by egotism.

O.B. became a legend in his lifetime, which is always a mark of distinction. He was a model for every sort of caricature, a constant subject for the invention of the quick-witted, and many of these items, though possibly fabulous, ring so true that it really does not much matter whether they are authentic or not. Internal evidence based on a thorough knowledge of the character to whom they are attributed is the only test which is worth anything : if they are really characteristic they should be accepted, and the story of O.B. returning to Cambridge after a delirious July in London among the eminent, and remarking quite casually that William II of Germany was one of the nicest Emperors he had ever met, is, by such a test, obviously authentic. Anyone who had known O.B. in moods when he was dead drunk with the strong wine of royalty, could not hesitate about passing it, and if it was not true, so much the worse for the truth. Indeed it is a tribute to his personality that so many tales were invented about him, for nobody troubles to make up stories about everyday people, nor would anyone listen to them if they did.

Of all the Classical Fellows of King's about this time, there was just one, and he of a younger generation and not of Eton, who worked conformably to the spirit of the bounty of King Henry VI, for in return for his board and lodging and Fellowship, he devoted himself entirely to the study of Greek. Those who lectured, those who taught, those who, like Mr. Nixon, looked over our weekly efforts in Latin prose or Greek Iambics were not scholars at all in any real sense of the word : their knowledge of these languages was of the same class as that of the twenty or twenty-five undergraduates who yearly took a first in the Classical Tripos. They knew the principal dates and main operations in the Peloponnesian War, they could translate passages of Greek and Latin into grammatical English, and they could turn passages of English prose into Greek that probably bore the same relation to classical Greek, as written in the age of Pericles, as the best Baboo does to plain decent English prose of the day. Like the Baboo clerk, who, when asked by his employer for what reason he wanted a day's remission from office work, replied ' The hand that rocked the cradle has kicked the bucket ' (the proper English for which is ' My mother is dead '), so these admirable preceptors of ours would produce the most remarkable patchwork of recondite constructions and unusual words snipped from Thucydides and Plato and neatly stitched together, and hand them to their pupils as models for classical composition. Had any of them competed in the Classical Tripos of the year they would probably have taken quite good degrees, but there their attainments ended, and their years of teaching had not taught them anything that differentiated them from their more intelligent pupils.

Their knowledge of Greek ended just about where Walter Headlam's began : his mind was Greek, and he kept on learning the lore of its ancestors. The fragmentary mimes of Herondas had lately been discovered, and on this new text he poured out a knowledge which was as far beyond that of the accredited tutors of the college as is some advanced treatise on mathematics beyond the scope of an ordinary school-teacher of algebra. Though he was of a rich and boyish humanity, he had also that queer aloof quality which develops in those whose life is centred on research, and he passed into regions where no calls or needs of the flesh could penetrate.

One morning, for instance, his water for shaving was not hot, so after breakfast he put a small kettle to boil over his spirit lamp, and as he waited for that, he sat down in the arm-chair where he worked and casually looked at a note he had made the evening before. It was about a change of rhythm in a Greek chorus, or perhaps it was a word in his Herondas, which occurred in no dictionary, but which he knew he had seen before in some scholiast on Aristophanes. But where was the particular book he wanted? His room was lined with bookshelves, books that he was using paved the floor round his chair, and the table was piled high with them. There it was underneath a heap of others on the table, and he pulled it out; those on the top of it tumbled to the ground. He put down his pipe on the edge of the table, and, as he turned the leaves, he found not just that which he was looking for, but something else he had wanted yesterday. He made a note of this on a slip of paper and picked up his pipe which had gone out. There were no matches, so he folded up the paper on which he had made his note, thrust it into the flame of the spirit-lamp and lit his pipe again. Then he found the passage he had originally started to hunt up. Awfully interesting: it was a slang word, not very polite, in use among the daughters of joy in Corinth during the fifth century B.C. These intelligent ladies seemed to have an argot of their own: there were several other words of the sort which he had come across. He became lost in this pursuit, his pipe had to be relit several times, and presently a smell of roasting metal brought him back for a brief moment to the surface of life. His shaving-water had all boiled away, and so he put out the spirit lamp. Later in the morning his gyp came to see if he wanted any lunch ordered for him : bread and butter and cheese would do, with a tankard of beer. These were laid and left in the next room, and he wandered there after another hour or two deep in his investigation. The sight of food aroused no association of desire, but he had a drink out of the tankard and, carrying it back with him, put it in a nest of books on his table. Presently more books got piled up round the tankard; he absently laid a folio note-book on the top of it, and so it completely vanished. Then he wanted more books from his shelves, in one of these excursions he stepped on his pipe and broke the stem. It did not matter for there were others about, but he forgot to look for them in the heat of this diverting chase. ' I shall write a monograph on the slang current in Corinthian brothels,' he said to himself.

It began to grow dark on this early close of the autumn afternoon. There was no electric light in those days, and he fetched a couple of candles and put them on the edge of his table. He was hungry now, and he gobbled up his bread and cheese, wondering what time it was, for his watch had stopped. Beer too ; he felt sure he had ordered some beer, but where the devil was it ? It should have been on his table with the bread and cheese. He looked everywhere for it, even in his bedroom, but it was nowhere to be seen. Then his razor, lying ready on his dressing-table, reminded him that he had not yet shaved. It was true there was no hot water, but cold water would do, and though it was rapidly

getting dark, he had not yet found any matches to light
his candles. But one ought to be able to shave in the
dark, he thought, for an action often repeated became,
as Aristotle said, an instinctive process, and it would be
interesting to see if he could not make quite a good job
of it. He made a fair job of it, there were a few negligible
cuts, and finding that he had a box of matches in his
pocket all the time, he lit his candles and went back to
the ladies of Corinth. Then his gyp came in to see if he
would go into Hall for dinner, or dine in his room : he
settled to have some cold meat here, but where was the
beer he had ordered for lunch ? The gyp felt sure he
had brought it, but evidently he was mistaken for there
was no sign of it. So he brought the cold meat and
another tankard, and with this comfortless refreshment
Walter Headlam pursued the ladies of Corinth till the
small hours of the morning. The missing tankard came
to light the next day.

He would work like this for several days on end
(the details of my description are in no way composed
but actually and collectively true), and then he was drained
of scholarly energy, and emerging as from deep seas
with some pearls of research, he busied himself with
social concerns and diversions till he could dive again.

One day he fell in love with an intelligent young lady
from Newnham, but he soon forgot about her, because
he went to a concert where he heard Schubert's
' Unfinished Symphony.' Instantly all became dross
except Schubert, and though he could not read a note
of music, nor play a correct scale, he sat hour after hour
at his piano, dabbing at single notes till out of them
he had extricated a short melody of four bars, which I
wrote down for him ; it was to be the air in the slow

movement of ' Headlam Op. 1.' Then he immersed
himself in Greek again, and again rising to the surface
came across a pseudo-medical primer. The study of
this convinced him that he had diabetes, and so sure was
he of this that he never consulted a doctor at all. He
had a tragic collection of unmistakable symptoms,
headache, fitful appetite, fatigue, and so there was no
doubt about it. He told me very seriously that he had not
long to live, and when I asked what was the matter with
him, he said in a hollow but resigned whisper ' Sugar.'

So we went to a race meeting at Newmarket, and
entirely bowled over with adoration for the splendour
and the speed of the flying hooves and the rhythm of
their galloping, he felt that he must instantly learn to
ride : for the moment the whores of Corinth were pale
to him. He ordered some elegant riding breeches and
hired a horse, and we set out along the Backs. One
of his feet slipped out of its stirrup, but in these first
moments of poise upon a horse's back, he did not think
it wise, in spite of advice and proffered assistance, to
imperil his balance by recovering it, and in consequence,
when his horse decided to walk into the shallow water of
the Grantchester mill-pool and drink, he slipped gently
out of the saddle and fell in. Then he thought he would
like to go for a drive, as a less hazardous method of commerce with horses, and he asked a friend to come out for
a spin with him. On arrival at the livery stables, a high
dog-cart was made ready for them, and Walter Headlam
asked his friend if he would do the driving. The friend
very properly replied that he had never done such a thing
in his life, and so he said, ' Nor have I,' and was instructed
that the reins went in the left hand, and the whip in the
right. A little way out of Cambridge, in trying to turn

a corner, he drove up a bank at the side of the road, and the dog-cart upset. As he flew out of it (still with the reins in his left hand) he was heard to observe, ' Damn : I shall never finish Herondas,' and alighted unharmed in a hedge.

Mr. Charles Waldstein (afterwards Sir Charles Walston), Reader in Classical Archaeology, was another of these Fellows of King's who was not quite like other people : King's was rich in variations from type. By blood of birth he was German, American, and Jew, and Sir Charles Stanford at a musical rehearsal of a Greek play, at which he had been irritated to the verge of insanity by Waldstein's continually interrupting the chanting of Athenian elders, in order to show them how to stand and move in truly Pheidian attitudes, exclaimed in a highly injured brogue, ' I wish that German-American-Jew would go back to his respective countries.' There was a coolness in consequence, or you might call it a heat. He was one of those fortunate folk to whom, for no particular reason, ludicrous things happen : thus he was a source of fearful joy as well as affection to his friends.

He belonged to an earnest and exclusive Literary Society called the ' Chit-chat.' Both dons and under-graduates were among its members, and we assembled in each other's rooms in rotation every Saturday night during term time, on terms of equality. The host for the evening provided claret-cup and hot buns and anchovy toast, and the Society owned a snuff-box from which, as a piece of ceremonial, we all took pinches. When the sneezing had died down, the secretary called upon the host to read a paper which he had written on some literary or ethical subject, and during the reading the claret-cup went quietly round. On one memorable

evening when Waldstein entertained the Society, he told
us that he had not had time to write down his lecture,
and so he addressed his fellow-members instead, on the
subject of 'Manners.' He stood in front of the fire in
cap and gown, and was full of glorious gestures. He lit
a cigarette and put it down on the chimney-piece, he
lit another and another and put them down on table-
edge or chair-back. An eloquence of sentences, faintly
Teutonic sometimes in construction, streamed from him,
sometimes they contained rather exotic words like
'cocksuredom,' and no one as yet knew with any precision what he was talking about. The atmosphere
grew a little tense, and the members of the Chit-chat,
sitting very demure and attentive, felt that it was not wise
to catch each other's eyes. There came a pause : the
lecturer slapped his forehead and confessed that he had
forgotten exactly what he meant to say on that topic.
So he launched out on something cognate, and then
remembered what he had forgotten and went back to it.
The exquisite grace of Greek sculpture—that was it :
it reflected the charm and the urbanity and the breeding
of that superlative race. Gentlemanly-ishness no less
than genius was characteristic of sculptor and model alike.
There was that statue of the Discobolus which illustrated
what he meant as well as anything, and he threw
himself into a semblance of the famous pose, and his
mortar-board cap dropped off. He picked it up. 'It's
no use,' he said, 'you should see me naked.' At that
intense moment when everybody might have been
statues too, so still they sat, Dr. Cunningham of Trinity
happened to be drinking claret-cup, and he burst. The
liquid squirted from his mouth and nose, he hooted
with laughter, and seizing his cap and gown he hurried

from the room. Through the open window he could be heard roaring and slapping his leg in the court below.

Like O.B., Waldstein was addicted to eminent persons, and the two competed in a sort of Royal Hunt Cup, or we might call it a boxing match. Royal visitors constituted the points scored by the antagonists. A Prince of the House of Greece came to lunch with Waldstein, and afterwards his host took him to see the Museum of Classical Casts, which would remind him of Athens. O.B. countered this by brandishing an English Royal Highness in Waldstein's face, and taking him to the Union, which would remind him of the Houses of Parliament. That required some beating, but Waldstein's blood was up, and one day there was a red carpet on the steps leading to his rooms, and the Crown Princess of Germany walked along it : this was the third round. It was very chic of O.B. to have no red carpet at all, when, in the fourth round, he landed a stunning blow on Waldstein with H.R.H. the Duchess of York, for her visit was thus quite private and informal. Upon this two or three undergraduates laid plans for having a fifth round, and knocking out both O.B. and Waldstein, the puny creatures ! They arranged that one of them who was short and stout should dress up in a black bonnet and a black silk gown and be seen to arrive at the porter's lodge at King's in a carriage and pair ; another of them who was slim and slight in build, would be sitting on the front seat, fashionably dressed as a young woman. There would be a bath-chair waiting at the porter's lodge. A hint as to the identity of the little old lady in black would already have been given to O.B. and Waldstein, so that it would be certain that they would be looking out of their windows, when the bath-chair, propelled by one of the conspirators, with the lady-in-waiting walking behind it, was wheeled round the court, to the entrance of a certain set of rooms in Fellows' Buildings, where another of the conspirators lived. But the courage of these ingenious young gentlemen failed them, and, as a matter of fact, this fifth and final round in the boxing match never took place. They feared they might be clapped into the Tower of London and shot for high treason.

To descend from thrones, there was a visit of Robert Browning to Cambridge, to which a memorable incident is attached. His admirers there had started a Browning Society (' There's a Me Society down at Cambridge,' to quote from one of the most brilliant parodies in the language, written by Jim Stephen), which met to discuss and elucidate the poet's more difficult moods, and he attended one of these meetings, but was said to be unable to throw any light on certain of the conundrums of his own making which were referred to him. There was present at it a young lady of Newnham College, who was a most enthusiastic member of the Society, and, greatly daring, she asked Mr. Browning if he would come to tea with her and a few friends at Newnham, and afterwards read some little piece of his own to them. He loved appreciation, and liked young ladies, so he said he would be delighted. There were waiting for him some dozen of eager adorers, and he was given his cup of tea (or it might have been cocoa) and a piece of muffin. Then his hostess, in a frenzy of diffidence and devotion, told him that she had woven a crown of roses for him, from which all thorns and unpleasant moistnesses had been banished, and might she have the extreme honour of placing it on his head. The poet most good-naturedly consented, and with trembling hands she deposited the decoration on that august brow. So there he sat, bland and ruddy, and slightly buttery from the muffins, with the crown of pink roses laid upon his white locks, and looking like a lamb decked for sacrifice. By his side was an occasional table on which were placed the volumes of his complete works, and opposite him on the wall there happened to hang a mirror. When tea was done he was asked to fulfil his gracious promise and read. None knew what he would choose : some hoped for a book or two of ' The Ring and the Book,' the more advanced for ' Sordello,' and some for ' Saul.' What he chose was the ' Serenade at the Villa,' and the young ladies (since there were not enough chairs) grouped themselves gracefully on the floor round those revered feet. He began reading from the book, but he found he knew the poem by heart and closed it.

> When the firefly hides its spot [said Mr. Browning]
> And the garden voices fail,
> In the darkness thick and hot—

And just then he raised his eyes and saw in the mirror the image of himself crowned with pink roses. He broke into a peal of the most jovial laughter. ' My dear young ladies,' he said, ' Shall I not read " The Patriot " instead ? It was roses, roses all the way.'

He came to dine one night with my parents in London : if the family had been allowed to commandeer the presence of whom they would, as guest, the vote would probably have been cast for him, for not only was my mother an ardent Browningite, but one of her daughters knew really prodigious quantities of his work by heart, and was willing, if anyone doubted it, to go on

repeating his poems till there could be no question about
her claim ; while one of the boys, a year or two before,
had devoted the money for a prize he won in some
athletic competition at school to the purchase of the six
volumed edition of his works, instead of buying a silver
cup with his own name enwreathed in *repoussé* ferns.   The
guest was immensely genial, he ate and drank and talked
with a juvenile pleasure, as if the world held many joyful
surprises for him still.   Then one of these pert creatures
asked him what he thought of Austin Dobson as a poet,
for there were strong differences of opinion in the family
about him.   He laughed, he sipped his port, and then
he said, ' Well, some people do like carved cherrystones.'
His audience approved of that, for they found it characteristic of one who in his entrancing ' Men and Women '
told you with huge gusto not what he thought, but
what fifty other people thought, and did not say a word
on his own account till the last poem of all.   Just such
a word he said on his own account that evening quite
at the end of dinner, and it is for that reason I am telling
the story, since to this day it stands in greater need of
interpretation than anything he ever wrote.   He guessed,
I imagine, that everybody wanted him to talk about
himself (so plain had the hints been), and now he asked
my father which class of his poems (as he had been so
kind) most appealed to him.   My father without hesitation said ' Your lyrics.'   Browning bounded in his
chair, ' Lyrics ? ' he said.   ' I've got deskfuls of
them.'

Here then we are confronted by the puzzle : what
has happened to those lyrics ?   After that evening,
when he said he had ' deskfuls ' of them, no further
volume was published during his life-time except the

one slim book 'Asolando' which came out actually on the day of his death, and since then there has been no posthumous publication of lyrics. Are they in existence still, slumbering in some forgotten cupboard of his beloved Palazzo Rezzonico? In this sad autumn of English poesy when the melody of its nightingales is mute, what would we not give for some staves of that lyrical song of the spring-time? It is surely possible that even now they may be found to make new magic for a new generation. Or (I have sometimes thought) did Browning only mean that in his brain there was still the bird of 'lyric love' ready to break into song? But if that was all, why did he say 'deskfuls'? That is surely too concrete a word to use for songs yet unwritten.

Certainly that volcanic spirit which 'loved well because it hated' was afire still beneath the surface-cooled age, and once again, at the very end of his life, it broke out again spouting lava and withering flame. For there had been published a volume of letters by the translator of Omar Khayyám, Edward FitzGerald; in it was one in which he wrote, 'Thank God Mrs. Browning is dead; we shall have no more Aurora Leighs.' It was a bitter cross-grained way to put it, but all FitzGerald really meant was that he did not like Mrs. Browning's poetry. He knew nothing of her, for they had never met, and there was no personal attack on her. But it was a crime to publish it during Browning's lifetime, for though the chance of his seeing it was small, the chance existed. He did see it, and instantly the old fire flared up. 'I felt as if she had died yesterday,' he said to a friend, and he published in the *Athenaeum* the following lines:

To Edward FitzGerald

I chanced upon a new book yesterday ;
I opened it, and where my fingers lay
'Twixt page and uncut page these words I read,
    Some six or seven at most, and learnt thereby
    That you, FitzGerald, whom by ear and eye
She never knew, thanked God my wife was dead.

Aye, dead ! and were yourself alive, good Fitz,
How to return you thanks would pass my wits.
Kicking you seems the common lot of curs,
    While more appropriate greeting lends you grace.
    Surely to spit there glorifies your face,
Spitting with lips once sanctified by hers.

It is impossible not to feel a certain savage satisfaction. There was the old man nearer eighty than seventy ; close on thirty years had passed since the death of his wife, but to him it was as if they had been but a watch in the night. Except possibly for the dedication of ' Asolando,' this was the last poem he ever wrote.

While O. B. in the later years of the eighties and still in the very zenith of his vivaciousness was becoming a legend at Cambridge, another very notable figure at Oxford, Dr. Benjamin Jowett, Master of Balliol, had already become a legend, though one of an exceedingly different sort. About him there was no kind of fatuousness (fatuousness withered in his presence) which made it easy to invent stories about him which would help the legend to crystallize, though Mr. W. H. Mallock, in that early and amazingly brilliant book of his ' The New Republic,' presented, under the name of Dr. Jenkinson, a portrait of him which was wicked just because it was so appallingly truthful in essentials. But the ordinary observer would never have ventured to concoct a story

about Jowett, for it would have rung false : the expert
would have detected it in a moment. For this reason
the Jowett-saga of the day can be relied on. It was
certainly true, for instance, that the orthodoxy of his
Christian faith was suspect (owing to his contribution
to 'Essays and Reviews') when he was appointed to
the Regius Professorship of Greek, though he was a
clergyman of the Church of England. He was therefore
asked whether he would sign the Thirty-nine Articles as
set forth in the Prayer-book, and he expressed his perfect
willingness to sign forty if they wished. Nobody could
produce a fortieth on the spur of the moment and so
Jowett asked for a pen. ' Give me a pen,' he said, and
signed all the Articles that there were. His style, in
his official dealings with dons and undergraduates alike,
was marked by this rather arid incisiveness ; when he delivered his terse ultimatums there was no more to be said.

He dealt in this way with my friend Dr. David
Hogarth, who, as a junior don at Magdalen, was in
charge of the production of one of Aristophanes'
comedies, which was to be performed by the undergraduates. Dr. Hogarth had cut out of the play certain
witty lines which bore on the Athenian code of ethics
with regard to boys—he just struck them out. The
Master heard that this had been done and requested
Hogarth to call on him. ' I hear you have been making
cuts in the Greek play,' he said. ' Aristophanes wrote
it. Who are you ? ' Again there had come to Oxford
under the leadership of Professor Blackie a deputation
from Edinburgh University, and the Master had mentioned to him a certain want of urbanity and polish
that he found about the visitors. Professor Blackie
genially replied : ' Oh, you mustn't think too hardly

of us, Master.' A still small voice answered him, ' We don't think about you at all.' This withering demeanour, not really representing the greatness of the man, was rather childish; intercourse with him was like being invited to taste a bottle of wine of noble vintage and finding it slightly corked. He liked snubbing harmless and well-meaning folk, and, had he ever known it, he would have found it very disconcerting to realize that these raps on the knuckles, so far from rendering him formidable, afforded the ingenious youth of Oxford a fearful joy. Like Whistler, they used ' carefully to exasperate him ' in order to add to the collection of those brilliant little gems. He often asked undergraduates of the College to breakfast with him alone, and sometimes he would not speak. In order to break the portentous silence, one of these young gentlemen, as he nervously chipped his bacon high into the air, threw a fly, and remarked that it was a fine day. Jowett said nothing whatever till his guest rose to go. Then he said, ' That was a very foolish observation of yours.' But he had contributed a treasure towards the legend.

Dr. Jowett liked promising young men (except Mallock), he liked lively visitors from outside, and he used constantly to entertain rather distinguished parties for the week-end at Balliol. It would do his friends good to see the Oxford mode, and it would do Oxford good to see poets and Prime Ministers. At these parties he had a very good idea of the duties of a bachelor host, and though he seldom or never laughed, he became companionable. One day he told a small intimate circle that there were three men to whom he owed a great deal, men who had moulded and formed his mind, and made him what he was. The first of these was Gladstone ; Gladstone's views on the Church were illuminating. It ought to be disestablished, and then sedulously cherished : also Gladstone's reverence towards the classics, especially Homer, had led the Master to a worthier appreciation of them. The second of these prodigious minds to which he owed so much was that of Darwin. Darwin's 'Origin of Species' had opened to him a new conception of ethics, it had revealed to him that the progress of mankind lay in complete resignation to the Divine Will and in obedience to the laws of Nature in conjunction with it. This was all terribly interesting, and no one wished to break the pause that followed, for it was supposed that some rare and deep upwelling of emotion had caused the Master's silence. Eventually one of the circle broke the silence (for he like everyone else was eager to hear more) and most sympathetically asked who was the third of those who had so powerfully influenced him. ' I've forgotten the third,' said the Master.

But he who had so often silenced others once made a man in difficulties speak. This occasion was in Balliol Chapel one Good Friday, for which day special psalms are appointed. There was no music and the officiating chaplain repeated one verse and the congregation the next. The first psalm had been finished : the chaplain gave out the second, but he could not find it in his prayer book. A sort of nervous myopia seized him, he turned his leaves backwards and forwards but still the fortieth psalm eluded him. Then came a penetrating little weary voice from the Master's stall. ' I waited patiently,' it said, and instantly the chaplain found his place. ' I waited patiently for the Lord,' he recited, ' and he inclined unto me and heard my calling.'

Jowett had no pretensions whatever to be a great scholar; he would have thought it imbecile to spend his time like Walter Headlam, who, like the 'Grammarian' whose funeral oration Robert Browning so nobly pronounced, would count any day well spent that had enabled him properly 'to base οὖν.' Jowett knew that οὖν meant, more or less, 'therefore,' and that was sufficient for him; why bother any more about a Greek particle? But he spent years of useful labour in his translation of the history of Thucydides, and of the dialogues of Plato, and produced exactly what he meant to produce, namely readable English versions of exceedingly interesting books, which gave very fairly the sense of the original. He did not set himself to solve the more human problems that arise out of Thucydides's narrative, nor did he attempt to reconcile, for instance, that historian's view of Alcibiades with Plato's or Plutarch's: his business was to provide intelligent English readers (not scholars nor specialists) with an admirable version in English of what Thucydides wrote. He took the utmost pains to find out which was the most reliable text, and having done that proceeded to translate it, freely but faithfully, into dry and weighty English, recognising, as he says in his introduction to the 'Dialogues of Plato,' that literal translation does not always give the English equivalent, and that the particles with which Plato bestrews his sentences are often not translatable at all. Strangely enough in a man who had spent so many years in studying Greek, he was by no means accurate, and knowing his frailty in this regard, he had his translation carefully revised by other scholars. Among these (though I think the Master does not mention him by name) was the poet Swinburne: probably

Swinburne was only an occasional reader of his proofs, when he was staying with the Master at Balliol. But there was a certain humour about the situation, for Swinburne had left Oxford without taking a degree, and there he was again looking over the Master's classical work for him. And the humour became even more manifest when he was engaged at his task. One morning the Master was in his study going through with their authors the English essays which the undergraduates had sent in for his perusal and criticism : Swinburne was sitting, with proofs of a Platonic dialogue, in a small adjoining room, the door between the two being open. It was the Master's habit sometimes to make rather withering remarks to these young essayists, and to-day one of his most biting observations was interrupted by a joyful crow of laughter from the next room and Swinburne's exultant voice exclaiming, ' Another howler, Master ! ' ' Thank you, Algernon,' said the Master meekly, and gently closed the door.

Of the kindness of his heart there could be no question, his loyalty and his generosity to his friends were invariable, but always masking that to the world was that metallic tang of his tongue which liked scoring cheap successes. Was it perhaps an attitude of defence on the part of one who shunned intimate contact, and who wore his heart not on his sleeve, but in his innermost pocket ? It had been hurt once ; the object of its adoration had been Florence Nightingale. Such a conjunction seems more like the fantastic situations in the pleasant game called ' Consequences ' than a romance of real life, for the imagination boggles at the picture of Miss Nightingale as the wife of an Oxford don, and, not less, at that of Jowett seeing that the lamp was trimmed.

CHAPTER VIII

THE focus-point of life for me had shifted from Cambridge to London and other places far more remote before my Cambridge days were over. The stream of those impressions which for three years had carried me along really heedless of what happened outside that adorable flood of friendships and games and rapt observations of Nixon and O.B., joined that of the world outside and the Cambridge current seemed to edge away into a very pleasant backwater. It was still delightful to leave the main stream and float quietly there under the bank, but all that had appeared so swift and strenuous now seemed leisurely, quietly eddying. I had won decent distinction in the Classical and Archaeological Triposes, and already there was a novel which I regarded as finished, written on loose sheets of foolscap, reposing somewhere in a drawer, till a year or two later I picked it out again, and wrote the second half of it. But for the present archaeology was the passion and for three years in succession Cambridge most amiably gave me grants and travelling studentships for the pursuit of antiquity. Chester and its walls, in which were embedded the tombstones of the Roman legions which had interested Mr. Gladstone, was the first field for research, and I spent three winters as a student in the English school at Athens.

What an enlightenment was there! Those dreary
hours devoted at Marlborough and at Cambridge to
learning irregular Greek verbs, to racking the brain for
crabbed scraps of phrases from Thucydides and Plato
for the decoration of Baboo versions of Greek prose
(thus earning occasional approving smiles from tutors),
were suddenly seen to be exercises, however mis-
begotten, to acquire the tongue not of a dead folk long
perished, but of the wondrous people who had built
the Parthenon, and whose spirits, still intensely alive,
wandered in its ruinous colonnade, sat on the mellowed
marble seats in the theatre, and rode in peerless squadrons
up the sacred hill of Acropolis, to do honour to Athene
on her birthday. The plane-trees and the *agnus castus*
had perished from the bank of the Ilissus and its stream
was dwindled, and the washerwomen scolded and rinsed
their linen by its shrunken pools, but it was here in very
truth that Socrates had sat and told young Phaedrus of
the chariots of the soul, and when his tale was done had
prayed ' Beloved Pan, and all ye deities that haunt this
place, give me inward beauty of soul, and may the outward and the inward man be at one.' My year of studying archaeology at Cambridge, and, above all, intercourse
with Walter Headlam and Professor Middleton, who
instead of lecturing gave me Greek gems and fragments
of red-figured vases to examine, had begun the vivifying
work, and now the dry bones of that arid valley of
education began to stir, and they came together, bone
to his bone, and were transformed into a host of swift
and comely presences. I do not mean to suggest that
every boy who is about to be taught Greek should be
taken out to Athens, before he learns his first declen-
sion, but merely to remark how dismal was the system

which, expunging all human interest and beauty from
a subject that is instinct with humanity and loveliness,
taught a language, and that the most flexible of all
human tongues, as if it had been a series of algebraical
formulae.   How willingly would those dry irregularities
have been learned if the imagination had first been kindled
by photographs of the temples of the beautiful people
and by reproductions of their statues : there would then
have been an incitement to know how the poets and
historians of the folk who made those things, talked
and wrote.   But at the time when I was learning Greek,
the methods of tutors resembled that of those who, by
making their pupils chop up dry faggots of wood,
hoped to teach them what was the nature of the trees
that once the wind made murmurous on the hillsides
of Attica.

Apart from its ancient inheritance, Greece in these
years just before the war with Turkey, which broke out
in 1896, was an astonishing little kingdom, the like of
which, outside pure fiction, will never again exist in
Europe, for fresh forms of democracy, constructive
and destructive alike, have rendered it obsolete.   It
was not rich, but it had great undeveloped resources,
and financially it had a far better credit than most
of the great European States of to-day, for the
value of its drachma (nominally equivalent to the
franc) stood at about thirty to the pound sterling.
Gladstone, the lover of Homer, had on the accession of
King George of Greece given back to it the lovely
Ionian Islands, and its independent status as well as its
exchequer was guaranteed by the Great Powers.   There
was scarcely a trace of the old Hellenic blood on the
mainland, so ruthlessly had it been overrun by Romans,

Venetians, and Turks, and the population of Athens and the towns of the Peloponnese was largely of that mixed blood which by way of a formula we call Levantine. Their merchants were very acute business men, a good match for the Jews and even the Armenians of the Eastern markets, and many had made large fortunes in Cairo and Smyrna and Alexandria. There was also in the northern half of Greece, especially in the country districts, much of the robust Albanian blood, and all over Greece there burned a strong national spirit justly proud of those stubborn ancestors who, seventy years before, had risen, under the leadership of Petrobey and the Mainats, and thrown off the damnable yoke of the Turks, kindling by that most heroic insurrection European sympathy with Hellenism, of which the immortal mouthpiece was Byron. He was regarded as a national hero, and his name was still known and honoured in the remotest parts of Greece. Once, travelling in the Peloponnese, when I came into sight of the Gulf of Corinth, my young mule-driver from Sparta doffed his cap, and pointed to the hills of Missolonghi, where 'our Byron died,' and where his heart was buried. He was very keen also to know about Queen Victoria, the report of whose amazing wealth had reached him. I told him that she was remarkably well off, and attempted to express the Civil List in terms of drachmas. He listened almost incredulous and said, 'I suppose she can have tinned meat every day.' His imagination could not picture a more sumptuous extravagance.

But the national spirit in Athens was prouder yet of its earlier ancestry: the people considered themselves to be the modern representatives of the race that had conquered the Persians and built the Parthenon,

and all the little Levantine boys were christened Agamemnon and Theseus and Epaminondas. They were
quite convinced that the whole world was in their debt
as being the lineal heirs of the ancient Hellenes, and
they permitted Germany and France and America and
England to excavate the classical sites, and restore to the
rightful heirs the treasures they unearthed. Schliemann
had dug up Mycenae, and the Central Museum at
Athens gleamed with the gold-studded swords and
decorations of their ancestor the conqueror of Troy.
Germany, too, had recovered the riches of Olympia
for their rightful owner, and the Hermes of Praxiteles
stood radiant on his pedestal : the French were permitted
to dig up Delphi and recover the bronze charioteer.
America, under Dr. Charles Waldstein, was doing its
duty at Argos, and England at Megalopolis. All these
efforts on the part of artistic Europe fostered the national
pride : by the favour of modern Greece the nations
were permitted to render their homage to it by giving
back to it its ancient glories. But Germany and England were rather shabby folk, for the one, having rescued
the marbles of Aegina from destruction, had taken them
off to Munich, and England had filched the greater
splendour of the Parthenon, at which, when *in situ*,
Turkish soldiers took pot-shots to see if they could hit
the nose of Zeus or the breasts of Athene. That the
frieze and pediments would probably have perished
had Lord Elgin left them there was not relevant ; he had
had the inestimable privilege of saving them, and now
England ought to send them back.

Further, it was the privilege of the Powers to establish the heirs of Agamemnon and Pericles in an inviolable
land, and to give them a reigning house of royal blood

to hold rule over Greece and the isles of the Aegean. Otho of Bavaria had been the first King, but his despotic methods were intolerable, and in 1862 a fresh King was given them, George I, then seventeen years of age, who was still on the throne in these years of the nineties. Greece, indeed, was furnished with a very well-connected royal family : their King was the son of the King of Denmark, and brother of the future Queen of England and of the Empress of Russia, his wife Queen Olga was the daughter of the Imperial Grand Duke Constantine, and their eldest son Constantine was married to Sophia, sister of the German Emperor. Europe had really done its best to give them a reigning family not unworthy of their ancient glories, and all these eminent personages with the best will in the world set themselves to be truly royal and thoroughly democratic.

The effect was inimitable. Athens, with its high-born princes, and its national pride, and its army dressed in Albanian costume (embroidered jacket, fustinella, like a ballet skirt, fez, white gaiters, red shoes with tassels on the toes like the seed of dandelions), its fleet of three small cruisers, its national assembly of bawling Levantines, and its boot-blacks called Agamemnon and Thucydides, was precisely like the fabulous kingdom of Paflagonia in the 'Rose and the Ring,' or some Gilbertian realm of light opera. King George lived in a monstrous white palace overlooking the square ; a bugler was stationed by the front door in the long portico of Doric columns who blew soul-stirring blasts in a great hurry whenever a royal personage emerged from within. Sometimes the royal personage was only a royal baby in its perambulator, and the slightly self-conscious nursery-maid hastened to convey her

charge into the garden away from these trumpetings
of advertisement. The affable King gave audience to
any foreigner who, through his legation, asked to have
a quarter of an hour's conversation with him, the Queen
was equally willing to talk to those of her sex, and
aspiring American ladies flocked to Athens because (as
one of them stated to me with the most engaging frankness) ' The royal family of Greece is the easiest royal
family to become acquainted with.'

Here was the democratic side : this open access was
useful to Greece, for it brought visitors, but Royalty
also asserted itself. These fortunate foreigners must be
suitably clad for their interviews : ladies who visited
Queen Olga must wear high evening-dress with a lace
mantilla or something of the sort on their heads ;
gentlemen who visited King George must be decked
in top-hats and frock-coats, but since few travellers
carried such articles in their luggage, they were permitted to wear dress-clothes and white ties. Hence
about eleven o'clock on a broiling morning one might
observe the pleasant spectacle of an obese pilgrim
emerging from the Grand Hotel in a dress suit (slightly
green in the strong sunlight), pumps and a straw hat,
and making his way across the small stony desert in
front of the palace for his chat. The King received him
in a room with a purple Victorian wall-paper sprinkled
with gilt stars, and he stood during the whole interview
see-sawing backwards and forwards from toe to heel.
That movement was as infectious as yawning, and it
was only by a strong effort of self-control that the pilgrim
prevented himself from following the royal example.
When a long catalogue of simple questions and answers
had been correctly repeated, the King gave a little bow

and the catechumen a low one, and he then left the
palace. If the bugler on duty was an ardent fellow,
he probably started tootling without waiting to make
sure who came out, and all the wayfarers and loungers
observed with well-merited sneers this attempt of a
man in dress-clothes and a straw hat to impersonate
royalty. He slunk back to the Grand Hotel past the
garlic-savouring congratulations of the porter, and,
having changed his clothes, sat down to his lunch with
its strange native menu of fried baby cuttle-fish and
stew of nameless meat and a bowl of curdled sheep's
milk. Stranger yet was the native beverage, a white
wine in which the flavour of the grape was imperceptible
below that of the resin which was lavishly mingled with
it. National tradition proudly accounted for this
monstrous concoction by affirming that in the days of
Pericles and Aspasia wine was stored in sheepskins
caulked with resin, and hence was derived the liking
for the taste of turpentine which their descendants
inherited. They liked what Pericles liked. King
George, however, was not sufficiently Hellenic to like
what Pericles liked, and had vineyards of his own up
at his country seat at Tatoi, where he made a very
decent wine called Deceleia, which was innocent of the
traditional ingredient, and he sold it at considerable
profit to the restaurants and hotels of Athens in bottles
bearing a label with the royal crown. Just so might
the King of England start a brewery at Windsor with
the lion and the unicorn on its label to distinguish it
from other brands.

Often on a Sunday afternoon there would be a
small compartment reserved on the steam tram that
ran between Athens and the shore of Phalerum ; it

stopped opposite the palace. Then came a prodigious
tootling from the bugler, and King George and several
of his family came out and walked briskly across towards
it. If they did not come at once, or if they loitered,
the driver touched the whistle, and they made better
speed and climbed quickly into their compartment so
as not to keep the lieges waiting. Had they not done so,
the driver, after this warning, would undoubtedly have
moved off without them, leaving them to wait for the
next tram or take a cab, and so they hurried. This
royal simplicity pleased the Greeks : that was what a
king should be. The Dowager Empress Frederick
of Germany, who was spending a long time in Athens,
waiting for the birth of the baby which her daughter
the Crown Princess was expecting, was very simple too.
There would be a quiet, comely woman plainly dressed
in black sitting all the morning on a fallen block of
column on the Acropolis, busy with her sketching. A
semi-circle of tourists and idlers stood round her, but
she did not mind that, and if they knew anything about
painting they would easily see that this lady was no
ordinary amateur, but an artist, as Lord Leighton once
told me, to be judged by professional standards. She
had little imagination, he said, she was a second-rate
artist, but, so admirable was her technical skill, she
could not be considered an amateur at all. So there
she sat very busy, and they all stood round her spitting
and smoking, till her gentleman, Count Seckendorff,
who had also been sketching, came and told Her Majesty
that the fiacre was waiting. He stood bareheaded as
he spoke to her, until she told him to be covered, and
so the crowd recognized who she was, and off they
drove in a little jingling one-horsed victoria.

One morning, casually, she sent round word to the English Legation, where I was staying, that she would like to lunch there, and though the occasion was quite informal, diplomatic etiquette seemed to demand that I should wear a frock-coat, of which I had no specimen. The butler therefore, a man of abundant presence, kindly lent me his, and as we went down to lunch, I suspected from the whispers and giggles that went on between the Minister and the Empress, that this sartorial secret was being divulged. And so it was, for as we sat at lunch she began to admire my frock-coat; she had never seen such a beautiful frock-coat, and how well it fitted. . . . Directly afterwards Sir Edwin Egerton had to go to see the King, and I was left alone with her, and had a glimpse, tragic and sudden and disconcerting, of the tumult that raged underneath that tranquil manner. She talked for a little about an uncle of mine, who had lived for many years in Germany, and of whom she was very fond. Then she was silent a moment, and suddenly broke out, ' But Willie is mad ! ' Again she paused, then pointed an emphasizing finger at me, ' I mean just what I say,' she cried ; ' it is literal : Willie is mad.'

To all of them Athens was a sort of holiday home, the Empress Frederick came to be with her daughter, the Czarina came to see her brother, the Princess of Wales to see her sister, the Czarevitch to see his uncle and his cousins, and all the Greeks thought they had come to render homage to the land of Hellenic culture. They could relax at Athens, and forget about their crowns, just as they relaxed at Copenhagen, and though, when a family gathering was going on, the bugler outside the palace was sadly overworked, for they all kept

popping in and out unattended to do their shopping,
and the demand for his music was incessant, they much
enjoyed these hours of ease. They romped and unbent;
one day a young Englishman who had the privilege
to sit and laze in the Royal garden heard the sound of
tripping feet and male laughter and female cries of
dismay, and round the corner of the rose-pergola where
he sat came King George, kicking in front of him what
had once been a hat. Behind him tripped the Princess
of Wales, shrilly protesting. 'I beg you not to, George,'
she cried; 'it is my hat: so rude of you!' The young
Englishman was in a *cul-de-sac*, he could not flee, and
presently he was apotheosized into an umpire. 'But
she had an ugly hat,' pleaded the King, 'and I did not
like it. So I took it off and I kicked it.' Then the
plaintiff stated her case. 'It was my hat and it was
so rude of him, and now I can never wear it any
more.'

This astonished umpire had lately been at Corfu
and now they asked him about his experiences there.
They had been rather remarkable, for he had been
bidden to call on the Empress of Austria, who at that
time had a big house on the island called the Achilleion.
He presented himself there, and was told that Her
Majesty was in the garden, and thither he went, conducted
by a great golden major-domo. Presently he heard
the boom of an intoning voice, and as it came nearer,
he perceived that it was reciting the majestic hexameters
of Homer. Then round a clump of oleanders came
the Empress dressed in Albanian costume, and behind
her walked her Greek secretary reading aloud to his
mistress, while she took the air, this masterpiece of
Greek literature. After a word of greeting, the visitor

fell in beside his hostess, the major-domo behind the reader, and to the sonorous music of the Odyssey, this remarkable phil-Hellene procession marched back to the Achilleion.

Then perhaps there was a State ball, but still the suspicion of *opéra bouffe* was there, for it seemed almost incredible that the man who had been kicking his sister's hat down the garden path was a real king, or that the woman I had seen coming out of the dentist's yesterday with a rueful face, and who now appeared resplendent wearing a girdle of emeralds so large that they seemed highly improbable, was a real queen : they were playing at being kings and queens and the emeralds were a stage property. The same sense that it was a toy kingdom over which they ruled was present everywhere. For this ball was in honour of the King's name day, and that morning there had been a review of troops in front of the palace : lusty and well-favoured men they were in their ballet skirts and tasselled shoes, but obviously supers. An incident had occurred which, though almost too extravagant even for comic opera, must have required a great deal of rehearsing, for a perfectly trained horse standing in a cab rank near by suddenly bolted, and charged straight through the flower of the Greek army, which scampered nimbly away behind orange trees and places of convenience. Right across the square it galloped amid the shrieks of the populace, and was stopped by a courageous boot-black who slung his blacking-box in its face. The army then re-formed again for the march past. The incident was recorded in the evening papers with much florid detail, in columns of Thucydidean prose, under the heading ' Zeto Epaminondas ' (' Here's to the health of Epaminondas '), that being the name of the boot-black.

Was it not also pure operetta that, when the Greek fleet of three cruisers was ordered to sail to the Peiraeus from Nauplia, where it was stationed, to salute the Russian squadron accompanying the Czarevitch Nicholas who was arriving on a visit to his uncle, it was found on the eve of this naval display that there were not sufficient stokers to enable the entire fleet to move together ?   Two ships therefore were brought into the Peiraeus, and as soon as they had anchored there, a con- tingent of stokers was bundled back to Nauplia, over- land, in order to bring the third cruiser.   So when the Russian fleet arrived, there was the Greek navy ready for it.

Patriotic pride and national sentiment are most admirable qualities ; no country can get far without them.   But it is possible to have too much of them, as of other good things, and they must be balanced by some sobering weight of sense, which in these early years of the nineties was sadly wanting in Greece.   It was not altogether her fault, for the Powers had done their best to spoil her, and they had, unhappily, suc- ceeded only too well.   They had given her back the Ionian Isles, they had guaranteed her loans, they had provided her with a Royal family which, in those days when Kings really counted, was closely allied with the ruling families of England, Germany and Russia, and the national pride of Greece, as embodied in the man in the street, never suspected (or at least instantly put such an absurdity out of his mind) that all these benefits had anything to do with the balance of power in Europe or with a check on Turkey, that ' sick man ' who, an English premier had once rather rashly stated, should be put out of his misery. The Powers (such undoubtedly was the opinion of the Greek cafés) were very properly paying by instalments the infinite debt which civilization and culture owed to the Hellenes. In reality the Powers had stabilized the kingdom of Greece with much the same object as they might have set up a clock-work mechanism to control the flow of water through the sluices of some reservoir.

Greece, not quite realizing this, felt she must make some gracious gesture of acknowledgment to the tributes paid her, and the suggestion was made that the Olympic games should be revived, and be celebrated at Athens. Athens took the notion up very warmly, for athletes of all nations would certainly flock there, in order to have the honour of competing with the Hellenes, whose forefathers had been the originators of contests in bodily prowess. Originally the Olympic games had been open only to those of true Hellenic blood, but Romans had been permitted afterwards to compete in them, and now they were to be thrown open to the entire world, after being in abeyance for fifteen hundred years. It was decided to include in the events not only such ancient feats as the throwing of the discus but newer athletic acts of physical valour like bicycling. The youth of Athens, not hitherto remarkable for bodily activities, instantly went crazy over athleticism, for Greece was challenging the whole world. Strings of young men in shorts trotted about the streets of Athens all day, occasionally bursting into sprints : they practised long jump and high jump ; they put weights, using large stones if they could not procure the standard instruments ; the extremely bumpy roads to Phalerum and Kephissia were thick with flashing bicycles, and one day I saw two stout and elderly gentlemen solemnly wrestling together, by the columns of Zeus Olympios.

But the blue riband of the games would be the race from Marathon to Athens, in commemoration of the day when Athens had hurled back the might of Persia, and Pheidippides had run from Marathon to the city with news of the victory, expiring as he panted out his message. The race would be run over the sacred soil (more or less) which Pheidippides had actually traversed. A patriotic millionaire renovated the ancient stadium, there was a running track round it, a space within the track for such events as jumping and discus-throwing, and tiers of seats, hewn of the marble from the bowels of Hymettus, were provided for spectators, and all was ready by the spring of 1896. The King performed the opening ceremony, the hymn to Apollo recently dug up at Delphi by French excavators was chanted in the Dorian mode, and the games began. There was a fair sprinkling of athletes from foreign countries, though there were few, if any, of the first class, and all these, in the popular view, contended with the Hellenes : it was *Hellas contra mundum*. There was a good deal of friction of one sort and another ; defeated Hellenes argued passionately with the judges, disputing their decisions, and threatening them with corporal violence, but the national pride, which was rather humbled by the result of most of the events, was amply restored by the Marathon race. It was easily won by a young Greek called Loues, who happily did not expire like Pheidippides, but reached the stadium in wonderfully good condition. So far ahead was he of all other competitors, and so phenomenal was the time in which he had covered

the twenty-five miles from Marathon, that there were
some ugly conjectures whispered about that he had
possibly been assisted by occasionally putting his hand
on the stirrup of the Greek cavalry officer who rode
beside him with words of encouragement. Without
doubt the suggestion was false, indeed it was refuted
next year when the victor once more proved very
definitely (as we shall see) his unrivalled power of speed
and staying. He was hailed as a national hero, he was
crowned with a wreath of wild olive by the King.
Pindaric odes were written in his honour, the munici-
pality voted him a free dinner every day till the end of
his life, and the Athens-Corinth railway a free pass, for
he had re-established for Greece the athletic supremacy
which had been hers two thousand years ago.

Late that year, arising out of Turkish barbarities in
Crete, there broke out the Greco-Turkish war. In
1897 the Turks invaded Thessaly from the north, and
high flamed the fiery spirit of Hellas. The Crown
Prince Constantine was appointed Commander-in-Chief
of the Greek armies, and went to the front. All over
Greece there raged a delirium of war-fever, the most
gratifying news was issued hot and hot from the press,
and though as yet there was no Turk within fifty miles
of Volo, the seaport in the south of Thessaly, excited
youths rushed into the cafés there carrying fezzes im-
paled on knives. They cried out that they had taken
these from the heads of the Turks they had slain, and
though everybody knew that this was rubbish, they
were much applauded. But at the front things were not
going so well; the Greeks were incapable of making
any sort of stand against the enemy, the Crown Prince
retreated from his headquarters at Larissa, and the

Turkish armies marched quietly on till at the end of a few weeks the whole of Thessaly was in their hands. Refugees from the Greek army—they could hardly be called deserters, for the army no longer existed at all— poured into Athens, and the first to arrive, easily distancing all competitors, was Loues, the winner of the Marathon race the year before. He had silenced for ever all doubts about his running.

The collapse was complete. Streams of homeless, penniless families poured into Athens on the heels of the army, though the majority of the Thessalian peasants, lacking means of transport, remained in their villages. The troops of the occupying Turks behaved to them with exemplary kindness and consideration, and their worst enemies were brigands of their own race, who overran the country. I had been commissioned to distribute the alms of an English fund for the relief of the Greeks in Thessaly, and, as it was quite impossible to move about the country without some small armed guard, I applied to the Greek government to furnish me with one.

Endless difficulties and delays ensued ; I was passed from one department to another, and despairing of getting anything done in Athens, I went up to Volo, where Edhem Pasha, the Commander-in-Chief of the Turkish forces, had his headquarters, and told him what the object of my mission was. There stood out the high breeding of the Turk ; he was delighted that any help should be brought to these poor villagers of the Greeks, whose soldiers had given him so little trouble, and he instantly provided me with the escort the Greeks would not give me for the relief of their own countrymen.

Then once more the Powers stepped in, and ordered

Turkey to evacuate this province of Thessaly which she now occupied, for she could not be allowed to increase her holding of European soil. In fact, the only result of this war, if it could be called a war, was that Crete was put under the protectorate of Greece. The Great Powers wound up the works of the toy-kingdom again, and it was soon ticking away as merrily as before.

CHAPTER IX

THREE GREAT LADIES AND OTHERS

THOUGH a very decisive thaw had melted the more ludicrous of the early and mid-Victorian frigidities years before the last and liveliest decade of the reign, there still remained the tradition of a certain splendour and dignity which expressed itself in the particular type of woman known as 'a great lady.' She is scarcely definable, though she was very easily recognizable—in fact she could not be mistaken for anything else —and she is now as extinct as the Great Copper butterfly. It is not that the intrinsic qualities which composed her have failed, for there are probably just as many women in London now who have them all, but it is rather that, even as the draining of the fens in Cambridgeshire deprived that noble butterfly of the environment and grazing ground in which its caterpillar thrived, so the breaking down of the whole Victorian setting of dignity and fine manners deprived these great ladies of the stage on which they so magnificently functioned. There were also material props and scaffoldings to that stage : great houses in London where they entertained were part of it, so too was the willingness of their guests to set themselves to the stately key. That is not the mode now : the thirst for immediate and lively amusement is more insistent, and publicity (to be heard and seen of

men, and to resound at restaurants) is a larger ingredient
in entertainment than it used to be. To give a dinner
at an hotel and take her party to a dance-club afterwards
would have seemed to the great lady a most extraordinary
proceeding ; she could never have been a figure at such
functions, though they were far less trouble and expense
than a dinner and a dance in her own house. Then
when a season of three months in London was over
she settled down fairly solidly till after Christmas in her
house in the country, and gave parties for her friends
with shooting for the men, and for the women drives
in landaus to points of interest in the neighbourhood.
Autumns in London, lip-sticking in public, winters on
the Riviera, the kippering of her arms and legs, bosom
and back on the sands of the Lido, and inability to remain
in one place for more than a week, were not habits of
the great lady. Above all, she was possessed of that
queer old quality called dignity.

Indeed it is far easier to get near the definition of her
by excluding what she was not, than by the inclusion of
what she was. She was not in a blazing hurry all the
time, she did not run a hat-shop or sit in the House of
Commons, she had no push, because there was nowhere
to push to, for as regards position she was there already
by birth or marriage or both, and the craving that everyone should know how much she was there could not
exist in her, for nobody could doubt it. Therefore
she did not permit, still less encourage, the public press
to regale its readers with chatty paragraphs about the
decoration of her 'boudoir,' the tiles in her bathroom, and the diet of her dogs, nor did she order her
dressmaker to show the author of the column signed
' Jezebel ' or ' Hermione ' the dresses she intended to

wear at Ascot. She did not want to be advertised or her doings daily to be mirrored, and she had no ambition (the odd, old-fashioned creature) that next morning every one whom she did not know by sight should be told how she had entertained a distinguished company to dinner, or that her guests sat at two round tables decorated with sprays of ' Aurora Borealis ' and ' Delirium Tremens ' from her greenhouses at Widdicombe Royal. There were others, effulgent and beautiful and fashionable creatures who liked that : their photographs appeared in all shop windows and they were called ' Professional Beauties,' and as they walked in the Park, people stood on the chairs to see them. But no ' great lady ' ever desired that sort of publicity, and Jezebel and Hermione might have died of starvation on the doorstep before they were resuscitated with such succulent domestic morsels as are now pressed on their jaded and fastidious appetites, for her private life did not concern the public. Unlike the hostesses of a later day (and, for that matter, many hostesses in her own day) to whose bountiful hospitalities London owes so much, she did not cadge and scheme to collect her glittering assemblies. It was enough that she gave a party, and instead of exerting feverish efforts to secure a galaxy, she had only to decide whom she was obliged to leave out owing to lack of room. She was not concerned with making a position for herself by enticing notable folk to her house, for the position was hers already, and she did her social duty by it. Sometimes it rather bored her, but she must play the part for which she was cast in the pageant. She had power, she mattered, and that was her unsought reward in the performance of her duties. With the disappearance of such women, there vanished every nucleus of social power, the very idea of which to-day is an antediluvian notion. 'Society' (in the sense of inverted commas) has so broadened out that, becoming quite flat in the process, there is not the semblance of a peak left. To suggest that anybody matters now, or wields any social power, would imply as complete a misunderstanding of modern conditions as would the failure to grasp the fact that in the eighties and the nineties there were in existence these great ladies who mattered very much indeed.

Three women out of many may be taken as instances of the vanished type which was possessed of an extreme distinction and wielded this effortless though obsolete power. In many respects they were exceedingly unlike each other, but essentially they had this classical but indefinable quality in common. The Duchess of Manchester, who became Duchess of Devonshire, was one, the late Lady Londonderry was another, the third was Lady Ripon, at that time Lady de Grey. All of them had to a very high degree a sort of regal personality, which could manifest itself in graciousness or imperiousness, but was always dominating, and all of them (though that had very little, if anything, to do with their greatness) had been at one time strikingly beautiful women. Lady Ripon retained that personal splendour to the end of her life. But beauty was only a casual, outward expression of that quality, indefinable as is a colour, which all can recognize but none explain, except by saying that it is itself. Certainly they were all extremely capable women, and we may take it that their high intelligence was a tool with which this quality worked. But it was not the same as the quality.

The Duchess of Devonshire was German by birth,

Countess Louise von Alten.   Those who knew her
when she was young said that no one who had not seen
her then could possibly tell how beautiful a woman
could be : it is the irritating habit of old people to say
that sort of thing, but early portraits of her seem to give
support to it.   As a young woman when she first came
to England, she used to take delight in walking alone
about the streets of London, a thing which was not done
then, especially by Duchesses, but it amused and interested
her, and a story of a little adventure that once happened
to her on one of these excursions, which she told of
herself, was evidently characteristic.   Naturally there
would often be a man hopefully following this radiant
and unaccompanied vision, and she gave one of these a
salutary lesson to leave her alone.   She had stopped to
look in at the window of some smart bonnet-shop, and
the hopeful follower asked her if she would not like to
have one of those nice bonnets.   She said she would
like one very much, and they went in together and she
chose one, for which the follower paid.   So, of course
he said he would carry it home for her, but she said he
must not trouble himself to do that, for they would send
it to her, and she gave her name, the Duchess of Manchester, and her address.   He would thus learn not to
pester respectable young ladies who were taking the air :
it would do him good. . . .

There was something (as may thus be conjectured) of
the unswerving relentlessness of a steam-roller about her,
neither kindly nor unkindly, but crushing its way on, and
flattening out the unevennesses of the road it intended
to traverse.   With the same quiet fixity of purpose, she
intended, should the day arrive when she was free to do
so, to marry her second husband, who was her devoted

admirer. But long before that day came, while he was still in the House of Commons as Lord Hartington, she made him pull his weight in the political world, and she appreciated very correctly what his weight could be. Under the spur of her ambition for him, he became one of the most powerful units of influence there, not because he was possessed of any very exceptional genius or had great political dexterity or because he was personally ambitious. Indeed it was exactly because he was indifferent to personal motives, because he had no enthusiasms (the happiest moment of his life, he was reported to have said, was when his pig took a first prize at some agricultural show) that she saw what a tremendous force he could become. He had no axe to grind, and that was why he could deliver such stunning blows with it. His bitterest opponents could not accuse him of self-seeking, because it was obvious that he wanted nothing for himself, for the man who in the course of nature will become Duke of Devonshire, and inherit colossal wealth and noble possessions has not very much that he can covet for himself among the vain trappings of the material world. So when, with his great position and very sound judgment, he made up his mind (which took time) on any political question, it was because he thought that such a course was right, and probity, when all is said and done, is the most valuable equipment in any career. It was largely she who made him use this weight: he could use it equally well sitting down. Sometimes, of course, when he was in office he had to stand up and make a statement of policy, uninspired always, but full of plain common sense, and always to be listened to as the conviction of a perfectly honest man with regard to the welfare of his country. No wizardry of speech, no

sophistically attractive argument liable to be torn to
shreds, no ridicule of his opponents, in the modern mode,
gave spice to these laborious pronouncements ; once
he yawned heavily in the middle of a statement, and
accounted for this lapse by explaining that what he was
saying 'was so damned dull.' He found it so himself,
and that was partly why it was impressive. Later, when
as Duke he came into his enormous properties, he preserved an engaging ignorance born of complete indifference as to what was his. A friend of mine one day
going down to stay with him for a week-end at Compton
Place near Eastbourne, left London in the morning in
order to ramble in the country and in especial to visit the
noble ruin of Pevensey Castle, which belonged to the
Duke. He told his host that evening what he had been
doing, and how deeply impressed he was by Pevensey.
The Duke was vaguely interested, but he had heard the
name before. 'Pevensey?' he said. 'Whose is
Pevensey?' But the Duchess knew.

Most people found her rather formidable, for she
could be unexpectedly ruthless in her ways. They
never quite knew, and so they were careful. One day
a couple of young men drove over from Gisburn to
lunch with her at Bolton Abbey. Afterwards she drove
them out in a waggonette with a pair of horses to see
the Strid, where the River Wharfe bustles down, swift
and deep, between narrow rocks. It was raining, a
cheerless day, but she would like a breath of air, and she
carried no umbrella, only a stick. As she was getting
back again into the waggonette, after having majestically
observed the Strid, one of the horses moved on a step,
then was checked again, and she was thrown forward on
to her knees in the carriage. Without a word she hit

her coachman smartly over the back with her stick, and
then seating herself said to her companions, 'As I was
just saying——.' On another occasion, when there
was some rumour about that Devonshire House was to
be sold, a friend, rather imprudently, asked her if it was
true. She said very drily: 'Yes, perfectly true. We
are proposing to live at Clapham Junction instead. So
convenient a train service.' This was the steam-roller
at work, neither kind nor unkind, but just crushing this
slightly impertinent obstacle. Later (for she lived to
be an old woman) she became the wraith of what she
had been, and still be-wigged and be-diamonded and
be-rouged, she was rather like the half-ruinous shell of
some castellated keep, with flower-boxes in full bloom
on the crumbling sills. She had had enough of it all
(and indeed she had had a good deal), enough of power,
which she had loved most of all, and of wealth and of
position: playing cards and race cards were the toys to
beguile the last lap of her superb course. She did not
care any more, and in the absence of external stimulus
she became almost a piece of still life, expressionless,
speechless and motionless. Up till the end that luck
which had always attended her, still held, for she knew
nothing of death when it came. She had a stroke while
at a race meeting at Sandown, and never recovered
consciousness.

Lady Londonderry was equally enamoured of
power, and had a far keener appreciation of its insignia.
She revelled in personal splendour, she frankly and
unmitigatedly enjoyed standing at the head of her
stairs when some big party was in progress, with the
'family fender,' as she called that nice diamond crown
gleaming on her most comely head, and hugging the

fact that this was her house, and that she was a
marchioness from top to toe and was playing the part
to perfection. She was of course far younger than the
Duchess and quite lacked the subtlety of the other.
She liked violence and strong colour, and sweeping
along with her head in the air, vibrant with vitality.
She did not plot or plan or devise, she ' went for ' life,
hammer and tongs, she collared it, and scragged it and
rooked it like a highwaywoman in a tiara, trampling on
her enemies, as if they had been a bed of nettles—and
occasionally getting stung about the ankles in the
process—incapable of leniency towards them, or of
disloyalty to her friends. She did not want to forgive
her enemies, nor did she want any peace-conferences
with them : she hated them with a genial sincerity, and
loved her friends without reserve. She was in the
great style and liked to know that the Talbot blood
which was hers, was described, by some mediaeval
Latin chronicler, as the most unbridled strain. She
had the stuff in her of autocratic empresses, the kindliest
heart towards those to whom she was well disposed,
and a vitality which, like a bracing wind to those who
can stand it, raised the vitality of any who were exposed
to it. But if they couldn't stand it, it merely flattened
them out. She lived on a plane of high-pitched sensation of the most catholic kind : sailing a small boat in
a gale of wind, the twelve o'clock Communion at St.
Paul's Cathedral, the state-coach in which she attended
the opening of Parliament, a loud noise on the organ,
all these were of the quality which gave her sustenance.

Naturally (being what she was) she wanted to
manage everything for everybody, and though she
would always do her best that her friends should get

their hearts' desire, she distinctly preferred that she should compass this for them in her own way. She was always very conscious of herself (a very different thing from being self-conscious in the usual sense of the word) and she continually remembered who she was : you might almost say that she impersonated herself (she was an inimitable mimic) with realism and gusto. Then in the middle of this exposition of her imperious will and her ebullient blood and her arrogant certainty, she would suddenly turn over a new leaf in this illuminated manuscript of herself, and you saw written there (in the margin and minutely) little tender things. A tiny instance must suffice though perhaps it may not seem so significant to others as to one who knew her well. The King had come to tea with her one afternoon and that evening she happened to be dressed rather early for dinner, and came into her drawing-room before her time, and saw that her house-maid was still tidying it up. The girl had not heard her enter and she was employing herself, duster in hand, in sitting down on all the chairs, one after the other. Lady Londonderry instantly guessed what was the purpose of these odd sessions, and pointed to one of the chairs. ' That was the chair the King sat on,' she said. ' Sit down on it.'

The third of these great ladies, Lady Ripon, had little in common with the two others, except that she was also of the grand style, superb in dignity and manner. Unlike the Duchess of Devonshire she regarded everything connected with politics with a sort of weary repulsion ; unlike Lady Londonderry she neither had nor wished to have a great London house for stately and magnificent entertaining. During the years of the nineties, she was still in the zenith of her youthful splendour. She was very tall, a full six feet, but of so matchless a grace that the effect was not that she looked tall, but that most other women looked squat. Her beauty was of the quality that can only be described as dazzling ; when she was there the rest appeared a shade shabby. They wanted a touch of the sponge or duster. She had a series of beautiful names : first she had been Lady Gladys Herbert, then she was Countess of Lonsdale, now in the nineties she was Countess de Grey, and presently became Marchioness of Ripon—who ever had such lovely names or so well became them? Henry James, who had a passion for nomenclature appropriate to the style of his heroines, could not have named her more aptly. At this time she had a smallish house in Bruton Street where she entertained with a touch of that apotheosized Bohemianism of which nobody else ever quite had the secret.

One such evening, though it must be nearer forty than thirty years ago, has its lights still brightly burning for me. It was the last night of the opera season, and Edouard and Jean de Reszke came on to a little party there. There were not more than fifty guests all told, the Duke of Cambridge was among them, and he, sitting on a very low chair, was sunk in the condition which hypnotists call 'light trance'; not asleep, at least not at all sound asleep, but slightly oblivious to external impressions. Then Alick Yorke came tripping in, with a little rouge and an eyebrow and a stupendous carnation in his button-hole, not much more than five feet tall. He looked up at his hostess who had done her hair in some amazing manner, piling it on the top of her head, while somewhere near the summit was a diamond crescent; indeed for once she looked almost too tall. Alick Yorke surveyed her critically, blinked up at the crescent, and with a little lisp he said, 'Dear Gladys, I like the way you've done your hair to-night. It gives you what you've always wanted—height.' Oscar Wilde came drifting largely along, and caught sight of some new arrival. 'Oh, I'm so glad you've come,' he said. 'There are a hundred things I want not to say to you.' Then Réjane recited 'La Poupée,' and after a few trifles of that kind, all rather informally bestowed, Lady de Grey, purely for a joke, said to Edouard de Reszke, 'Won't you sing something?' He, instead of answering her according to her folly and saying he hadn't brought his music, said, 'But certainly I will, though I have never sung in so small a room. I will sing you " Le Veau d'Or " from " Faust." ' He had a prodigious volume of voice when he chose to open it out, and now he sang 'Le Veau d'Or' as loud as he possibly could, and the windows rattled, and the crystal festoons of the chandelier quivered. He sang it with extravagant operatic gestures, parodying himself, with an eye all the time on the Duke of Cambridge, but he never disturbed the light trance. And then Jean de Reszke, fired by this noble exhibition, and slightly jealous, said, 'But I want to sing too. I will show you how I sing the " Preis-lied." ' So he found two footstools and placed them in the middle of the room, and insecurely perched on them proceeded also to parody himself. He sang it as he always sang it, but with some absurd exaggeration of gesture and caricature of the way he took his high notes. Never was anything quite so ludicrous, and before he had finished his singing there was not, quite in the Victorian manner, a dry eye

in the room except those of the Duke of Cambridge. . . .
Bohemia in excelsis : Bohemia in tiaras.

Now possibly Réjane might have recited at a party
of the Duchess of Devonshire's or of Lady Londonderry's
for some colossal fee, and just possibly the de Reszkes
might have consented to sing there, but there was no
one but Lady de Grey for whom they would have
rollicked like this, just for the fun of it.   They were
not stars at this remarkable party, they were merely
her guests in the *milieu* which they all loved.   At heart
she was Bohemian, while socially a great lady on a
pinnacle which, in the eyes of the world, was higher
than any other.   But the pageant of her existence was
to her merely a painted background.   It was pleasant
to have it there, and probably she could not have done
without it, but it was only her setting, and did not make
her life, for she had far too much ability and brains to
be content with it.   She hated politics, she did not
care for such pastimes as cards, her mind, though
exceedingly subtle and perceptive, was not of the blue-
stocking order that can immerse itself in literary or artistic
study, and she abhorred the high-brow.   Her husband
was one of the best shots in the world, possibly quite
the best, but to entertain parties all the autumn at her
father-in-law's house at Studley Royal was wearisome-
ness, for she had not the smallest interest in sport.   She
was essentially urban, she yawned in the country,
and the ' vernal wood ' provided her with no impulses
or ecstasies.   She disliked any form of physical exercise,
though when bicycling became for a brief space one
of the fashionable crazes of the nineties, she took it up
for a while.   But she did not want to trundle through
rough country lanes, and listen to the cuckoo.   It was

fun sometimes in the evening, when there was no traffic in the City, to skim over the asphalted ways with a few friends and return to a supper party, but she soon had enough of that. All such things with which many women fill their lives, her own distinction, her own pinnacle in the world, the never-ending round of social engagements were all trivial to the eagerness of an unsatisfied though not dissatisfied mind. She wanted a definite ' stunt ' to occupy her, and a year or so before that party of hers about which I have spoken she had found it in the opera. Opera was urban, there was the touch of Bohemianism about it, and its pageantry and artifice suited her sophistication.

At this time in London it was languishing in an incredible tawdriness. Rossini and Donizetti and Gounod were the chief masters in the repertoire of Covent Garden, and the performances were ill-rehearsed, ill-staged, and interpreted by a wretched orchestra and squalling singers to shabby and sparse houses. Once it had been a great institution in the days when Queen Victoria and the Prince Consort came to the Haymarket to hear Mario and Grisi or Jenny Lind, and since then had been great singers such as Adelina Patti, but it had fallen from its high estate and the whole affair, both in front of the footlights and behind them, must be revitalized. Opera must be made the fashion : boxes must gleam with the jewels of beautiful women, and the stage must resound with glorious voices singing noble music. About music technically Lady de Grey knew nothing, nor was she musical in the sense that it was a need of her nature. She could not, without aching weariness, have sat out a symphony of Beethoven unless she had been a personal friend of the composer or the conductor. But now

when in this regeneration of the opera, which was
mainly due to her, great artists flocked to London,
Edouard and Jean de Reszke and Ternina and Melba,
her friendship with them gave her stunt a living
interest which mere music did not possess for her.
It was her beloved Melba who was enchanting all the
gleaming boxes with her flawless singing as Mimi,
and it was Jean de Reszke who *ritterlich* as no other
Lohengrin had ever been, came down the Scheldt,
and bade farewell to his swan. And when he called
for his swan again to ferry him away, there was no
longer any such catastrophe to be feared as had once
been presented in the shabbier days to the astonished
stalls, when, after the knight had taken his place again
between its wings, the swan did not glide away on its
motif as Wagner had directed that it should, but remained planted very firmly in the centre of the stage.
The orchestra held on as long as it could to the final
chord, by which time the swan should have made its
exit, and various tuggings and wheezings of ropes behind the stage were heard, but the bird heeded them not.
Then, with a smart explosion, the head and neck of the
swan broke off, and flew into the wings, as if discharged
from a catapult, leaving a decapitated bird and an agitated
knight to be tugged away by a workman in shirt-sleeves.

Nor were surprising musical accidents to be expected
any more from the orchestra. Richter conducted the
Wagner performances; he had worked at Baireuth
under the Master's tuition, and the orchestra, swayed by
the spell of his magic wand, became the voice of one
melodious presence. The quality of the singers also,
who equally responded to the inspiration, was, irre-
spective of the great primos and primas, far finer than

that at Baireuth, and Richter frankly said that it had always been his belief that Wagner's music would one day return to Germany, sung and not barked and yelled, and now he knew that it would be England who set the example. 'The Ring,' 'Tristan,' 'Meistersinger' and the rest (not of course 'Parsifal') were nobly given, and it was here at Covent Garden that Ternina, the most peerless artist of them all, sang her swan-song as Isolde and thereafter was mute. That night I was with Lady de Grey in her box, and for the first time opera profoundly moved her, for she knew that her friend Ternina would never sing again. And never was the Liebestod sung as she sang it then : she sang it quite privately, bending over Tristan's dead body, and at the end she died herself to all that had been life to her.

It was not that Lady de Grey made sure for herself that the swan's neck in Lohengrin was robustly joined to its body, or that she swung in the Rhine maidens' trapezes, or tried Jean de Reszke's voice, or criticized the wood-wind in the orchestra, or told Hans Richter that he must go to bed if he was to be fresh for 'Siegfried' next day, or even insisted that her friends should take boxes at the Opera and wear their tiaras, but it was directly due to her that this regeneration of the opera took place. She wanted it, she intended to have it, and hers was a personality that usually got what it wanted. Somewhat similarly, as one of his staff told me, Lord Kitchener sat at the War Office in the early days of August 1914, and rapped with his knuckles on the table and said 'I want a million men' until he got them. That was the effect of his personality : and it was thus that Lady de Grey sat in the centre of the web in touch with it all. Seemingly rather effortless but appreciative, she was actually the initial and effective force. An apparent casualness was her chief weapon; she would do no more than mention how magnificently Melba had sung last night, and how pleasant it was to see so many friends in the full tiers. In reality she was taking endless trouble, though it looked (she did it so easily) as if she was merely leading the life of pageantry that was natural to her. She had a house now down at Coombe, easy of access from London, people came down there to have tea and stroll about and dine, and it seemed almost accidental that on the evening when the Princess of Wales came down to dine with her, it happened to be an off-night at the opera, and in consequence Melba and Jean de Reszke were there too, and so after dinner there was a little singing. It was not so easy to hear either of them except at the opera, for Melba only took one private engagement a year when she sang at the house of Mr. Alfred de Rothschild for a suitable sum, and Jean's appearance at a private concert was just as rare. Those folk therefore who were privileged to hear them like this in mufti were very apt (and with good reason) to tell everyone how marvellously they had sung, and that was very good for the opera, while the divine choristers had been delighted to sing for the Princess of Wales. Such an entertainment seemed quite casual and fortuitous, though as a matter of fact, these parties gave Lady de Grey torture-hours of anxiety, so desperately keen was she that everything should go swimmingly, and all her guests enjoy themselves. Above all it was done privately; the searchlights of the Press never succeeded in getting Coombe on to the illuminated area, nor did 'Hermione' and 'Jezebel' ever recount how they had chatted with friends on Lady de Grey's lawn, and saw her smoking a cigarette out of an amber holder. She completely evaded the limelight, and though she immensely enjoyed entertaining her Royal guests, and having the evening stars to sing to them, she had not the faintest desire to let the public know all about it. In this respect she differed from Lady Londonderry, who loved driving in the family coach through crowded streets to the opening of Parliament. If Lady de Grey had ever dreamt of attending such a function, she would certainly have gone there in a four-wheeler with the blinds down. Nothing was more alien to her than the desire to astound the citizens by her splendour or regale them with news of her parties : she would as soon have done conjuring tricks with a rabbit and a pack of cards in Piccadilly Circus. She did not think of them as 'canaille' or anything of the sort, but like Dr. Jowett she did not think of them at all.

It was inevitable that since she was not musical she should have tired of her creation when it was finished. She had done what she set out to do, but that was not primarily to enjoy a first-rate operatic performance any night during the season, but to clean and wind up this shabby old clock and set it going and striking the hours. The greatest singers of the time appeared here now, Wagner was sung here as nowhere else in the world, and, perhaps hardly less of an achievement, the house now on a gala night or on a Melba night was a scene of almost barbaric splendour, and that too was part of her creation. She had no sort of sympathy with the indigent music lover (not being a music lover herself) who wanted his opera cheap, for if he wanted that he could go to Germany, and she would have

sickened at the thought of the stalls being invaded by
men in Norfolk jackets, or of the *foyer* being peopled
by short-skirted women smoking cigarettes : her opera
at Covent Garden was not for such, it was an expensive
piece of luxury for the wealthy. For English composers and English singers, similarly, she had no sympathy at all : she thought of them vaguely as people
who wrote and performed oratorios in cathedral towns.
By nature and taste she was very cosmopolitan, and,
like most cosmopolitans, she preferred foreign products
to native; opera to her connoted something coming from
abroad. But the relentless years ticked on, the velvet
of the voices of the two de Reszkes began to show signs
of wear, and like wise men they did not outstay their
warning. She took less trouble now over what she
had inaugurated, the business part of it was in excellent
hands, and she did not care to take up new singers and
play the gorgeous Bohemian godmother over again.
But when the Russian ballet appeared in England her
interest in the affairs of Covent Garden swiftly revived.
This form of art was new to her, it was violent, it was
intensely artificial, it was exotic and Bohemian, vivid
as a gorgeous butterfly, and it excited her in itself in
a way that music had never done. But there was no
proselytizing to be undertaken here, for it took London
by storm. Then came the war, and she discarded
ballet and opera and the whole of her past modes of
life like worn-out toys. She showed what noble stuff,
what humble zeal for service lay below her pageantries,
and up till the time when a disease, cruel and hideous,
wholly incapacitated her, she spent every day and all
day in the management of the military hospital in
Waterloo Road, capable and tender and beloved.

Time, the mere lapse of it, performs the function of a telescope; through its extended tube one perceives things at a distance in very clear shape and outline, whereas more recent happenings, for the scrutiny of which no such telescope can be used, are often far more fluid and undetermined. They have not yet 'set,' they shift and slide under the eye, various lights, which confuse as well as illuminate, play upon them, and they have not yet undergone that quasi-crystallization which more remote, more documented objects have acquired. The latter have somehow shed the topical trappings which dangle irrelevant issues before us, they appear in a drier and more distinct light, and their main outlines, focused through the telescope of time, are firmly fixed. Unfortunately the telescope has two ends, and the observer may be applying one or the other one to his eye (he never knows which for certain) and the objects he brings into its focused field may now appear to be bigger than they really were, or very much smaller. The clumsy fellow in fact never can be quite sure whether he is exaggerating or whether he is missing a larger significance than the objects appear to him to possess. He can only give an account of them based on what he believes himself to see, and perhaps these figures of great ladies here presented were not so remarkable as through his telescope he fancies them to have been, nor perhaps was Mr. Gladstone so cosmic and overwhelming a personage.

But they and others like them persist in appearing larger than those contemporary figures which now occupy their positions and offices, and he insists that the late Lord Salisbury also belonged to the larger breed. Other Prime Ministers have steered the country through

far more perilous waters, and far vaster responsibilities
have lain on their shoulders than ever burdened the
statesmen of the nineties, but the sight of Mr. Asquith
going down to the House of Commons in the early days
of the war or of Mr. Baldwin knocking out the ashes of
his pipe seemed less striking symbols of the majesty of
imperial affairs than Mr. Gladstone waving his umbrella
to arrest a cab, or Lord Salisbury labouring on his
tricycle through St. James's Park in the early hours of
the day. His was the grand style, something Elizabethan, and he wore his office with the same indifference
as his Garter robes, and that very indifference, the
naturalness of it, was impressive. One admirable
instance of it was when he consulted my father about
some appointment. There were two candidates discussed, whom we will call Mr. Smithson and Mr. Jameson,
and my father recommended Mr. Jameson. Lord
Salisbury acquiesced, and said he would make the appointment. A day or two later my father had occasion
to write to the Prime Minister again on the matter,
referring in his letter to the newly appointed Mr.
Jameson, and received the following reply :

I do not know which of our memories was wrong, but
I thought it was Smithson not Jameson we had agreed upon.
Both are Liberal M.P.s. Unfortunately before I received
your Grace's letter, I had sent in Mr. S.'s name to the Queen.
But I daresay it will do as well.

That surely was in the grand style : all Liberal M.P.s
were clearly much the same sort of person, and if, in
addition, their names were so very similar, who could
be expected to distinguish between these dim specimens ?
And in any case, whoever was responsible for the confusion, it could not much matter which of them was

appointed. But behind this superb indifference to such minor accidents in patronage, there was a very stubborn obstinacy from which it was very difficult to move him if he thought the question was really important. The Queen also could be equally immovable if she too had made up her mind, and on one occasion certainly she was too much for him. For the Bishopric of Durham, one of the very greatest positions in the Church, had fallen vacant, owing to the death of Bishop Lightfoot in 1890, and the Queen, after consultation with my father, had felt sure that the right man for the post was Bishop Westcott. But Lord Salisbury, who as Prime Minister had to make his recommendation to her, refused to put forward his name and told her so. He added that ' he had been looking into some of Westcott's works, and thought he would be unsuited to Durham.' Though there was a humorous side to the picture of Lord Salisbury adopting the rôle of the conscientious theological student and, after purchasing and perusing Westcott's 'Gospel According to St. John,' deciding that the author was not fitted to occupy an important See, there was a deadlock of an embarrassing kind. He was determined ' not to be pushed,' the Queen was equally averse from being pulled, and she therefore prepared to remind him, quite in the style of Queen Elizabeth, that ' when all was said and done she was Queen of England.' She told Sir Henry Ponsonby that ' she intended to prevail,' and asked Lord Salisbury to come down and see her at Windsor. The interview took place (Queen Bess and Burleigh over again), and though we can only guess what she said, the effect was that the Bishopric of Durham was at once offered to Westcott.

On the other hand, in a year's time another bishopric fell

vacant, that of Winchester, and once more the Queen and
her Prime Minister could not agree as to the appointment.
She wanted Dean Davidson of Windsor to be appointed
to Winchester, for she had an immense opinion of his
wisdom, and he would thus take his seat at once in the
House of Lords ; also Windsor and Osborne were both
in that diocese.   She wrote two strong letters to Lord
Salisbury on the subject, but he would not hear of it,
though he was willing to offer Rochester to Dean
Davidson : he assigned reasons which the Queen thought
' most extraordinary.' So she wrote to my father
asking him to back her up and, without allusion to her
wishes in any way, to express a hope that Lord Salisbury
would appoint Dean Davidson to Winchester.   She
thought this independent recommendation would have
great weight.   But it proved to have none whatever,
and Lord Salisbury had his way. . . . He was a master
of ironic humour : one of his notable phrases, very
thoughtfully delivered, was ' the Draconic character
which usually marks philanthropic legislation.'   Again,
when he was asked for what sort of reason he had appointed Mr. Alfred Austin to be Poet Laureate in the
place of Lord Tennyson, he is reported to have said
(again with thoughtful candour) ' I don't think anybody
else applied for the post.' His opinion both of the
candidate and of the office to which he had presented
him could thereby be accurately gauged.

My family were deeply interested in this appointment,
for a short time before it was announced the poet had
stayed with us at Addington.   In anticipation of his
visit we had acquainted ourselves with some of his
pieces, and these had filled us with a horrid joy.   We
soon saw that he as well as his work was worth study,

for at dinner he told us (as already recounted) about his talks with Tennyson and how he had found fault with certain of his lines, and how Immortal Bard had confessed that these criticisms were just. That was promising, it boded well, and I am afraid we formed the design of drawing out Mr. Austin when he came to the smoking-room that night and getting all we could out of him. But there was no need to put this treacherous scheme into practice, for Mr. Austin poured himself out, of his own spontaneous uncorking, with a fullness and a foam that our clumsy handling could never have accomplished. He laid himself down, all five feet of him on the sofa, and as feast-master directed a wondrous symposium entirely about himself; *ipse fecit*. He told us how he had once been an occasional leader-writer to the *Standard*: forty-five minutes was the time it took him to write one of these leaders on whatever subject was required. Mr. Bryce was once staying with him, and very rashly expressed his firm conviction that nobody could write a leading article in forty-five minutes. Oddly enough there arrived at this precise moment a telegram for Mr. Austin in which the Editor of the *Standard* requested him to supply him with a leader on some particular subject without delay. He went at once into his study, and Mr. Bryce, having noted the time, sat in the garden to wait for him. As soon as Mr. Austin had finished his article, he went out to show it to Mr. Bryce. There it was complete, and Mr. Bryce looked at his watch. ' To be quite exact, forty-three minutes,' he said. ' I could not have believed it.'

But leader-writing was a mere toy (continued Mr. Austin), a piece of child's play, and when the *Standard* offered him £3000 a year to become a regular writer for

them, he could not entertain the idea. Then he wrote
two novels : ' they were dreadful rubbish,' he said, and
at that our faces fell, for this was not the Ercles-vein we
wanted. But presently we were comforted, for Mr.
Austin began to tell us of ' It.' ' It ' was the poetic
inspiration. Sometimes It left him altogether, and when
that first happened he was terribly upset, for he feared
that he would be able to write no more poetry, since he
never wrote a line except when It directed him. But
he-had learned since then that, though It might leave him
for a while, It always returned, and so he waited without
fretting or attempting to produce uninspired stuff, until
It came back. ' It left me once,' said Mr. Austin, ' after
the second Act of " The Human Tragedy." I had just
written the lines—

> As for the twain they vanished in the rattle
> Of jolting tumbrils and the joy of battle—

when It went. I could write no more and so I put my
pen away and waited. Then It came back and I went
straight on. Let me see : how does the third Act
begin ? Can any of you remember it ? ' Of course it
was on the tips of all our tongues, and we snapped our
fingers and said, ' Tut ! how stupid ! ' But then Mr.
Austin luckily remembered it himself.

Now this noble evening occurred after Lord
Tennyson's death, and I have a suspicion that Mr. Austin
had already sent in his application to Lord Salisbury,
for when, in a rather thoughtless manner, we hazarded
guesses as to the successor of Immortal Bard, he preserved
a very tactful silence. Great was our joy when the
appointment was gazetted, for now we all felt sure that
It would be with him when some imperial occasion

demanded that the heart of England should make itself
articulate.   These bright hopes were splendidly fulfilled,
for in 1897 Mr. Austin published that remarkable poem
'Who would not die for England?' (Sub-title Whip-
pingham-Sandringham, February 1896).   It brought
up to date the duties of the national bard to the Royal
House, which Mr. Austin thought had fallen into
arrears, for in its comprehensive stanzas it deplored the
recent death of a member of the Family; it recorded the
poetic vision of 'veiled Fate like muse inspired,' addressing the cradle in which lay the infant Prince of Wales in
those lines beginning ' Another Albert shalt thou
be,' and it paid the following tribute to the memory
of the Prince Consort who had died thirty-five years
before—

> Sweetest Consort, sagest Prince,
> Snows on snow have melted since
> England lost you : late to learn
> Worth that never can return :
>
> Learned to know you as you were,
> Known till then alone to Her !
> Luminous as sun at noon,
> Tender as the midnight moon :
> Steadfast as the steered-by Star :
> Wise as Time and Silence are.

We felt that It had been strongly functioning when such
lines as these were born, and waited eagerly for more.
The Jameson Raid inspired a fugitive composition,
and It was surely there when Mr. Austin wrote :

> They went across the veldt,
> As hard as they could pelt,

To him, too, is ascribed, though with what certainty
I know not, a wonderful couplet concerning the national
suspense during the illness of the Prince of Wales in
1870 : the internal evidence strongly supports the
theory.

> Across the wires the electric message came,
> He is no better, he is much the same.

That sounds very like It : that sounds like Mr. Austin
at his very best.   He never wrote a line except when
It was directing him, and he never fell below the standard
of what he considered his greatest work, ' The Human
Tragedy,' from which (as it has been suffered to fall
into an ill-merited oblivion) I must allow myself one
more quotation.   The poet is describing (under It)
how the rejected Godfrid receives a letter from the
mistress of his heart :

> He tore it open with a trembling hand,
> And with a greedy eye its message read,
> Written, it seemed, in haste and quickly scanned :
> ' I write to tell you my last news, instead
> Of leaving it to gossip's busy hand.
> I am engaged and shortly shall be wed.
> Congratulate me, won't you ?   All here send
> Their best regards.   I fear that I must end.'

All these gems, incredible but authentic, gave fresh
impetus to our scheme of bringing out a slender volume
(suitable for a Christmas present) called ' Leaves from
the Laurels of the Poets Laureate ' which should entirely
consist of precious fragments from the official bards
of England.   Laureate the Reverend Laurence Eusden
would lend us those striking lines in which he
addressed George II on his coronation :

> Hail mighty Monarch, whom desert alone
> Would without birthright, raise e'en to the Throne.
> Thy merits shine conspicuously nice,
> Ungloomed by contiguity to vice.

and Tennyson should contribute :

> O darling room, my heart's delight,
> Dear room, the apple of my sight,
> With thy two couches soft and white,
> There is no room so exquisite,
> No little room so warm and bright
> Wherein to read, wherein to write.

and Wordsworth should tell us how

> And five times to the Child I said
> Why, Edward, tell me why !

With these promising samples to show, I once submitted the scheme to our beloved Edmund Gosse, who gave it his high approval and promised an enthusiastic review. But he begged me to include among these gems a poem written by a housemaid of his wife's, which, he maintained, in the matter of triumphant bathos was quite up to the mark of our Laureates. No doubt she would have been laureated had it not been for her misfortune as regards sex : ' Besides,' said he, ' think of Sappho : you would not leave Sappho out of a Greek anthology : so do not be so narrow . . .' This young lady had no time to do her menial jobs among slops and soap-dishes for she was busy writing poetry, and Gosse pleaded with his wife not to dismiss her, for poetesses (see Sappho) stood outside the laws that applied to the common rabble. But she continued to write so much poetry and to empty so few slops that at length Mrs. Gosse would stand it no more, and gave her notice. She took her manuscripts with her, but when her room was being made ready for her meaner successor, it was found that she had overlooked one precious leaf on which was written the quatrain which Gosse implored me to include among the jewels of the Laureates. It was an ' Address to the Moon,' and ran as follows :

> O Moon, lovely Moon, with thy beautiful face,
> Careering throughout the boundáries of space,
> Whenever I see thee, I think in my mind,
> Shall I ever, oh ever, behold thy behind.

' It is bathos,' said Gosse, ' of purest ray serene, and incidentally it contains the statement of a profound astronomical problem.'

But our volume was of Laureates only, and though recognizing the quality of these lines, I could not include them any more than I can include in it certain gems that Mr. Gerald Gould, poet and critic, has lately given us. On him the mantle of Elijah has fallen, and though I know Mr. Austin's style very well, I should certainly have attributed to Elijah such lines as—

> And now we have a boy—like me, they say :
> Also I think a little bit like you ;

or the even finer conclusion to a poem about Lancelot and Guinevere :

> The eyes and cheeks of her grew hot,
> The hands and mouth of her grew dry :
> Her heart was clamorous for reply,
> But asked not, and was answered not ;
> Till in a sudden dreadful shout
> His passionate ' Guinevere ' rang out
> To meet her pitiful ' Lancelot.'

That's the true stuff, and I would that it was eligible
for my book. Perhaps an appendix. . . .

Edmund Gosse was of that rare breed, a natural
and instinctive man of letters, and English literature
will always be in his debt for the acuteness and sanity
of his critical faculty. The particular quality of it is
rather hard to describe : I may perhaps get nearest it
by saying that he was not appreciated in America. He
wrote one book, rather a cruel one, of first-rate merit,
'Father and Son,' and one poem called 'Tusitala,'
addressed to R. L. Stevenson, which will live long
in English anthologies, but he had neither that tragic
grip on life nor that deadly seriousness of aim out of
which alone arise masterpieces. As he himself said in
one of his graceful poems, 'I hold it best in living to
take all things very lightly,' and he had no taste for
'the singeing and the smoke' the struggle and the
suffocation of soul in which great original writers
constantly labour. Nor did he really care for the fruits
of such portentous travail, nor for what we may call the
blasting masterpieces of literature, works like the
'Divine Comedy' or 'Wuthering Heights,' or 'The
Brothers Karamazov.' Though he had a sincere
reverence for such and for the genius of the huge
brooding minds which made them, he did not devote
himself to the study of such large movements. In
many ways he was more like a tremendously intelligent
child who, playing on the sea shore, did not concern
himself with the sweep of the great tides, but splashed
ecstatically in the less menacing ripples with the keenest
of eyes for the adorable jetsam they flung up. He was
not at ease nor at his best in the presence of high tensions,
they made him feel uncomfortable, as if a thunderstorm

was brewing. So, skipping lightly from their neighbourhood, he devoted his taste, his knowledge, his
acumen to less cosmic phenomena. It was not that
he liked the second-rate in literature, for no one disliked
it more, but he liked the first-rate in its less violent
manifestations. Though it took a Pheidias to conceive
and execute the great presence of the Parthenon, it
also took a very great artist to paint an Attic vase or
carve a fine intaglio, and the vase and the intaglio were
more to his taste, first-rate work on a small scale. He
would never have dreamed of writing a commentary
on Isaiah, but he could bring to light all sorts of hidden
charms in the work of excellent though minor prophets.

There were the roaring masterpieces : anyone who
had a taste for being roasted alive might go and impale
himself on a spit in front of these sombre furnaces, but
for himself he preferred the cool and pleasant glades and
gardens of literature, its smoking-rooms, its libraries,
its firesides and arm-chairs. But he did not pass
mere hours of dozings and relaxations among these,
he was extremely active and wideawake in such surroundings, exercising to the full his powers of penetrating observation. But there was nothing to be said
about the more torrid masterpieces ; he was not equipped
for them, but for conveying in a light and urbane style
the most entertaining suggestions and speculations
about less perilous stuff, and in this field he was quite
unrivalled. Should you happen to be in need of very
accurate information based on dry scholarly research,
there were no doubt many safer guides than he, but if
you wanted the brilliant gossip of an amateur on a
subject, there was no one so stimulating. Thus, though
as a critical historian he made no important contribution

(except perhaps in his life of Donne) to literary knowledge, he gave you by means of that dancing will-o'-
the-wisp light of his, both in speech and written word,
a constant galaxy of enchanting glimpses. For some
years before his death he wrote a weekly review in the
Sunday Times, which exhibited his method and style
of criticism at its very best, urbane and cultivated.
His first object, always apparent, was to put himself
in sympathy with his author, and then, turning himself
into a delightful Master of the Ceremonies, to introduce him to his reader as a charming fellow. Like
all good critics he was always advocate rather than
judge, and never found it worth his while to assume
the black cap or thunder from the critical Olympus.
His object as a critic was to point out what was to be
praised; there were plenty of myopic reviewers who
could see nothing beyond motes in their author's eye
by reason of the beam in their own and triumphantly
detected small misprints or lapses of grammar. Most
of all he detested an attitude of pompous self-assertive-
ness in a critic, that pontification with tiara and *sedia
gestatoria* and its flatulent pronouncements. Gosse
never called attention to himself when he spoke of other
people's books. He chatted in his arm-chair, but
anyone could see how sound his critical faculty was.

His companionship had all the charm and the stimulus
of his writing, wit and humour and a most delicate
and airy perception of the ludicrous. Occasionally,
a little wariness was needed with him, for something
went awry, some sensitiveness of his was stung, something offended him, and he would suddenly dry up, and
sit glaring glassily through his spectacles and bow
silently with a slightly acid smile if a remark was

addressed to him.   Mrs. Gosse knew perfectly how to
deal with such a mood, for the symptoms were clear
to her, and if he was really vexed she would let him be
and divert attention from him ; if she saw that his disturbance was superficial she would say in a comfortable
voice, ' Edmund is being tiresome, just poke him,' and
the glassy aspect melted, and at once he was the joyous
talker again.   He had known with a revelling Bos-
wellian intimacy most of the great literary figures of
his day, and would tell you how Swinburne came to
him one morning chuckling and twitching and snapping
his fingers.   ' Emerson will be surprised,' he said ' to
receive the letter I wrote him last night, for I reminded
him that he was a debilitated and now toothless ape,
who, once hoisted into prominence on the shoulders
of Carlyle, now spits and gibbers from a platform of
his own finding and fouling.' [1]   He had been intimate
with R. L. Stevenson from the time of the gallant
invalid days of his youth, and to the end of his life had
a boy's hero-worship for him, not only and perhaps
not chiefly as author (for I think that some faint doubts,
instantly suppressed, occasionally assailed him as to
whether R. L. S. was quite so supreme a master as he
always maintained), but as the most entrancing personality he had ever come across. ' The gods had come down
in the likeness of men,' and he was to Gosse the most
radiant of all his memories.

Or he would tell you how the late Lord Houghton
had been present at a dinner given to George Curzon
by his friends, to congratulate him on his appointment
to one of his earlier political posts.   Lord Houghton

---

[1] This was Swinburne's account of his own letter to Edmund Gosse. The
actual wording of it, I believe, differs slightly.

had got very drowsy, as sometimes happened, during the speeches that followed, and woke up just as the hero of the evening, now in the middle of a suave and polished oration, was assuring his admirers that any success that had come to him was entirely due to his having made it a rule of his life only to associate with his intellectual superiors. This was a very apt and pretty compliment to everybody present, and they gently preened themselves on being his associates. But Lord Houghton saw it in another light. 'By God!' he exclaimed, 'That wouldn't be difficult,' and the unerring tact of the future Viceroy of India prompted him to pursue that line of thought no further.

Unlike most people who talk exceedingly well and many who talk exceedingly badly, Gosse had never the slightest desire or tendency to monopolize. He much preferred that the ball of conversation should be thrown backwards and forwards, and when it came to him he made his brilliant catch, and instead of retaining it, threw it lightly away to some other player. Of the three wittiest talkers I have ever known he stood midway in habit between the two others, namely Harry Higgins, who in later years, owing to an operation on his throat, spoke only in a whisper and did not join in general conversation, and Oscar Wilde, who also seldom joined in general conversation because he conducted the most of it himself. Of the three, for sheer wit in making *mots* and in comments, *obiter dicta*, always sharp as a needle and possibly Rabelaisian, Harry Higgins was without rival. He did not, like Gosse, keep the ball of conversation in the air, he did not, like Oscar Wilde, hold the table entertained with spoutings and eloquence and amazing fireworks, but in that confidential whisper there came from his lips, as from the mouth of the good little child in the fairy tale, a pearl or a gem each time he opened them. It was quite inimitable : nobody else had the secret of those ludicrous and humorous thrusts. There was once, for instance, in connection with the Opera Syndicate of Covent Garden of which he was the business manager, a question as to the engagement of a very notable lady to sing there, and to him fell the task of discussing with her the terms for her appearance. Notable as she was as a singer, with a fine though not a superb voice, she was perhaps even more notable (in fact she had a European reputation) for her beauty, her temperamental nature, her charm and her broad-minded views. When the question arose as to the terms of her appearance, she asked a really prodigious sum—a sum, so it seemed to him, out of all proportion to her quality as a singer. So with infinite tact and politeness, he whispered to her, ' But we only want you to sing.' . . . One night I met him on the steps of the Garrick Club, and he suggested we should dine together. A particularly odious book of reminiscences had just come out in which the author had published the current private affairs of his friends with a good deal of malice and mischief, and the victims were justly furious, but rather vociferously so : everybody had anathema to hurl at him, even if he had said nothing particularly objectionable about them. As we sat down at our table Harry Higgins said to me, ' Have you read that brute's book ? I've looked at the index, which is the same thing, and found I was mentioned seventeen times. So I turned them all up and saw that on each of these occasions he had been to dine with me. Now what right has the man to tell the world that ?

It's monstrous : I've been trying to conceal it all my life.' . . .

Lady Randolph Churchill, whose friendship will always remain so dear and vivid a memory to me that sometimes still I find myself thinking that I must remember to tell her some witty trifle I have heard, had something of the same swift aptness. She once asked our most pungent critic and dramatist to spend a week-end at her house. He had lately been lifting up his voice against the practice of week-end parties, and, scenting advertisement, he scribbled a refusal on a post-card with the query, 'Why this assault on my well-known principles about week-ends ?' Instantly she seized a telegram form and wrote on it, 'I know nothing about your principles, but hope they are better than your manners.' One night she was playing bridge with me, and after hectic hours of hard work she won exactly a shilling. She greedily seized it. 'Is all that mine ?' she said. 'Someone will want to marry me for my money.'

Of the third of these witty men I will tell presently.

CHAPTER X

TWO SCANDALS

THERE were, during the period of the nineties, two scandals accompanied by trials in the law courts, both of which produced an immense sensation and a din of public hooting. The first of these, which was the more openly and vehemently discussed, was the Tranby Croft affair in 1891. The second, to the sequel of which is attached a remarkable literary interest, was the trial of Oscar Wilde four years later. To both of them I have a little material not generally known to contribute.

With regard to the first, the main facts, briefly stated, were as follows. The Prince of Wales (subsequently King Edward VII) went to stay at Mr. Arthur Wilson's house, Tranby Croft, near Doncaster, for the St. Leger meeting in September 1890. There was a large party in the house, most of whom, after dinner on the first evening of his visit, amused themselves with a game of baccarat. There were counters denoting various sums of money up to ten pounds, which, as usual, players purchased at the beginning of the game, and accounts were settled at the end of it. The counters used were the property of the Prince of Wales, and the game was conducted in the ordinary manner. It was entirely the concern of the people who played it, but owing to an unfortunate incident that occurred on this and the next evening, there developed out of it a most prodigious scandal.

On the first night they played at a make-shift table, and during the progress of the game Mr. A. S. Wilson, a son of the house, observed, so he thought, that his neighbour, Sir William Gordon-Cumming, Lieutenant-Colonel in the Scots Guards, was cheating. He whispered what he had seen to Mr. Berkeley Levett, who was sitting on his other side, and who was a subaltern in the same regiment. They then both watched him, and again saw him cheating, withdrawing or augmenting his stake, under cover of his hand, according to the value of the cards he received. When the game was over Mr. Wilson told his mother the same night what had occurred, and next morning also told his brother-in-law, Mr. Lycett Green, who told his wife. There were thus five persons already who knew about it. As there would probably be a game of baccarat again on the second night, Mr. A. S. Wilson procured a table of more convenient shape, on which it was hoped that cheating would be impossible. Though at the subsequent trial all these five persons denied that there had been any agreement between them to watch Sir William, in order to see if he would cheat again, they all did watch him, and though there may have been no agreement to do so, such was their intention.

Now that was not a very pleasant thing to do, and assuredly none of them could have liked doing it. A party of friends and of guests in the same house was to sit down to a cheery little game of cards, and all the time, *au-dessous des cartes*, there would be going on this grim piece of criminal investigation. Some men, no doubt, would have felt that whatever course was taken, it must not be that, for detective work among friends would have appeared to them a prohibitively ugly business. Moreover, in acting thus, they omitted to consider that, supposing on this second occasion they saw nothing to confirm their suspicions, there would always have been left in their minds the belief that this man had cheated the night before. They could not possibly have rid themselves of that notion, and while additional evidence would convict him, the absence of it would not (in their minds) have really cleared him, for two of them were perfectly certain that they had seen what the five now, though without a formal agreement to watch, were on the look out for. On the other hand it was very difficult to know what else they could do. It would have been useless to have taxed Sir William with having cheated the night before, for he would have denied it, even as he subsequently did when they had obtained a far higher degree of certainty than they at present possessed. It would have been equally useless, as regards the object they had in view if their suspicions were confirmed, to arrange that there should be no more baccarat that night, for the suspect would then have been free to continue his practices, and that they were determined, if his guilt was established, to stop.

So on this second night they sat down again to this damnable friendly game of baccarat: the Prince of Wales, as on the night before, took the bank. All five of the observers saw that on more than one occasion Sir William put his stake close to the line which is drawn round the table and separates the counters that are staked from those the player has in hand. If he got a good card, he supplemented his stake, if a bad one, he withdrew it or a portion of it. Their suspicions ceased to be suspicions at all, for they were convinced of the truth of them.

Next day, after further confabulation, those who had watched told Lord Coventry and General Owen Williams, who was a close friend of Sir William Gordon-Cumming, what they had seen, and it was decided first to tell Sir William and then the Prince of Wales, who up to this point knew nothing whatever about what was going on. This was done. The Prince then interviewed Sir William in the presence of Lord Coventry and General Owen Williams, and afterwards those who had seen the unfair play. They all regarded a man who cheated at cards as a pest and an intolerable danger to his friends, and they determined to stop his card-playing. With the Prince's concurrence he was sent for and given a choice of two alternatives, and a declaration was written out in which he promised on his word of honour not to play cards for money again. If he would sign that, the committee promised him on their part that the matter would go no further, and that no one outside themselves should ever know about what had occurred. If he refused to sign, no such secrecy would be binding on them. Thereupon, though protesting his innocence, he signed the declaration, and it was witnessed by ten persons, of whom the Prince was the first signatory. The declaration was then put in the hands of the Prince, who sent it up to his private secretary in London, by whom it was placed, unopened, among his personal papers.

Some member (or possibly members) of this committee, who had obtained Sir William's signature on the definite promise that the matter would never be

heard of again, must have given this pact away, for
before the end of the year, he received an anonymous
communication from Paris, which showed him that the
secrecy had been violated. A more odious treachery
can hardly be conceived, and the victim of it brought
an action for defamatory scandal against Mrs. Arthur
Wilson, Mr. A. S. Wilson, Mr. and Mrs. Lycett Green
and Mr. Berkeley Levett, who were, it will be remembered, the five persons who on the second night had
observed his play, and, in consequence of what they saw,
had told Lord Coventry and General Owen Williams,
who in turn told the Prince. Sir William cited the
Prince to appear as witness, and when the trial took
place in the following June 1891, he took his place in
the witness-box, and was examined by Sir Edward
Clarke, counsel for the prosecution. It was not a
pretty company to appear in : one of his friends had
cheated at cards (so ran the defence), several had par-
taken in a friendly game to make sure that he was
a swindler, and of the ten signatories, one certainly
had broken his word of honour that he would never
divulge what had passed. Human nature being what
it is, a secret shared by ten persons is precariously placed,
and in this case it did not preserve its balance for long,
but the individual traitor is none the less ugly for that
reason. According to an ingenious theory, lately
advanced by an eminent solicitor, there was no such
traitor, but it was observed next day at the Doncaster
races that Sir William was looking anxious and depressed, and that the rest of the party, notably the Prince,
had no converse with him. From this (it is argued)
suspicion was aroused that something very unpleasant
had taken place, and the true story gradually took shape.

A fatal objection to this theory, apart from the remarkable clairvoyance required, is that the entire Tranby Croft party dispersed next day, in consequence of a death in the family, and that not a single one of them went to the races at all.

At the trial the evidence which most told against the plaintiff was the fact that he had signed this paper promising never to play cards again, and that was certainly most awkward, for this did not look like the conduct of an innocent man. His explanation was that, though innocent, he wished at any personal sacrifice to keep the Prince's name out of the affair. This view his counsel Sir Edward Clarke believed to be true. Sir Edward Clarke also argued that if the Prince of Wales and General Owen Williams had believed that Sir William had cheated they were bound to have reported it to the military authorities, and this they had not done. He inferred therefore that the Prince had not believed him guilty. A juryman, however, asked the Prince whether he believed him guilty or not, and the Prince said that he had no option, in the face of such support, to do otherwise. For the defence there was the impregnable argument that five persons, and those his friends, were sure they had seen him cheat on more than one occasion, and unless there was some monstrous and incredible conspiracy on their part, or unless they were all the victims of a collective hallucination, there was no explaining it away. The verdict was exactly that which might have been expected, and the case was given for the defence.

The scandal that followed was colossal. Not only in England but abroad the Press teemed with it. A German comic paper produced a cartoon showing the

great door into Windsor Castle, surmounted by the Prince
of Wales's feathers and the motto ' Ich Deal.' French
papers had columns of far more acid matter, and the
Prince's private game of baccarat became the business
of the whole world : you would have thought that
baccarat was the sin that could never find remission.
It was all very unpleasant, but what really mattered was
the universal disgust of the English Press. The incident was made the occasion of the most virulent attacks
on the Prince : Stead, in his *Review of Reviews*, applied
the test of the ' Prayer Gauge.' He calculated with
ruthless arithmetic how many times in the various
churches of the United Kingdom prayer had been offered
during the last fifty years on behalf of the Prince of
Wales since the day of his birth, and how many people
had sincerely said ' Amen,' and drew the conclusion
that the baccarat scandal had been the only answer
vouchsafed from on high to these millions of petitions.
If the Prince himself had been detected cheating, he
could not have been more savagely sentenced. In
particular all papers of a serious or religious turn,
especially Church papers and Nonconformist papers,
trumpeted their horror, like great moral elephants
piously running amok. They told their readers that
the Prince carried gambling counters with his Royal
device wherever he went, that he insisted that the party
should join him in high play : that his host at Tranby
Croft would never allow gambling in his house, but
had been obliged to yield to the Prince's wishes : in a
word he was made scapegoat for all that had happened
and all that was invented, and was denounced as the
ringleader in that odious vice of gambling which was
undermining the morals of the country. He was

exposed to an unparalleled tempest of abuse, and, owing to his position, he could not say a single word on his own behalf, though, as it turned out, he had plenty of very just observations to make. Doubtless in these attacks there was much genuine indignation that the heir to the throne should have been mixed up in so unsavoury an affair, but it was obvious that in these attacks there was a great deal of insincere gusto. It was not every day that a leader writer in the *Camborne Chronicle* could lecture so exalted a personage, and he felt a smug Pharisaical satisfaction in joining loudly in the booing and thanking God that he had never played baccarat himself nor even whist for money. But other more responsible journals felt the same, and *The Times* published a leader at the end of the trial, which, in conclusion, expressed regret that the Prince, as well as Sir William Gordon-Cumming, had not signed a declaration that he, too, would never play cards again. *The Times* in those days wielded an influence which no group of papers can rival to-day, and this expression of its opinion might be taken as the voice of all serious and respectable people who had read the account of the trial. Though the Prince had known nothing about the cheating and the watching, it was he who drew the barrage fire of all these moralists, and publicly, owing to his position, he must be dumb. And then, privately, he spoke.

One morning when the hooting was at its shrillest, my father received a message from him that he would like to see him at Marlborough House. My father already knew that there was something brewing, for the day before he had received a telegram from the Prince's private secretary, when he was in the country, asking him to make an appointment, but this had been followed by a cancelling telegram. Now, on this second invitation, he went straight off to Marlborough House, and the Prince, without any ado, stated his business. He had seen that the whole of the religious and Church Press was condemning him ' as a gambler and worse,' and he believed that my father had been instigating this campaign. He therefore wished to discuss the whole matter with him in person, and give my father an opportunity of affording him an explanation.

At that moment two highly exasperated people faced each other. How the Prince had got hold of the notion that he had been doing anything of the sort is quite unexplained, and my father had no curiosity to enquire into that, but contented himself with telling the Prince that there was no truth of any sort or kind in the accusation. He had on the contrary been particularly careful neither to say nor write a single word of comment on the whole business and had forbidden any discussion of the case in his own house. What he thought about it was a very different matter, and that was his own concern, but he would be delighted to tell the Prince, if he wished, what he did think, or if His Royal Highness preferred, he would write him a letter about it. He had considered before now whether he had not better do so, but decided that while there was so much virulent and unwarrantable language flying about, he had better wait. But there was not the faintest justification for what the Prince had supposed.

They then discussed the whole affair. The Prince was eager to state to an old friend of his who was also head of the Church, what he had to say in answer to the fierce attacks made on him in the Church papers.

He strongly affirmed that he was no gambler, that gambling, as he understood the word, was hateful to him, but that playing cards for small sums was no such thing. But he would never try to put down betting, there was a national instinct for betting, and every small boy in a grocer's shop put his sixpence on the Derby. 'Very bad developments that leads to,' said my father. 'Certainly it does,' said the Prince, 'but there's no harm in playing cards for money in itself. And one of the first men I ever played cards with was Bishop Wilberforce.' At which, I imagine, they both smiled.

The Prince then spoke of certain points in these attacks which had been made on him, which he particularly resented. The Press howled with horror at the idea of counters belonging to him being used at this game of baccarat. 'They say that I carry about counters, as a Turk carries his prayer-carpet,' he said. 'But the reason why I carry counters is to check high play. High sums are easily named, but these counters range from five shillings to five pounds,[1] and that can hurt nobody.' Probably that did not much appeal to my father as an argument, for he hated all betting on principle. But admitting, as most would do, that there is no harm in people playing cards for such sums as are well within their means, the contention is a very sensible one. Counters, if you play baccarat, are as necessary to the game as a pencil and a scoring-sheet at bridge.

The second point of which the Prince justly complained was the statement, freely made in the Press,

[1] My father evidently made a mistake in his account of this interview, for, as came out at the trial, the counters ranged up to ten pounds.

that his host disapproved of cards and forebade them in his house, but that in spite of that the Prince had insisted on playing. He now affirmed that he had been absolutely unaware at the time that Mr. Wilson had any objection to games of cards being played in his house, and that when, in consequence of these statements, he had enquired into it, he had found it was not true. Mr. Wilson had never forbidden cards in his house, and the only foundation for his supposed prohibition was that when his sons were quite young, just growing up, if he found them playing recklessly he said to them, 'You don't understand the game, you don't play it properly, and I won't have you play it.' On that alone was founded the accusation that he himself had insisted on playing baccarat against his host's wishes.

It was quite evident then that in these points of which the papers had made much the Prince had been the victim of malicious and repeated slanders in the Press, and he said that if such things were believed of him, the whole country would be against him. They then settled that my father should write him a letter, putting before him, better than could be done in a conversation, the views of sensible and serious men who were not disposed to join in shrieks, for the whole scandal had deeply shocked many whose opinions must be treated with respect. 'Very well,' said the Prince, 'we will consider that settled. And we're old friends.' And as such they parted.

My father therefore wrote the following letter :

SIR,—The utterances of various religious bodies have been so painful and ill-judged that I am anxious to assure Your Royal Highness more explicitly than seemed possible in our conversation, how entirely erroneous are any assertions that

I had in any way countenanced or encouraged such tone of criticism.

These utterances were well calculated to advertise the various speakers and their ' connexion,' but equally well calculated to defeat any serious object beyond low political aims. And my attachment to the person and honour of Your Royal Highness is so heartfelt and of such long standing that it would give me the acutest pain to think that you supposed I sympathized with their proceedings. The Church has, I am sure, felt throughout that if there were a word to be said about the Tranby Croft affair it must be said in a perfectly different spirit and manner.

I cannot say how grateful I was for the two points which Your Royal Highness impressed on me as the *facts*. They have been useful to me. But I should ill repay Your Royal Highness's kindness as regards my own loyalty, if I did not in a few words assure you how keen and anxious has been the feeling in the Church roused by the controversy, and how many and keen have been the representations made to the Bishops and leading men of every order. It is not the way of the Church to be vociferous, but whatever touches the throne and those near it, touches the Church and affects the peace of its best members.

Some twenty years ago it was made evident by discussions in Parliament and outside that the evil of intemperance among working classes and women was growing intolerable. It is not too much to say that what intemperance was then, gambling is now, and I was not surprised to hear Your Royal Highness express yourself as abhorring the spirit of it. It is proving itself the hopeless ruin of young and old among the poorer classes. All alike who, without holding any absurd views as to minute acts, are in earnest on the subject would be encouraged and their hands strengthened if you would take any natural opportunity which might present itself of saying what you said to me, while fully distinguishing what is innocent from what is bad. Your Royal Highness is foremost in all movements for the good of the working classes and the poor, and never more so, I am sure, than in the present

year. I do earnestly venture to say that the least thing said
or done (without forcing the occasion but taking it as it came)
which would show the people what your real mind is in respect
of these thoughtless but most dangerous habits would do a
world of good and evoke a world of good feeling.

The Prince answered this with great friendliness,
formally stating the views he had expressed at the interview, but declining, perhaps wisely, to make further
utterance on the subject of gambling. His letter is given
in full by gracious permission of H.M. King George V.

> R. Yacht 'Osborne,'
> Cowes, August 13, 1891.

MY DEAR ARCHBISHOP,—Your kind letter of the 10th has
touched me very much as I know the kind feelings which
prompted you to write to me on a subject which we have
discussed together and which you are aware has caused me
deep pain and annoyance.

A recent trial which no one deplores more than I do and
which I was powerless to prevent, gave occasion for the Press
to make most bitter and unjust attacks upon me, knowing
that I was defenceless, and I am not sure that politics were
not mixed up in it. The whole matter has now died down,
and I think therefore it would be inopportune for me in any
public manner to allude again to the painful subject which
brought such a torrent of abuse upon me not only by the Press,
but by the Low Church and especially the Nonconformists.

They have a perfect right, as I am well aware, in a free
country like our own to express their opinions, but I do not
consider they have a just right to jump at conclusions regarding
myself without knowing the facts.

I have a horror of gambling and should always do my
utmost to discourage others who have an inclination for it, as
I consider that gambling, like intemperance, is one of the
greatest curses which a country can be inflicted with.

Horse-racing may produce gambling or it may not, but.
I have always looked upon it as a manly sport which is popular

with Englishmen of all classes, and there is no reason why it should be looked upon as a gambling transaction. Alas! Those who gamble will gamble at anything. I have written quite openly to you, my dear Archbishop, whom I have had the advantage of knowing for so many years.

Again thanking you for your letter and hoping you will enjoy your holiday.

Yours sincerely,
ALBERT EDWARD.

It is impossible in the light of the above interview and exchange of letters not to feel the utmost sympathy with the Prince of Wales. Not only had the Press made savage capital out of this incident, but it had libelled him, making public statements about him which were definitely untrue, but to which he could not reply. He had been execrated as a gambler, who was determined to have his baccarat whatever his host's feelings were, and whose luggage, according to comic prints, chiefly consisted of boxes of gaming counters, but his reiterated statement that he was not a gambler and that he abhorred gambling carries complete conviction for its sense and sincerity. A game of cards for such stakes as he and his party had been playing, was not, according to his view, gambling at all. Gambling was playing for stakes which a man could not afford and had no business to risk, and this view must surely commend itself as sound to anyone who has played domestic bridge for a shilling a hundred. Gambling is not an absolute term, nor is it to be defined by one fixed set of figures. It is a question of proportion, and while a bet of a sovereign on the Derby is culpable gambling on the part of a man whose wages are thirty shillings a week, it would be a ludicrous misuse of language to call the same bet gambling if made by a man who had ten thousand a year. The use of alcohol furnishes an excellent parallel, for drinking only becomes a vice when it is indulged in to excess, and the question of excess is part of a personal equation, similar to that concerning stakes at cards and the income of the player, and no one but a faddist could object on principle to a man taking a glass of wine with his dinner. The rigid moralists of the Nonconformist Press had failed to appreciate this, and their homilies based on a misconception of the case, and decorated with ripe juicy falsehoods, must have been intolerable to the Prince. He had been put in pillory for the whole of the ugly story, the cheating and the watching, which took place before he came into the affair at all, and a private game of baccarat in which he was perfectly at liberty to indulge in a friend's house resulted in these attacks from which he was powerless to defend himself. And all the time his views about gambling and about horse-racing would have commended themselves to at least ninety per cent. of reasonable folk. But reasonable folk had no opportunity to hear what he had to say, and until the supply of gossipy inventions ran low, the Press continued to regale the public with these morsels. They felt that they had been given a real glimpse, more lurid than the most sumptuous imaginings of Ouida, into the private life of exalted personages, and the shock they professed to have experienced was certainly spiced by a high degree of enjoyment. It was not so pleasant for those more immediately concerned, and a letter which Queen Victoria wrote to my father, later in the same year, in reply to his felicitations on the engagement of Prince Albert Victor of Wales to Princess Victoria Mary of

Teck, our present Queen, perhaps faintly reflects what she thought about it all.

Osborne,
Dec. 21, 1891.

MY DEAR ARCHBISHOP,—I must thank you very much for your kind letter, and congratulations on the engagement of my dear grandson Albert Victor to Princess Victoria Mary of Teck, which promises to be a happy union. 'May' is a charming girl, with much sense and amiability and very *un*frivolous, so that I have every hope the young people will set an example of a steady, quiet life, which, alas, is not the fashion in these days. The wedding is to be at St. George's Chapel, on the 27th February. I hope you will perform the ceremony.

In conclusion, let me ask you to accept the accompanying card and with best wishes for Christmas and New Year for yourself and family.

I am,
Ever yours affly,
VICTORIA R. & I.[1]

II

The second of these two scandals which caused such a commotion in the nineties was the trial of Oscar Wilde on a criminal indictment. A very remarkable literary interest, both directly and indirectly, attaches to it and to the savage punishment to which he was sentenced, for they were among the causes which combined to establish his reputation as a writer and a dramatist, and caused it to soar, especially in Germany and Italy, to a height which it is most improbable that it would ever have reached otherwise.

Up till that year, 1895, he had written (apart from the plays of which I shall speak presently) little that had

---

[1] By gracious permission of H.M. King George V.

attracted serious attention. His poems had enjoyed a
very great success when they were first published, but
they had long been forgotten, and of the rest ' Dorian
Gray ' and the ' Happy Prince ' had been his only books,
at the time of his tragic debacle, to pass into a second
edition. He used to say, with a charming gaiety, that
while the first editions of most classical authors were
those coveted by bibliophiles, it was the second edition
of his books that were the true rarities, and even
the British Museum had not been able to secure copies
of most of them. In England there was a small but
very enthusiastic band of artistic and literary folk, who
saw in him the greatest genius of the age, but outside
England he was absolutely unknown as a writer, whether
in prose or poetry, while the English critics treated
his publications with the scantiest contempt. ' Dorian
Gray ' had been fiercely attacked, but otherwise they had
hardly troubled to point out to an indifferent public the
feeble and ineffective plagiarizations in his poems, and
the tawdry glitter of his prose.

This was not very discerning of them, for there
were far more noticeable qualities in his work than
plagiarization and glitter ; these were its defects and
not its merits, for in spite of the glitter there was brilliance
and in spite of the plagiarizations a truly original note.
Nobody else could possibly have written his ' Decay of
Lying ' or his ' Critic as Artist,' which were the gems
in ' Intentions,' but neither the taste of the literary
public nor that of its directors perceived that these two
dialogues, though possibly only trifles, were little masterpieces of airy wit and mockery, and had a very individual
quality of their own. A live voice spoke in them.
Then, about 1890, when Wilde was getting on for forty

years old, he turned his hand to comedy for the stage
and not for the study, and in the next four years wrote
'Lady Windermere's Fan,' 'The Ideal Husband,' 'A
Woman of no Importance,' 'Salomé,' and 'The
Importance of Being Earnest.' 'Salomé' was written
in French; Sarah Bernhardt had undertaken to produce
it in London, and it was actually in rehearsal when the
censor of plays for the Lord Chamberlain's office, in a
spasm of feverish conscientiousness, refused to license
it. The reason for the refusal of the licence was that it
presented on the stage Biblical characters, and that was
sufficient. The four other plays were brought out in
London. George Alexander had a notable success with
'Lady Windermere's Fan'; the two following it, 'The
Ideal Husband' and 'A Woman of no Importance,'
had a moderate success, but none of them was considered more remarkable than the majority of theatrical
pieces which had a fair run. They were neatly constructed, they were light and witty, but they contributed
nothing new to the history of dramatic art. Then in
February 1895, a few months before his trial, 'The
Importance of Being Earnest' was produced, again by
George Alexander, and that was far more notable than
anything that had preceded it. The critics, for the most
part, still thought scorn of his work (indeed their sneers
had become fixed like Kundry's laugh), for they had
made up their minds about him, and nothing that he
wrote could alter their verdict, but the public signified
its high approval, and stalls and gallery alike revelled in
this very amusing piece. It scintillated with witty fireworks and characteristic fantasy, it was constructed with
brilliant and farcical ingenuity, it was admirably played,
and though the critics called it rubbish, the playgoers

whispered ' Sheridan.' Mr. Bernard Shaw, it must be remembered, had not then come to the rescue of the English stage, and audiences had not yet been taught to think, but were satisfied with being amused. Then suddenly the scandal flared up, the author's libel action against Lord Queensberry melted into the criminal prosecution of himself, and what was to be done with the play ?

Mr. George Alexander was in a difficult position, and very gallantly he attempted a solution which was in the true spirit of Victorian reticence and unconsciousness of anything disagreeable. Both for his own sake and that of the author he did not want to withdraw a popular play that was running strong, but it was unwise to flaunt outside his theatre the play-bills which advertised ' The Importance of Being Earnest by Oscar Wilde,' for people might not like to come to see the work of that wretch. So with a high ingenuity he caused the offensive name of the author to be pasted over with opaque strips of fair white paper, and thus his patrons could come to see ' The Importance of Being Earnest ' without unpleasant associations being aroused ; they could enjoy this amusing, anonymous piece, and refrain from wondering who the author was. This was truly Victorian, and quite after the pattern of the Duchess of Beaufort admiring the picture of her husband's mistress, and calling it a fancy portrait. But already such lofty reticence was a little out of date ; besides, the public had learned from the baccarat scandal what entertainment can be derived from scapegoats and moral indignation. Or Mr. Alexander had not hit upon the precise brand of Victorianism that was required to meet the situation, and his sense of the importance of being tactful did not meet with the success it deserved. The play could not be saved, and he had to take it off.

The crash then with regard to Oscar Wilde as author, dramatist, and citizen was complete. It was years before any play of his was staged again; his books were withdrawn from library lists; the sale of them, such as it was, ceased altogether, or was confined to those who collect gruesome relics, and critics and public alike thought that they had heard the last of the ways and works of a man whose name must not even be mentioned in polite circles. Yet had not this landslide of ruin buried him, it is more than possible that by now he would have been forgotten. For his plays which were the most successful of his productions had never been produced abroad up till then and they have since proved very disappointing in English revivals. They have aged rapidly and become out of date, their wit to us seems tight-roped and acrobatic, and now no one in England will listen to them. His ruin, however, which everyone thought had consigned him to an execrated oblivion, was one of the chief factors out of which should develop a fame which he had never previously known.

The whole tragic business sprang from that act of inconceivable folly when (his life having been what it was) he brought a libel action against Lord Queensberry for leaving at his club a calling-card on which he had written the words which constituted the libel. Then in the witness-box, when being cross-examined by Mr. Edward Carson, he made the further deplorable error of being flippant, and though he was both dexterous and witty, this was a ghastly mistake. He said that he put the society of charming young men as even more pleasurable than the privilege of being cross-examined by an elderly Queen's Counsel : when asked whether iced champagne was a favourite drink of his he acknowledged that it was, though strictly against the doctor's orders, and when Carson rapped out 'Never mind the doctor, Mr. Wilde,' he said 'I don't mind the doctor.' It was all very amusing and there were roars of laughter, but the entertainment was madly out of place and most prejudicial to him, for these answers were given to questions which clearly had a very ugly significance, and a more unsuitable occasion for jests could not be imagined. But he was still intoxicated, even in that sobering experience, by his megalomania : he saw himself as a man of fashion and of genius strolling amateurishly into the witness-box, and in this brilliant extempore manner making the ministers of the law the disconcerted butts of his wit. It was a bore to have come here at all, but it would soon be over, and though he might miss an amusing luncheon party or two, how he would keep the dinner table in convulsions of laughter at the expense of Mr. Edward Carson !

For three days the trial lasted, and then the prosecution was withdrawn and the jury gave the verdict in favour of Lord Queensberry as having proved justification for the libel. Other trials followed, for such was the nature of the evidence of which he had made a jest that the Home Office ordered a prosecution against him for indecent offences. At this second trial the jury disagreed, and the Home Office under the direction of Mr. H. H. Asquith instituted a third. He had already lost friends, position and reputation, his career, as far as could be foreseen, both as author and playwright, was finished, but the law had to take its course. At that third trial he was convicted, and the judge passed on him the most severe sentence that the law permitted. That probably reflected the bulk of public opinion in England, and a plebiscite would have approved any amount of trials in order to obtain a conviction and the severest sentence possible. The wave of retribution towered and curled over and smashed him ; he had been made a scapegoat, and now the wretched animal was dragged ceremoniously off into the salt desert of tribulation. He was ruined, disgraced and bankrupt, and the moral sense of the hooting public sang Hosanna. But the actual offence for which he was condemned was not in most European countries a crime at all, since public indecency was not alleged, and in consequence of the repeated trial followed by this relentless treatment, there began to awake instantly in Germany and Italy an interest in him and his work. Most of this work had been accessible to the world for several years, and some of it for twenty, and hitherto it had not aroused abroad the slightest sympathy or even curiosity.

The second factor which contributed to his fame was the publication, during Oscar Wilde's lifetime but after his release, of the ' Ballad of Reading Gaol,' which he had written when in prison. It sprang directly from his catastrophe, for if we may judge from his previous poems, it seems unlikely that he had got it in him to write it before. No one could fail to be impressed with that wailing from the wilderness, for technically it is a masterpiece, ranking high among the finest ballads in the English language, and through it runs the venerable inspiration of bitter suffering.

The third factor, arising from the newly-awakened interest in him abroad, was the performance in Germany,

in the year 1901, of his one-act play 'Salomé.' It had
been banned by the Censor in England on the eve of its
appearance on the stage, its publication in book form
had been hailed by the critics with a more than usual
measure of abusive contempt, and though his French
(in which language it was composed) had satisfied
Sarah Bernhardt, it was far from pleasing those who
knew so much more about the language than she. One
critic translated some of the lines for the benefit of
English readers so that they might judge for themselves, but his rendering of Salomé's cry 'C'est de ta
bouche que je suis amoureuse, Iokanaan' by 'It's your
mouth I like, John,' was really not quite fair on the
French. But now 'Salomé' was selling largely in
Germany, and its production on the stage was received
with the greatest enthusiasm. Richard Strauss made it
the libretto for an opera, and we must suppose that the
blood-lust and savagery of the music was held to hallow
it, for the Censor subsequently relented, and allowed it
to be seen at Covent Garden. Following its production
in Germany, it was translated into and acted in most
European languages, its bibliography is almost as long
as the text, and to-day it and Oscar Wilde's other plays
are given in Germany more frequently than the works
of any other foreign dramatist.

The fourth and the most potent factor of all in
establishing the fame of a modern author who was
rapidly becoming classical, first abroad, and now also
in England, was the publication in 1904, after the
author's death, of the book to which the editor gave the
title of 'De Profundis.' It is part of a far more substantial manuscript which Oscar Wilde had written
while he was still in prison, and which was as direct a

result of his tribulation as was the 'Ballad of Reading Gaol.' It records in admirable and at times masterly prose, rather intentionally purple in places but always of great dignity, the effect that his bitter punishment had had on him ; how he accepted it without complaint, fear or reluctance ; how he realized that he must grow to be worthy of his suffering instead of considering it an indignity ; how he must, at the sacrifice of all else, keep love alive in his heart ; how, owing to this spiritual awakening, a new hope had been born out of his anguish ; how Christ is to be found in all art and in all romance. Though some readers were astonished that this enlightenment had brought him no sense of regret for the misery he had brought on others as well as himself, and that he regarded his past life merely as the due development of his own nature, the book made an enormous sensation, passing through edition after edition, for the scapegoat, by the miracle of love and the study of the Gospels, had transmuted the salt of the desert into an exceeding sweetness, and rested content beside the waters of comfort. It had an immense sale in England, and the translations of it in Europe, and, while arousing the most poignant sympathy with the author, it established him as a classic.

It was Mr. Robert Ross, Oscar Wilde's executor, who brought out this book, and before proceeding to the real history of it, it must at once be stated that there was never a stricken and disgraced man more lovingly and unselfishly ministered to than was Wilde by this devoted friend. But the book itself, 'De Profundis,' in the form in which it was given to the world by Mr. Ross, is the most gigantic literary fraud. In his preface, he refers to 'instructions' he had received about the publication of it from Oscar Wilde (though he does not give the smallest hint as to what those instructions were) in which, addressing Mr. Ross, Wilde alludes to ' De Profundis ' as ' my letter,' and goes on to say how grateful he is to the Governor of the prison for his permission 'to write fully to you, and at as great length as I desire.' The plain inferences from this are that this letter was addressed to Mr. Ross, and that it was published (more or less) in its entirety.   But both these inferences are incorrect.   ' De Profundis ' was indeed a letter in the sense that it began in the ordinary form of a letter, ' My dear——' ; but it was not addressed to Mr. Ross at all, but, by name, to Lord Alfred Douglas, and little more than half of it (if as much) was published at all.   But to publish the whole of it was obviously impossible, for the omitted pages contained tirades of the bitterest vindictiveness against Lord Alfred, bringing against him a farrago of preposterous accusations.   Not only would a libel action against the publisher and the editor have been the well-deserved and immediate result, but the text, if complete, would have entirely defaced the sublime impression produced by the rest, and, instead, have presented one far less edifying though of a unique and tragic interest.   Since, then, complete publication was impossible, Mr. Ross made these elegant extracts (for they are indeed no more than that) though he knew that they must convey an absolutely different picture from that which the author actually painted.   Oscar Wilde, in these extracts, revealed himself to Mr. Ross as humbled and softened and sweetened by suffering, as having love in his heart and love only, whereas the whole letter would have shown him as still harbouring resentments the most petty and the most unjust against the man to whom it was really addressed. I do not say that those published sentiments (some of them of an almost infantile simplicity) were not sincere, but the bitter and vindictive moods with which the entire letter abounded were certainly just as genuine.

Finally, after making his extracts, Mr. Ross, in order to render himself secure against any immediate disclosure of the whole, presented the complete manuscript to the British Museum, with the proviso that it should be sealed and sequestered there until the year (I think) 1960, by which time, presumably, both he and Lord Alfred Douglas, against whom it brought accusations which no doubt could have been proved libellous, or at any rate mistaken, were dead. Possibly he received instructions in this sense from Oscar Wilde, but in that case it is impossible to understand why he did not say so in his preface, and thus justify his action.

Again if Oscar Wilde had intended that this bitter and vindictive letter of his should be presented to the world as this patchwork of sweetness and spiritual illumination, there cannot possibly have been any reason why he should not (with Mr. Ross's help) have brought it out himself, when he published the ' Ballad of Reading Gaol,' unless he desired a posthumous sanctification of himself. But this is frankly impossible ; *poseur* in many ways he was, but that sort of pose was not one that could have appealed to him in any mood. He could feel the attraction of many attitudes, but that of a saint in a stained glass window which he would never see would always have seemed grotesque to him. Indeed, on Mr. Ross's lines an editor would be almost justified in omitting the negatives in certain sentences of his text, and thus reversing their meaning, if he thought that the moral tone of the whole would be thereby improved. No doubt he thought it his duty as literary executor to secure the best possible sale for a most remarkable manuscript, which, without substantial omissions, could not be published at all ; he may also have said to himself that these fulminations of abuse did not represent Wilde in his true light and were only moods of passing passion. But there comes a point when ' *de mortuis nil nisi bonum* ' merges into ' *de mortuis nil nisi bunkum,*' and the version of ' De Profundis ' as given to the world does not represent what Wilde entrusted to him. Though he wrote every word of what Mr. Ross published, he wrote in that same document so much besides and in so different a spirit, that the omissions cannot but be held to falsify the whole of it. In the absence of further evidence, it is, in fact, scarcely credible that the instructions to which Mr. Ross vaguely alludes in this misleading preface to the book, enjoined on him to do what he did.

It is difficult also to understand the mental processes of the authorities of the British Museum, who accepted this bequest under the condition of sealing it up for more than fifty years. Presumably they were acquainted with its contents, for we cannot suppose that they accepted a sealed gift without acquainting themselves with it, and they therefore knew that it abounded in violent and bitter accusations against a man who, when the period of its privacy was over, would be dead and therefore unable to reply to them. No doubt they saw that the manuscript was a masterpiece of writing, and both was then, and would be in the future, of great literary interest, but would they, on the same principle, accept a manuscript, let us say, of Mr. Bernard Shaw's, which contained a brilliantly written account of the terrible wrongs he had suffered at the hands of Mr. Rudyard Kipling, with the stipulation that it should remain in sanctuary there until some future date when Mr. Kipling would no longer be able to defend himself? Whatever Oscar Wilde's unknown instructions to Mr. Ross were, even if he told him to deal with this manuscript exactly as he did, it is hard to comprehend how it was given harbourage on such terms. By law, of course, it is impossible to libel the dead, but it may by such measures be easy to give unwarrantable pain to descendants of the dead who are living.

It may be asked how I can vouch for the vindictiveness of the complete manuscript and for its incongruity as a whole with the extracts which have been given to the world. The answer is very simple, for there are in existence, as is now known, copies of the holograph which reposes in the British Museum, and I have studied one of these with the greatest care. It is a marvellous and a terrible piece of writing; stony-hearted would he be who could read unmoved the account of that dolorous way, but it is not the work of one who has been made regenerate by suffering, nor can anybody who has read the whole of it think that the published portion is a legitimate abbreviation of it. It is the exceeding bitter cry, *de profundis* indeed, of a very gifted, a very sensitive and a very self-conscious man, who has bartered his birthright and who, tortured by loneliness and privation, *imagines* love and beauty (as set forth in Mr. Ross's extracts) springing from such fiery experience as had been his. He could see himself in imagination wandering on the hills of Galilee, beholding the lilies how they grow, and learning humility and charity from the words of Christ, and recognizing in Him the type of the supreme artist. No doubt those aspirations were quite sincere, but then, with pen not yet dry, he indited blistering reproaches against the friend he had loved, taxing him with perfidy and ingratitude, and denouncing him as the cause of his own ruin. Then the venomous stuff, omitted by Mr. Ross, was spent (but it had been as sincere as the other), and now he took up his pen again, and forecasted how, on his release, he would be a very lonely man and friendless, and how he would hide himself from the eyes of the scornful in secret valleys where he could weep undisturbed. Nature would hang the night with stars for him and cleanse him in great waters, he would sleep in the cool grass in summer and in winter under the lee of a hay-stack. . . . But even as he wrote that he must have known that he had no intention of sleeping under hay-stacks and that he was indulging in forecasts which he was quite incapable of fulfilling, for tribulation had not changed his tastes. He was drawing an imaginary portrait of himself, and though soothed and self-intoxicated by the beauty of the phrases and paragraphs that flowed from his pen, barred till now when the privilege of writing was restored to him, he only pictured such impulses. It was the passion for writing a fairy-tale, and not for living it which possessed him.

His manuscript was finished before he left prison, but he never sent it to the friend to whom it was addressed and who still remained ignorant of its existence: eventually it passed into Mr. Ross's possession. Phantasmal became to him at once, now that he was free, the self-induced dream which had peopled his cell with bright presences, and touched its drab walls with the colours of an opal, and he knew that he was unchanged. No miracle of grace had been wrought in him, skilly and solitude had not cured him of a psychological abnormality for the indulgence of which he had suffered as a criminal, but which, owing to that same abnormality, he could not himself think of as morally wrong ; nor had he in ' De Profundis ' even hinted that his nature had undergone any sort of conversion to the ordinary tastes and passions of mankind. Prison life and all he had suffered there had been a punishment, savage in the extreme, for offences against the law, and neither those who framed that law nor those who inflicted that punishment can possibly have supposed that it would do anything more for him than torture him. Presently he sought the arc lights of Paris cafés in preference to the shimmer of stars, and cleansed himself not in Nature's great waters, but in innumerable tumblers of absinthe. For a while his brain and his perceptions were clear enough to record in the immortal verses of the ' Ballad of Reading Gaol ' the eating of the iron into his poor tortured soul, and we owe to his anguish a wonderful poem. Prison and its enforced abstinence had renewed him physically for the time, but morally he was not changed, and soon, with the removal of discipline, the slime of intemperance and perverted passions gathered upon him again, till the wheels of his soul were choked with it. No decent man can feel anything but sheer pity and sympathy for one so gifted and so brittle and withal so lovable.

From his youth it had been a passion with him to be conspicuous and stand in the limelight, and for the sake of that he had always laughed at ridicule and held contempt in scorn. He had passed through his undergraduate years at Oxford with credit and distinction, taking a first in his schools and winning the Newdigate prize poem, and he had there come under the influence of Ruskin. The Slade professor had told some of the young men that they wasted their time and energies in playing games ; let them exercise the vigour of their bodies to better purpose, and make a road instead of making runs, and he would talk to them as they cut sods and plied pickaxe and wheelbarrow. A well-made road, so ran his message, was a thing absolutely and divinely beautiful ; it was a highway in the wilderness and a path in the desert. Though Oscar Wilde had never wasted a moment playing games, he went out with the road-makers, and listened to Ruskin. But the road did not get very far, for the flannelled fools went back to wickets and the muddied oafs to their goals, and it came to an end in the middle of a field.

Then coming up to London Oscar Wilde worked at his poems and at journalism, and presently espied in the aesthetic movement which had grown out of the pre-Raphaelite school, with Ruskin as its prophet, a far more promising chance of limelight than road-making. He consecrated himself High Priest of the cult, and anointed himself its king, and dressing himself, in the service of beauty, in a velvet coat with cut steel buttons, knee breeches and white stockings and brandishing a sunflower in his hand, he speedily attained notoriety. These antics drew on him the favours of the comic press, but to make any mark, however ludicrous, was infinitely better than making none. He extended his operations by a lecture tour in America, and spoke to amazed but limited audiences about the beauty of life and of William Morris's furniture. But even outside his own country this prophet was not received with honour, while in it the opera ' Patience ' from which so much might have been expected, as an advertisement, called attention to the wit of Mr. W. S. Gilbert rather than to the object of his satire. Similarly his journalistic duels with Whistler only made the public perceive what a droll person Mr. Whistler was. Wilde went on writing, though making, as we have seen, no great mark for himself, until the success of his plays brought the limelight full on him.

He was widely known already as a very brilliant talker, but this was something more substantial, for there was fame and there was money, and it was as the man of genius and fashion, careless and gay, witty and elaborate, that he loved to appear in those halcyon days of the early nineties. He envied that particular *insouciance* which he thought to be the habit of those who have been brought up in certain traditions, and he aped the manner of it, without having the instincts that render it natural. There was no more of the flamboyant charlatanism of sunflower and velveteen breeches, a garb of ultra-conventional propriety best fitted the man of the world who happened also to be a consummate artist. He played his part without the slightest touch of pomposity (for the *clou* to it was this care-free gaiety), but with a child-like zest and gusto. Every morning his hansom was waiting for him to be at his disposal all day, and in he stepped with his shining hat and his cane and his great tie-pin and his frock-coat, and his earliest errand was to a fashionable florist's, where there was ready an immense buttonhole for himself, and another slightly smaller, as was meet, for the decoration of his driver. He often stayed at the

Savoy Hotel, for Tite Street, where his wife and
children lived, was a long way off, and he gaily
explained that he could not go home that night because
he had forgotten the number of his own house,
though he knew which Whistler's was. Besides,
to stay at the Savoy was part of the make-up of the
character which he played with such huge enjoyment :
it gave him a naïve and costly delight to write to a friend
and tell him that he had got a new sitting-room and
that his bill for the week was prodigious. It was part
of the fun to throw money about, and to point out how
beautifully, as if to the heedless manner born, he was
doing so. He lunched at some suitably distinguished
table, entrancing his hostess's guests by his wit, or perhaps he lunched at the Café Royal, and sent for the *chef*
afterwards to compliment him on his curry. The festival
would be prolonged with liqueurs and innumerable
cigarettes and marvellous talk, till the winter's day was
on the wane. Then he would dine at Kettner's, drinking
oceans of the most admired brand of champagne that
could be procured, looked in perhaps for an act of one
of his own plays, prominent in a box to be seen of all
men, and then it was time for supper. He took his
own Dorian Gray as his model, and saw in himself the
exemplar of the truly delectable life, denying himself
no pleasure, full of wit and laughter, rejoicing in heedless extravagance, even adopting the ancient kings of
Ireland as his ancestors to give birthright to this regal
sumptuousness, and by some strange lack in just perception believing that he was realizing for a drab world
the ancient Greek ideal of the joy and beauty of life.
Nothing could have been less like what he was doing,
for the Greek genius for exquisite living was founded

on physical fitness and moderation in all things, while he based it on the unbridled gratification of animal appetites. He took Plato's ' Symposium ' as the text for his life, but expurgated it by omitting all that Socrates stood for, which was continence and the sense of the sacredness of beauty. Effortlessly, cursorily (such was his pose at the time) and with the ease of casual conversation he scribbled the plays that filled his pockets with gold. A few weeks of airy work saw each complete, and he shook them from him like the drops of water the wild duck shakes from his feathers as he rises for his flight.

These triumphant and ludicrous progresses with buttonholes in a hansom, this life with its gorgings and drinkings, its very various companionships, its luncheon parties and its laughter, its largesses of jewelled sleeve links and gold cigarette cases, its Dorian Gray pageantry in which he was the principal figure, sound in the telling of them more like the antics of one dressed up for some preposterous charade than the normal behaviour of a man of fashion leading the delectable life, and they were conducted, it must be remembered, on the smoking sides of a volcano which might burst into eruption at any moment. He was doubtless the victim of a monstrous megalomania ; he thought himself a man apart, exempt from the laws that govern others, and set above the thunder. He says as much, indeed, in ' De Profundis,' speaking of himself as one ' who stood in symbolic relation to the arts and culture of his day, and acknowledged and felt so to be ' : he compares himself to Byron, though Byron, he notes, was symbolic of things less vital and permanent. He tells us, for his own greater splendour, that his father

and mother 'had bequeathed me a name they had
made noble and honoured not merely in literature, art,
archaeology and science, but in the public history of my
own country, in its evolution as a nation.' But in truth
these are all figments of his egotism, for Sir William
Wilde was a surgeon of possibly doubtful reputation,
and his wife a highly theatrical and second-rate poetess,
and they neither of them had anything more to do with
the national evolution of Ireland than Oscar Wilde himself. He believed himself to be the Lord of Life and
the Lord of Language, and as such he might order his
goings as he pleased, and the world would only gape at
and applaud his radiant hedonism. Mayfair was his
washpot and Piccadilly was glad of him. The desire
to appear magnificent is no doubt a quality common to
both sexes, but these gewgaws, these glittering trappings
and millineries of which he, like Dorian Gray, was so
much enamoured, point perhaps to a feminine trait in
him, which is not without significance.

Yet it seemed almost right that any vain excess or
extravagance should be condoned in so lavish a maker
of mirth who talked as he could talk. It was no wonder
that his brilliance should dazzle and intoxicate himself
as well as his listeners. It soared and sparkled, it was
ἀνήριθμον γέλασμα, it passed into shadow and grew
serious, and then its gravity cleared again as some bomb
of absurdity exploded in the middle of it; and so ingenious was he that he could, when challenged, defend
the most outrageous of his paradoxes. Like Vivian
in his 'Decay of Lying,' he was prepared to prove anything. He loved a string of jewelled phrases in his
spoken word as well as in his writing, and if possibly
they sometimes sounded like a recollection of Walter

Pater, as perhaps they were, who cared so long as the
Pied Piper continued to flute ?   How like was his talk to
the play of a sunlit fountain !   It rose in the air constantly changing its shape, but always with the hue of
the rainbow on it, and almost before you could realize
the outline of this jet or of that, it had vanished and
another sparkled where it had been, so that you could
hardly remember even the moment afterwards, what
exactly it was that had enchanted you.   Like all talk, it
is completely unreproducible, for gesture and voice
had no small part in it, and, essentially so, his own glee
in what he said.   Mr. Laurence Housman, in his
admirable sketch, called ' Echo de Paris,' may perhaps
recall to those who heard Oscar Wilde talk something
of the manner of it, but even then it lacks the colour
and the personal element which gave it individuality.

Or he told stories, but of these again the narrator
was a part.   The first time I ever saw him he recounted
to me some miracle play which he had lately seen in
the south of France acted by peasants, and if, as I feel
sure was the case, he improvised the whole, what did
that signify ?   The charm of it lay not in what he might
or might not have seen in a booth near Napoule, but
in the peerless narration of what he had probably invented.   Talk in his mouth was not as with Whistler,
a rapier making shrewd and telling thrusts and always
gleaming with menace : for the heedless butterfly had
as sharp a sting as any wasp, and indeed he was less
like a butterfly than an aeroplane dropping bombs,
bright little delicate bombs, full of mustard gas.   Oscar
Wilde, on the other hand, was always genial, he was
lambent but not burning, he neither barked nor bit, his
gaiety was not barbed for wounding, and his laughter

(except when he spoke of America) was always kindly.
Behind the brilliance of his talk, behind and infinitely
more charming than his poses, in those days before his
bitter ruin came on him, was an extraordinarily amiable
and sunny spirit which wished well to every one, and the
sense of that gave him a charm that many of those who
distrusted him and found him sinister were unable long
to resist. Months before the crash came, there had
been unpleasant mutterings and whispers about him;
he was bloated and flabby in person, his dandifications
were rather terrible, but then the charm of his talk began
to work, and in how short a time even those on whom
these other things made a disagreeable impression were
disarmed by the wit of it, and the geniality from which
it flowed.

That same gaiety of good humour marks his critical
work, especially when, as in 'The Decay of Lying,' it
is cast in a conversational form. He pokes fun at the
most admired literary reputations of the day, but with
so light and laughing a touch that none could be hurt,
and his ridicule had no sting in it, like that of Whistler
or of George Moore, who in his 'Confessions of a
Young Man' goes round his bookshelves with a little
bottle of corrosive acid, which he drops first on this
volume, then on that, and sets them all smoking. . . .
Oddly enough, though he had so keen and just a sense
of the music in spoken or written words, he had absolutely no sense of music itself, being practically unable
to distinguish one tune from another. But, as the
apostle of beauty in all its forms, he was bound to
profess an appreciation of music, and his total ignorance
of it did not prevent him from speaking of the 'passionate, curiously coloured fantasies of Dvořák': the

phrase pleased him, for Dvořák seemed a likely person
to write curiously coloured music and he embodied
it in one of his dialogues. Again he wrote of those to
whom life wears a changed aspect because they have
listened to one of Chopin's nocturnes, or, having heard
some one speak of the deferred resolutions of Chopin,
he would refer, not very felicitously, to the 'deferred
resolutions of Beethoven,' which does not make very
good sense. But music always presents the most in-
sidious traps for those who regard the appreciation of
it as a social equipment. Once at a concert I sat next
to a woman who had a tremendous reputation as a
music lover : it was meat and drink to her. An item
on the programme was Beethoven's 'Appassionata,' to
which she listened with clasped hands and steeped far-
away eyes. She had heard no doubt that a sonata
consists of not less than three movements, but no one
had told her that in the 'Appassionata' the second and
the third movements are played without a pause between
them. So when the third movement had been finished,
and all was over, she thought (so naturally) that there
had been only two movements, and recalling herself
from her rapt intensity she whispered to me, 'And now
for that heavenly third movement.'

But indeed I am not sure whether Oscar Wilde's
most individual conversational gift was not that well-
spring of nonsense, pure and undefiled, which perennially
flowed from him. He announced with great gravity
that he was very busy just now on a small volume of
ethical essays, moral tracts they might be called, which
was designed to fulfil the needs of thoughtful people of
small means, who wished to give their friends little
tokens of good-will at Christmas time. The Bishop of

London had kindly consented to write a preface in which he expressed the hope that these little trifles would carry their message of sadness into many otherwise hilarious homes.   The book would be published at the price of one guinea, and would be No. 1 of the 'People's cheap guinea series of Great Thoughts.'   The first of these ethical essays (just completed : that was why he was late for lunch) had for its subject ' The Value of Presence of Mind,' and it took the form of a parable—There was a play being performed at a West London theatre which was proving exceedingly popular : boxes, stalls, dress circle, gallery and pit were always crammed, and the queues for the cheaper places extended to Hammersmith.   In fact, he added, the play was at Hammersmith. One night during that tremendous scene in which the flower-girl of Piccadilly Circus rejected with scorn the odious proposals of a debauched Marquis, a huge volume of smoke, intermixed with flames, poured out of the wings.   The fire-curtain was instantly let down, and the audience rose in panic, and rushed to the exits of the theatre.   They shoved and pushed, skirts were trodden on, and dress-shirts irretrievably injured : they were all mad to get out, and there was serious danger that in this wild stampede some of the weaker might be trampled on.   Then in front of the fire-curtain there appeared the noble figure of the young man who was the true lover of the flower-girl.   His voice rang out (as they had heard it before that night) and commanded the attention of these panic-stricken folk.   He assured them that the fire had already been got under, and there was no danger any more from that.   The only danger now to them was that with which their own unfounded panic was threatening them.   Let

them all go back to their seats, and recover their calm.
So ringing was his voice, and so commanding his
gestures that they ceased to crush round the doors and
returned to their places, leaving the exits free. The
brilliant young actor then leapt lightly down over the
footlights and ran out of the theatre. Not a single
other person left the place alive, for the flames poured
in from every side and they were all burned to death.

Such nonsense was rich in decoration of phrase:
sometimes, as above, it was highly dramatic, for who
could guess the dénouement of this moral tale till it
was divulged or fail to be entranced with it when it
came? Sometimes it was sheer nonsense, unharnessable
to any idea. He was arranging a symposium and hoped
I would come to it. 'Everything nowadays is settled
by symposiums,' he said, 'and this one is to deal finally
with the subject of bi-metallism: of bi-metallism
between men and women.' . . . Again, he had just
been introduced to the lady he was to take down to
dinner and his hostess had impressed on him the solem-
nity of the occasion, and had told him that flippancy
of any sort would be sadly out of place. For his partner
was a serious woman and expected everybody else to
be serious too. She was also highly intellectual, and
had lately published a long novel, which at that time
was supposed to have delivered a staggering blow to
Christianity. As they descended the stairs to dinner
arm in arm on this wintry night, she said to him:

'What terrible weather we are having,' which was
surely a very judicious opening for serious talk.

To this he replied with great earnestness: 'Yes, but
if it wasn't for the snow, how could we believe in the
immortality of the soul?'

This sounded most promising ; at the same time she was a little puzzled.

'What an interesting question, Mr. Wilde,' she said. 'But tell me exactly what you mean.'

'I haven't the slightest idea,' he said. . . .

Or he would find himself in some week-end house party of athletic tendencies, and agreeable occupations for Sunday afternoon were being discussed at lunch. Everybody wanted to be out of doors, and to play some game. There was golf, there was tennis, there were boats on the river for those who could row, and water in the river for those who could swim. When asked to say what he would like to do, he sighed :

'I am afraid I play no outdoor game at all, except dominoes,' he said. 'I have sometimes played dominoes outside French cafés.'

Once at the end of one of his admirable stories, which he said he had made up that morning, some well-informed creature asked him if it was really his own : had it not appeared a year or two ago in the *Mercure de France* ?

'Very likely indeed,' he said, 'but I believe it came originally from the Dutch. I made up another, too. Once upon a time. . . .'

One did not know whether to revel most in the apt absurdity of the reply, or the scholastic mentality of the questioner. The latter resembled that of the seriously minded small boy who after earnestly watching Mr. George Robey preparing to play golf on the stage, and getting held up by a piece of adhesive paper which stuck to the face of his driver, and his ball and the back of his hand, turned to his mother and said, 'Mummie, is Mr. Robey a *good* man ? ' That had precisely as much to do with the entertainment as had the question whether one of Oscar Wilde's stories came out of the *Mercure de France*.

His witty gaiety never left him even in the darkest days, for when the late Lord Haldane, who held very strong views about the brutality of his punishment, went to see him in prison and recommended him, now that he had so much leisure, to embark on some considerable work, he plucked up at once, and said he was preparing a small volume of table epigrams.

Such, apart from that side of his life for which he so bitterly paid, was the manner of his days in the early nineties. Later, after the crash, he asserted that nothing of these pomps and social successes had been of any worth to him compared with his art, but then he also said that he had only given his talents to his art, and had devoted his genius to life and to talk. The two statements are irreconcilable, and it is probable that the latter was nearer the truth. He did not live the life of one to whom the call of art is supreme, for he must have known that such a manner of existence as his was suicidal to an artist. He made phrases to justify it : he said that the artist should realize every mood, and gratify himself in every desire in order to render himself complete, but he knew that he was only making the shallowest excuses for his own uncontrollable appetites. Then straight from his treading of 'the primrose path to the sound of flutes' he passed into the grim isolation of his cell. That phrase, which is his own, and is applied by him to the years we have been speaking of, conveys the image which he formed of himself as the central figure or at least the hierophant of the god in some Bacchic pageant. But unless ruin had thus come upon him, it may justly be doubted whether the artistic and literary world, especially of Germany and Italy, would ever have begun to take that interest in his work which has led to his now being considered a classic. It was that which woke their interest in him, and it was that which made out of an exceedingly witty trifler the poet who wrote the 'Ballad of Reading Gaol.' Perhaps it was the harrowing of his soul which created the power, or perhaps it only turned it up, as the plough of woe cut its way through the grosser soil of his nature. It may have been merely dormant hitherto, while he devoted his wits and delightful gifts to the service of self-indulgence and trivial success, but in those years of anguish and solitude, he found himself, only, alas ! to lose himself again when he was free. When the crash came, there was never a man so bitterly mocked and execrated as he, but out of the number of his real friends, who knew what lay below his follies and his vices, there was none who failed to stand by him. There is much to be said for judging a man by his friends.

CHAPTER XI

REBELS

ORTHODOX English artists, who had won for themselves a recognized position as Associates of the Royal Academy or as Academicians, enjoyed during the sixties and seventies and eighties a period of unique commercial prosperity : never before or since have they found it so easy to sell at high prices the works which were hung on the line in the annual exhibition at Burlington House. The lean years were over in which Constable could not find a purchaser for his landscapes, and Victorian art, as we know it, was at the zenith of its popularity. It seems impossible to us now, so complete has been the slump in the work of most of the artists then so much admired and eagerly purchased, that the tide will ever again return to float off the hulks of those stranded masterpieces, and yet who would venture to make any pronouncement concerning the artistic tastes and fashions of the future? Who, twenty years ago, would have been so rash as to prophesy that Mr. Epstein's statue of Night would be erected outside the underground railway instead of inside it? Even Presidents of the Royal Academy itself may have their most solemn dictums disproved, for when Lord Elgin brought home from Athens the marbles from the Parthenon frieze and pediments,

Benjamin West, P.R.A., made an official examination of them and pronounced that these statues and reliefs were not Greek work at all but late Roman.

But no doubts ever troubled those eager purchasers and admirers when year by year they saw the line at the Royal Academy filled with masterpieces. How glorious were those walls, the whole wide acreage of which, up to the very ceiling, was inlaid, as neatly and completely as a finished jig-saw puzzle, with the pictures that had been judged worthy to hang there! Even a place at the very top where distance and foreshortening made one of moderate size appear like a glazed postage stamp, conferred a cachet on its exhibitor, for it had been hung at the Royal Academy, and the artist's friends turned their telescopes on it, and congratulated him on the honour. But the line was the Holy of Holies; there (at one time or another in those halcyon days) were exhibited stags in the mist by Sir Edwin Landseer, R.A., or some dogs, or some ptarmigan under a rock. There were Highland cattle standing knee-deep in the heather by Mr. Davis, R.A., and quantities of sheep by Mr. Briton Riviere, R.A., portraits by Herkomer, battle-pieces by Ernest Crofts, Greek youths and maidens reclining on marble benches, and reading to each other from rolls of manuscript, with glimpses of a blue, blue sea through pink flowering almond trees, by Mr. Alma Tadema, family parties having tea in the garden beneath an ivied wall, or young ladies, suitably unclad for medical examination, visiting a shrine of healing, by Mr. Poynter, interminable surfaces of the English Channel by Mr. Moore, and of Bible history by Mr. Herbert. All these pictures were painted by artists who knew their business and had got a sense of line

and colour, and they had given them appropriate titles ;
the ' English Channel ' by Mr. Moore was ' Britannia's
Realm,' and Mr. Alma Tadema's picture was a ' Reading
from Homer ' and Mr. Crofts's ' The Retreat from
Moscow.' Nothing could be more like the sea than
' Britannia's Realm,' nothing more like marble than
the translucent benches on which Greek youths and
maidens sat and read Homer to each other, or more
like ivy than the tidy creeper that covered the wall
where the family party had tea.

Of course, there were among them pictures which
we still believe, and which we think that future generations will believe, to be of the first rank. Millais, for
instance, was exhibiting then, but no one would class
Millais among those whom we call Victorian artists
any more than they would class Whistler among them.
But it was of these true Victorians that the line was
as full as is a railway line of wreckage and corpses after
some terrible accident. Perhaps some may be resuscitated, but for the present most of those admired works
still seem to us as dead as anything can possibly be.

Then somewhere on the line there was the greatest
annual masterpiece of all, which was known as ' the
picture of the year.' I vividly remember the ' Slave
Market ' by Mr. Long, R.A., which attained this distinction, and he sold it for £6000, which was precisely
the sum for which, not many years earlier, Ruskin could
have bought for the nation Tintoret's picture of the
Crucifixion in St. Cassian's in Venice. It was too much
for the nation to pay for one of the world's masterpieces, but Mr. Long's ' Slave Market ' found a ready
purchaser. The blue riband of the Academy was
probably awarded on the day of the Private View, when

the smart and privileged crowd in frock coats and
bustles and waists were really more intent on pictorial
art than on each other.   They clustered, they broke up,
they formed again, and soon they arrived at the verdict
which the popular taste generally endorsed, when next
day the gallery was open to the public.   It was always
an exceedingly well-painted picture, but it was always
by one of those artists whom we now consider typically
Victorian.   The most famous of all the series was
undoubtedly ' The Derby Day ' which was exhibited
in 1858 by Mr. Frith.   It was not only the most popular
picture of the year, but for many years the most widely
known picture in England :   there was not a coffee
room in any inn that had not a print of it.   The coaches,
the gipsies, the fortune-teller, the sky, the bookmakers,
the horses were all rendered with the most minute
finish, every quarter-inch of the picture was in focus :
you might say it was an infinite number of little pictures
put together with extreme skill.   It was bought by the
nation, and Oscar Wilde in a voice full of reverence
asked if it was really all done by hand.   Mr. Frith
followed it up by the hardly less famous ' Railway
Station.'

Victorian art reached the zenith of its popularity
in the eighties, during which decade Sir Frederic
Leighton was President of the Royal Academy.   He
was himself a most accomplished artist of that school,
and in person an incarnation of it, picturesque and
urbane, and highly finished.   Even if he had been no
artist, there could not have been found an apter
figurehead, but as it was, his pictures were among the
most admired of all.   ' Wedded,' ' Psyche ' and ' Hit '
were undoubtedly pictures of the year.   Modern art

became so popular, that perhaps what Edmund Gosse (speaking of the work of Miss Marie Corelli) once called 'the taint of popularity' was partly responsible for its decay. Yet the fact that an artist is popular need not necessarily imply that he is worthless, any more than the fact that an artist is not thus tainted is a proof that he has distinction, and Miss Corelli possibly had this in her mind when she replied to Mr. Gosse's criticism by pointing out that though her works might be tainted with popularity, no one could offer such an unfavourable comment on his.

But if these Victorian masters were thus tainted with popularity, M. Gustave Doré was positively crawling with it. He made a larger fortune out of his paintings than any artist in the whole of the history of the world, and, incredible as it may seem now (and doubly incredible if his pictures were exhibited here again), he had a permanent gallery of his works in Bond Street called the Doré Gallery, where for many years, winter and summer alike, his prodigious canvases were on view. In his unregenerate days he had made illustrations for Balzac's ' Contes Drolatiques ' the sight of which, so dreadful was their drollery, had made Ruskin physically sick. But the Doré Gallery was not of such, there were sacred subjects on an enormous scale, there was one of Christ leaving the Praetorium, another of the entry into Jerusalem, another of angels hovering above the arena of the Colosseum, where in the dusk lay the bodies of Christian martyrs lately killed by lions. The lions had been interrupted at their meal by this disconcerting vision, and prowled uneasily about. . . . It was not for a few brief weeks in the summer, as at the Academy, that this gallery was open, but all the

year round the turnstile clicked to the shillings of the
serious. Before the most important works there was
a row of chairs and, if you were lucky, you could slip
into a vacant seat and reposefully drink in the solemn
thoughts produced by these masterpieces. They had
all the technical merits which were characteristic of the
period, even the Pre-Raphaelites admitted the careful-
ness of their execution and the sublimity of their subjects, and in terms of paint, they were exactly on the
level, in terms of ink, of the novels of Miss Marie
Corelli, in terms of the stage, of the dramatic art of
Mr. Wilson Barrett, and in terms of the pulpit, of the
sermons of Dr. Farrar, then Archdeacon of Westminster. All these in their various lines were admirable
technicians, since technique means the ability to render
precisely the effect that the artist wishes to produce,
and the source of their inspiration as of that of Victorian
art generally, was that species of sentiment and feeling
which we now call sentimentality. We detect below
the prismatic brilliance of the surface a certain oiliness,
as when a motor, which has been gently leaking, covers
the asphalt of the street with the hues of a rainbow.
But no such oiliness was perceived then : the colours
seemed to be laid on the hard black asphalt, which
stood for power. ' Very par'ful ' was a common term
of praise for Victorian masterpieces, and the rest were
' perfectly sweet.'

But from far back in the Victorian epoch there had
been a fellowship of artists in revolt against the smug
conventions which in their opinion rendered all modern
art quite futile and meaningless. This was the school
of the pre-Raphaelites which was founded in the forties
by Holman Hunt and John Everett Millais. Dante

Gabriel Rossetti joined them so soon afterwards that
he may be counted also as a founder. The whole
history of the progress of Art is, necessarily, a history
of revolts against conventions, but the rebels, we may
remark, are of two classes. One of these consists of
hooligans whose delight is merely in smashing, but who
have nothing else to offer in place of what they consider
worthless. The other class is of those whose iconoclasm makes room for something worthier, which they
profess themselves ready to supply, and of such were
the pre-Raphaelites. They held that up till the year
1848, Raphael had been the last of the inspired painters,
and their aim was to bring Art back out of the wilderness
where commercialism and charlatanism had driven it.
They formed a Brotherhood with this end in view, and
every Brother on admission had to subscribe his name
to their creed. This creed consisted of a list of thirteen
names, some of which were distinguished by various
numbers of stars or asterisks, in the manner in which
Baedeker's guide-books point out the degrees of excellence in the notable objects which they recommend
the tourist to visit. Jesus Christ (in this creed) received four stars ; the author of ' Job ' three : Raphael,
Coventry Patmore, Elizabeth Browning, the author of
' Stories after Nature ' and Longfellow one each, while
the remaining names, undistinguished by stars, were
those of Newton, Bacon, Michelangelo, Joan of Arc,
Pheidias and Tintoret. Then followed the declaration
to be signed by all members of the Brotherhood :
' There exists no other immortality than what is centred
in these names.'

The ground was thus very conveniently cleared for
future operations. Shakespeare, Dante, Leonardo da

Vinci, Holbein, Titian, Velasquez were not of the
stuff which merits immortality, though Longfellow and
Mrs. Browning were held worthy, and the Brotherhood set to work to produce pictures of the starred
class and to ally to itself other artists who had within
them the seed of immortality.   Their aims were of the
loftiest, their pictures were to be inspired by moral as
well as artistic beauty, the utmost finish and accuracy
in detail must be bestowed upon them, and the subjects
must in themselves be of an elevating character.   Keats's
'Eve of St. Agnes,' for instance, was pronounced by
Holman Hunt to be a fit subject for a picture, 'because
it illustrates the sacredness of honest, responsible love,
and the weakness of proud intemperance,' and the same
process of moral selection inspired his own 'Converted
English Family sheltering a Christian Missionary from
the Druids,' his 'Triumph of the Innocents' and his
'Light of the World.'   He also regretted that Millais
had not chosen a better subject than 'Two Lovers
whispering by a Garden Wall.'   Their creed and their
practice in fact were the precise opposite of the artistic
principles of to-day, for to-day an elevating subject is
enough by itself to damn a picture, while if it has not
got that fatal defect, the fact that it is painted with care
and finish is sufficient.

Other Brothers joined them (indeed Rossetti discovered immortals with an almost embarrassing fre-
quency), Woolner, the sculptor, Ford Madox Brown and,
most notable of them all, Edward Burne-Jones.   To these
must be added William Morris, whose aim it was, in an
annexe of this great hall of regenerated art, to produce
beautiful books, and to restore beauty to modern
domestic life.   Chairs, tables, tapestries, carpets, glass

and wall-papers, were to shed their Victorian uglinesses
and be replaced by work of exquisite design and honest
manufacture, made of vegetable dyes and seasoned wood,
that should be a durable joy in daily life. William
Morris was also their poet, and for prophet they had
Ruskin, who with the full force of his authoritative
eloquence proclaimed the splendour of the new dawn
now beginning to light the face of the Artless earth.
Like them he held that, with the exception of Turner's
landscapes, no divinely-inspired works of art had been
produced since the sixteenth century. Rembrandt he
regarded with unfeigned horror, Claude with contemptuous ridicule, the great English portrait-painters,
Reynolds, Romney and the rest, were mere nonentities,
but he saluted Burne-Jones as the direct and immediate
artistic heir of Giorgione and found the true Hellenic
spirit incarnate again in him.

Now the Royal Academy had always been the throne-
room, so to speak, of English Art, and to appear on its
walls was a kind of presentation at Court, conferring
on the aspirant a definite certificate of artistic soundness
and respectability. But in the late seventies the pre-
Raphaelite school made the Bolshevist move of setting
up a Court of their own, and of pledging themselves not
to submit their applications to the Lord Chamberlain of
Burlington House at all. Sir Coutts Lindsay, a wealthy
banker, and himself an artist of moderate merit, opened
for them a rival Court at the new Grosvenor Gallery in
Bond Street, where their work would be the principal
feature, and here year by year were mustered the forces
of the rebels and their defiance of the obsolete Victorian
traditions. This first exhibition also contained Whistler's
' Nocturne in Black and Gold,' about which before long

much more was to be heard. In spite of the defection
of Millais from their ranks, and the death of Rossetti in
1882, their cult, this new religion of Art, spread rapidly,
and when in 1888 the Grosvenor Gallery was closed,
another centre was found at the New Gallery, so that
there was no break in the public exhibition of the pre-
Raphaelite ideal. To believe in it and to profess it
became a stamp of artistic sensibility, and a season ticket
to the New Gallery was a sort of documentary certificate
to that effect. There the elect would feed their souls on
Rossetti's collected canvases, full-blown matrons with
their sumptuous shawls, their downcast eyes, their great
red lips, their full white throats, and the finished furnishings of their surroundings : there, too, were companies
of Burne-Jones's wan and willowy maidens, exquisitely
painted, who faltered up and down the Golden Stairs, or
sadly observed their perfect features in the Mirror of
Venus. Certainly all trace of Victorian convention was
banished, not a single specimen of the well-groomed Highland cattle, nor a grouse nor a birch tree nor a glimpse of
the English Channel was to be seen there, nor a portrait
of any chairman of City Companies, but it might be
questioned if with this extinguishing of the smoky wick of
banal Victorian convention, there had not been kindled
another flame which might become just as conventional as
the other. For whether these new types were statuesque
or diaphanous, whether they were well nourished or
highly anaemic, they all wore an air of remote inhuman
melancholy, and whether they had clad themselves in
pearls and purple, or in dim draped muslins, they wore
inscrutable masks. No gleam of intelligence, no spark
of humour, no hint of joy or healthy animalism ever lit
those brooding or downcast countenances : they seemed

completely taken up with the task of being beautiful and sad, each sundered from her companions (for there were very few men among them) in a cell of her own, where she fed on her own world-weariness and perfect features. An anti-cyclone of mournfulness lay heavy on them, and it was not as if 'the soul with all its maladies' had passed into them, but as if the soul with all its qualities had passed out.

But the school, with Ruskin for its indefatigable prophet, became a sort of religion to the highly cultured : they quite agreed that since Raphael no artist worthy of the name had arisen, and some were not so sure about Raphael. Then, as Oscar Wilde remarked, Nature elbowed her way into the charmed circle of Art, and began reproducing the types which the two most notable pre-Raphaelites had invented, and Rossetti's Junos and Burne-Jones's wan women (the latter in swiftly increasing numbers) were often seen about the London streets, especially in the neighbourhood of the New Gallery. It became fashionable in cultured circles to be pensive and willowy. Indeed the aesthetic cult of the eighties was largely derived from the pre-Raphaelites, ladies drooped and were wilted, and clad themselves in Liberty fabrics (useful also for the ties of similarly minded males) and let fall over their eyes a tangle of hair, through which they miserably peered. *Punch*, week by week, was full of them, but they were not an invention of the comic papers, and scarcely an exaggeration : they actually existed in considerable numbers, until in the manner of other fashionable stunts, the glow of the aesthetic movement as a free translation of pre-Raphaelitism into life, began to grow as wan as its practitioners. It was better to look at Burne-Jones's pictures than to

look like them, for women found that it did not really
suit them to be haggard and sad, and Englishmen seldom
care to make themselves conspicuous by outrageous
breeches.

Besides the pre-Raphaelites and that sort of Brocken
spectre of aestheticism (with Oscar Wilde for its very
substantial showman) which emanated from them, there
was another school of art in London, though not English
in origin, which consisted of one unique and peerless
master without pupils, and quite without other propa-
ganda than that supplied by his own pugnacious wit.
This master, of course, was James McNeill Whistler,
and rich indeed was he in masterpieces of Art and entertainment. He strongly distrusted and disliked Oscar
Wilde personally, as I was told by Mr. William Heine-
mann, (one of the few friends with whom Whistler
never succeeded in quarrelling), and when he came back
from America and continued, though aestheticism had
faded away, to lecture on Art and generally resume his
sacerdotal functions, Whistler lost no opportunity (rather
he made them with untiring industry) of mocking him
and his pretensions and his poems and his poses. To
him, as to most other people who expressed their views
about Art, Whistler wrote the rudest letters, com-
municating them to the public Press, and in his own
phrase ' carefully exasperating ' them. He ordered
the poet, in the most summary manner, at once to
return to Nathan, the theatrical costumier, the befrogged
and befurred coat in which he had seen him walking
that afternoon, and not desecrate the streets of ' his '
Chelsea got up as a blend of Kossuth and Mr. Mantilini.
To that sort of attack no reply was necessary, for it
resembled the elementary methods of small boys who

chalk up on a wall ' Billy is a Fool,' but what was more serious and damaging was when Whistler accused him of appropriating his own theories about Art, and retailing them as original reflections in his lectures. It was in vain that Oscar Wilde, in answer to such attacks, pleaded that the only original ideas he had ever heard Whistler utter were those on his own merits as an artist, and that these shrill shrieks of plagiarism from impotent lips would interest nobody, for they afforded the readers of the *World* the highest entertainment, and indeed his denial was much more impotent than the accusations, which appeared to be well founded. In fact Whistler shooed him off the premises of the House of Art by the back-door. His contention was that nobody who was not himself an artist had any right to pronounce on subjects of art, and though that point of view may be contested, he was perfectly right to ridicule Wilde's lectures (except such parts as were plagiarized from him), for some of them, those given in America, have since been published, and, as George IV said of Shakespeare, they are indeed sad stuff. Besides, Whistler personally disliked him, and he saw that his poison fangs were fully charged when he engaged with him. Not even Wilde's appreciation of his wit (which usually softened him) had any effect here, and when Wilde applauded some swift repartee of his with an admiring ' I wish I had said that,' Whistler immediately answered, ' You will, Oscar, you will.' And he probably did.

It is strange that both these men whose brush and whose pen earned, before many years were out, such very large sums for those who possessed the pictures of the one, and the copyrights of the other, should both have passed through the bankruptcy court. Whistler extracted a drop of very characteristic glee from his experience, for when proceedings were imminent, he hurriedly painted and left in his studio for public auction an appalling canvas called ' The Gold Scab.' It was an unmistakable portrait, as far as the head was concerned, of the amiable Mr. Naylor-Leyland for whom he had decorated the celebrated peacock room, and who, he thought, should have paid him a far higher sum than that for which he had contracted to do it. So by one of those ' dainty ' revenges of his, again reminding us of the street boy who chalks up rude remarks, he left this ghastly effigy to be put up for sale with the rest of his belongings. There poor putty-coloured Mr. Leyland sat, monstrous and leering and playing on his piano. His face was human and easily recognizable, but his arms and legs were thin and scaly like the legs of birds, and out of the interstices between the scales oozed golden sovereigns. That would teach him ! Unfortunately for the success of the dainty revenge, the picture attracted no attention at all at the sale ; instead of completely withering Mr. Leyland it found its way into a dusky corner of some inconspicuous curiosity shop in Chelsea. There, several years afterwards, my friend Mr. G. P. Jacomb-Hood, himself a distinguished artist, chanced to see it, and recognizing the master's hand, bought it for a few pounds, and learned the history of it from Whistler. The sum which it eventually fetched when he sold it to an American collector would have gone a considerable way to avert the bankruptcy. But then Whistler had much enjoyed the savage painting of it.

His selection of a butterfly for his emblem and his signature was an odd choice : never was there an insect so armoured and aggressive, and every page of the

' Gentle Art of Making Enemies ' testifies to its native ferocity. Never did Whistler flutter idly in the sunshine and lightly sip the honey from the flowers, or settle with spread wings on a stone, unless he was engaged in making a lithograph on it. He worked with the untiring passion of the inspired artist, and in the intervals buzzed angrily in the limelight and bit and stung the unfortunate flowers on which he alighted. He could not stand a word of criticism, and anyone who ventured to say that any etching or painting of his was not a masterpiece was instantly pilloried and pelted. The joy of a Billingsgate battle, as well as the sacred duty of punishing all whose views on art were so heretic, no doubt inspired him, for Whistler never felt at peace with himself unless he was in the middle of some acid squabble with somebody else. It was a game to him, and his rules were that he was allowed to kick and scrag his opponents, but they must not retaliate, and being, like most folk who thoroughly enjoy hurting other people, extremely sensitive himself, he bitterly resented any rejoinder as being against the rules. To Whistler's mind this was as if a school-boy about to be chastised plucked the birch rod from his outraged preceptor and administered what he had been designed to receive. It was not always that he got the best of these encounters, for the mere gesture of putting out his tongue at somebody was so enjoyable that he forgot to use it for the more articulate purpose of argument, and to criticize a man's top-coat is not really a logical refutation of his depreciation of one's artistic abilities. He published the cream of these correspondences in that ' dainty ' book ' The Gentle Art of Making Enemies,' and never did he paint a more masterly portrait than that which he there executes

of himself, for never did a style better express the writer
of it.   He stings, he bites, he is absolutely convinced
that he has made an end for ever of his victims, and all
the time he figures himself as the heedless butterfly that
flutters over the margin of his pages, though he draws
it with fingers trembling with passion.   But too much
of the writing which he thought so dainty is a mere
cocking of snooks, and a far more pleasing and paying
device was to print, by way of advertisement, in the
catalogue of one of his exhibitions of etchings, all the
foolish things which the critics said about him, and leave
it at that, for they really dug their own graves better than
he could.   In fact he never dug their graves at all, so
busy was he kicking what he believed to be the corpses
of those whom his wit had slain.   And printing their
rubbish was good business too (never had there been in
the whole history of entomology so business-like a
butterfly), for all sorts of people who cared nothing whatever for etchings, but liked these pea-shooting contests,
flocked to the exhibition in order to get the catalogues
which contained the butterfly's ' latests,' and thus they
paid for exhibition and catalogue too, since the catalogue
was only on sale inside the turnstiles.

Though a most serious artist, Whistler, like Wilde,
culled honey not in the sunlight but in the limelight,
and he was full of devices to secure for himself its utmost
effulgence.   This habit of his led to the inference that
whatever he did was inspired by these motives, which
was not always the case, for the butterfly could be in
deadly earnest, even when he was construed as being
most farcical.   Nothing was further from his intention
than farce when, in consequence of highly acrimonious
happenings, he challenged Mr. George Moore to a duel,

sending his seconds in due and classic ritual to convey to him the bloody invitation. What led up to this dangerous proposal was the affair known as ' The Baronet and the Butterfly,' the baronet being Sir William Eden. It was a case of a picture and a payment, such as before now had occurred with the butterfly, and the climax had been when Whistler was ordered by a French court to deliver the picture of Lady Eden which he had already destroyed, and to pay a fine. Mr. George Moore had concerned himself with the whole business in a manner that seemed unfriendly to Whistler, and in reply to a very unpleasant letter from the butterfly, had published his answer in the *Pall Mall Gazette*, twitting Whistler with his age. This must be considered as a personal insult, and Whistler's challenge to a duel at once followed.

The crisis was truly interesting and indeed it was not farcical, for surely these were two firebrands, each burning to scorch up the other. Mr. George Moore had vividly described his own sanguinary temperament in his ' Confessions of a Young Man,' and told his readers how a ' beautiful young lord ' had been impertinent to him. There had been an argument and the beautiful young lord had struck Mr. Moore's face with his finger-tips, and Mr. Moore had hit him on the head with a champagne bottle, and had left this party in Curzon Street with the determination to fight him. He was a marvellous shot, too, he had constantly broken dozens of plates consecutively with his unerring revolver : besides, as Mr. Moore frankly tells us, a duel, for which he was so perfectly equipped, would get him a great notoriety. So he scoured the place for seconds, and met with grievous disappointments, for one of his friends

was going abroad and another was in the country, and
a third had to bury his father. Eventually the bereaved
son came to England, but he and Mr. Moore talked art
instead and so the challenge was never sent out at all,
since Mr. Moore so rightly preferred art to bloodshed.
But now the situation was far more dangerous, for there
was Whistler in deadly earnest, and, more fortunate than
Mr. Moore, he had found his seconds, and delivered
through them his message. What would have happened
if Mr. Moore had accepted the challenge we cannot tell :
probably friends would have intervened, but Whistler
was no *farceur* in matters of honour and he would
certainly have appeared on the scene of carnage. But
Mr. Moore's common sense prevented matters coming
to extremes, for he so rightly saw that a serious writer
and a serious artist cannot in any state of reasonable
civilization go about shooting at each other, for they
have to do their work. So he treated this sanguinary
proposal with silence, and went on with his book.

But through all his vindictive gaieties and bitter jests,
which the public generally at that time appreciated far
more than his pictures, Whistler the Butterfly was capable
of deep personal devotion. He loved his mother and
his wife and his art. Years before he had proved that
in the famous action for libel which he had brought
against Ruskin in 1878. At the very first exhibition at
the Grosvenor Gallery which was devoted to the work of
rebels from the Royal Academy, and in particular of the
pre-Raphaelites, there had appeared his 'Nocturne in
Black and Gold,' and in the trial his sense of the dignity
of the artist quite outshone his wit. Ruskin in his
criticism of the pictures in the Grosvenor Gallery had
pounced on this wonderful canvas and had accused

Whistler of being an impudent coxcomb who had had the effrontery to fling a pot of paint in the eye of the public, and ask £200 for the mess. With just the same sincerity and despatch with which he challenged Mr. George Moore to a duel, Whistler brought a libel action against Ruskin, and the account of it (which should be read with Whistler's marginal comments) seems to us now like some sheer parody of judicial administration, comparable only to the Bardell trial in 'Pickwick.' Ruskin was unwell when the case came on, and did not appear in person, and his chief expert witnesses, to support his plea of justification, were Mr. Burne-Jones (who hated the whole thing and only appeared out of loyal affection for Ruskin) Mr. Tom Taylor, art-critic and editor of *Punch*, and Mr. Frith, who had painted 'The Derby Day.' Whistler was asked by the Attorney-General how long it took him to 'knock off' that Nocturne; his picture of 'Battersea Bridge,' now in the Tate Gallery, was brought into Court and Mr. Justice Starleigh (I think the pseudonym by which he was known to the world was Huddleston) asked him which part of the picture was the bridge, and whether the things on the bridge were intended for people, and whether that was a barge below the bridge. Whistler professed himself much encouraged by the judge recognizing these objects, though what the point of the questions was, except to impress on the jury that the judge did not think much of Whistler's work, is difficult to understand. Then the Attorney-General asked Whistler if he could make him see the beauty of the Nocturne, and Whistler looked at his face and then at the Nocturne and back again and said he was afraid it was quite impossible. So in his address to the jury the foiled Attorney-General went back to the picture of

Battersea Bridge and asked whether the bridge was a
telescope or a fire-escape, and, if those were horses and
people on it, how on earth were they to get off again ?
He said he had looked out the word ' coxcomb ' which
was part of the so-called libellous matter, and found that
it meant a man who made jests professionally. So
Whistler could not complain of that, since his pictures had
afforded such unrivalled amusement to the public. But
when he asked him whether he thought he was justified
in asking £200 for a picture which had taken him, as he
had confessed, only a day and a half to execute, Whistler
jested no more, but, with the utmost dignity, said that
he asked that not for a few hours' work, but for the
experience of a lifetime.

Farce, one would have thought, could hardly have
been made to go further, but the witnesses for the
defence duly accomplished this difficult feat. Burne-
Jones, who, it must be repeated, hated to appear at all,
was true to the doctrines of the pre-Raphaelites and
said that, though the Nocturne was pleasant in colour, it
lacked the detail and finish which were essential to every
serious work of art. It was therefore not a serious work
of art but only one of the numerous failures to paint
night, and considering how much careful work by British
artists was priced much lower, it was definitely not
worth £200. Apparently it made no difference who
painted a picture, or what magical inspiration lay behind
it ; two days' work, whoever did it, could only result in
a ' sketch.' So then a Titian, with more jokes from the
judge, was brought into court and Burne-Jones pointed
out what finish meant.

He was succeeded by Mr. Frith, who had painted
' The Derby Day ' and who, almost necessarily, could see

nothing whatever in either the 'Nocturne' or 'Battersea Bridge,' and finally Mr. Taylor, the third of the expert witnesses, said that these pictures of Whistler's 'only came one step nearer pictures than a delicately tinted wall-paper.' Farce then could go no further, and the jury brought in a verdict for Whistler with one farthing damages : this farthing he wore ever after on his watch chain. Technically he had been libelled, but actually he had suffered no damage, for his picture was worthless. Yet if anyone had bought that Nocturne of which Mr. Frith and Mr. Justice Starleigh thought so poorly, at the price the coxcomb (though Mr. Ruskin should not have said so) had asked for it, and sold it not many years later, he could have enjoyed from the safe investment of the proceeds of his sale as large an annual income as the capital he had expended on it. But tastes and values are always varying and we must remember, *per contra*, that many of the works of the most admired Victorian artists would not to-day fetch the annual dividend which their purchase price, if similarly invested, would bring in.

Whistler, then, like the pre-Raphaelites, was in rebellion against the official school of English art, and in both there was such deadly singleness of aim that they could not really recognize any merit in the contemporary work of others. But the pre-Raphaelites, unlike him, had no taste for public polemics on the subject of art, nor did they desire to attack and scarify any critic who did not agree with them : all they wanted was passionately to pursue their heart's desire in the creation of beautiful things, and they cared nothing what anybody thought about their work, provided Ruskin and the Brothers approved. No touch of jealousy ever marred their concord; Burne-Jones

believed that Rossetti was the greatest genius of the age,
Rossetti introduced Burne-Jones into the artistic world of
Holland House as being the same, and Holman Hunt knew
that they all were. Topsy in his suit of butcher's blue
with his hands deeply stained from the vats of vegetable
dyes, declaimed the last instalment of the 'Earthly
Paradise' (which was the greatest poem in the world)
while Burne-Jones on the top of his studio ladder was
busy with the beard of King Cophetua. On Sunday
morning there was breakfast at the Grange, and others
of the like-minded dropped in. One said he was late
because he had been to see a most magnificent picture
by Sir Joshua Reynolds which a friend had acquired.
'Sir Sploshua,' said Burne-Jones, and that was the end
of Sir Sploshua. Or when work was over, they would
go round to Gabriel's house on the Chelsea Embank-
ment and admire the new wombat in the back garden.
Perhaps Rossetti would be writing a sonnet or perhaps
Mrs. William Morris would be sitting to him, but
whether at the Grange, or at Chelsea, or at Kelmscott,
there was always the same boyish enthusiasm as in the
old days at Red Lion Square, and the same conviction.
sincerely held by each and openly expressed, that the
work of the others was of the supremest merit. Burne-
Jones's pencil, when not seriously employed, was as
humorous as Edward Lear's, and on half-sheets of
paper he drew 'Pleasures of the Plain,' or Rossetti's
wombat, or caricatured Morris holding up a brimming
glass of wine, as a design for a stained-glass window.
The two were for some years in partnership, Burne-
Jones making designs for windows and tapestries, which
Morris executed. The accounts of the firm were kept
by Morris, who was the business partner as regards
production, and on the margin of the account-books

Burne-Jones would comment on the fact that gentlemen
in the liberal professions were usually paid not in pounds
but guineas. A delicious joyousness in life generally
and its inimitable humours possessed them in the intervals
when they were not at their easels and looms. Just as
Whistler put into his work all the tenderness, as in the
portrait of his mother and of Carlyle, of which his nature
was capable, and excluded from it his entire store of
waspishness and irritability, so Burne-Jones put into
his pictures all his seriousness and sense of the sacredness of beauty, and reserved for his friends his romping
sense of fun, Puck-like sometimes, but lambent and
living.

Art was to him a secret garden peopled with figures in
whom the pulses of life were quite arrested, and a picture
was to him as he fashioned it, the presentment of some
dream of romance seen in a light that never shone on
sea or land and wholly visionary. Herein lay his weakness and his strength; his weakness in that he shut off
from art any leakage of human stuff, whether gay or
tragic, that came from the stock-pot into which the woes
and raptures of humanity are shredded, and so to many
eyes his work is no more than friezes of sexless maidens
with here or there a youth wholly epicene ; his strength
that he pursued with the unswerving purpose of the true
artist and with unerring hand his own vision of the
beautiful. Always he sought the stillness of the valley
of Avilion, unvexed by the loud winds of life and its
snow and its hail, and basking in a sunshine so subdued
that it never casts any sharpness of shadow, while those
who dwell therein are more remote than the moon from
all the frets and the glories of living folk. Once only,
on that incomparable canvas ' In the Depths of the Sea,'

did he aim at emotional action : there we see an undeniable woman, though a mermaid, who is triumphantly bearing down to a subaqueous bridal the body of a man. Otherwise he always eschews anything like drama in his pictures ; they represent moments of what he called ' lyrical quiet,' and it was for this reason, as he himself stated, that he would not paint the awakening of the Princess, in his 'Briar Rose.' It would have been dramatic, and therefore discordant with the quiet of the rest of the series.

These pictorial rebels had been joined by artists who worked in other mediums, and who were also in revolt against Victorian convention. George Meredith was one of these, and he had a room at Rossetti's Tudor House, where also Swinburne lived, off and on, for a couple of years. This association had its drawbacks, for however purely burns the flame of art, it is not very wise for such highly strung folk to live together, since they are certain to grate on each other's sensibilities, and though they all, in the true pre-Raphaelite fashion, believed in each other's genius, that was not sufficient to secure domestic serenity. Indeed it matters very little on the score of harmony whether you appreciate the genius of the man who morning by morning sits opposite to you at breakfast, provided he does not fidget and sips his tea in a becoming manner. But, as Rossetti told Edmund Gosse, ' Swinburne used to get on my nerves by dancing all over the studio like a wild cat,' and Meredith on a highly critical occasion vowed that he would certainly have kicked Swinburne downstairs had he not foreseen what a clatter his horrid little bottom would have made as it bounced from step to step. So disagreeable a forecast surely betokens a very rich

incompatibility, and a further and final quarrel took
place at the Garrick Club, where they were brought
together for purposes of reconciliation. Meredith was
in temporary charge of the *Fortnightly Review*, and Swinburne asked him why he had been sent only £10 for a
poem which had appeared there. Meredith replied that
this was what he himself got for his own poems. Upon
which Swinburne, deeply insulted, slapped his face, and
that was the end of all things.

But Swinburne's friendship with Burne-Jones, to
whom he dedicated ' Poems and Ballads,' was heated by
no such friction, and their intimacy was close and unbroken throughout these unedifying and lyrical days
when Swinburne's frail fingers were plucking such music
from the lyre of English speech as had never been heard
before, and will never be heard again till another master
of ' beautiful things made new ' comes over the hills
of the dawn. He was only a man by pseudonym :
some Greek Bacchanal or inspired spirit born of the
Aegean Sea and nourished on the honey of Hymettan
bees had wrapped itself, as with a cloak, in human form,
and found it difficult to adapt itself to the modes of the
later civilization. He would drive down in a hansom
to Burne-Jones's house at Hammersmith, with a newly
written poem of portentous length in his pocket, and
his arrival was often made known by shrill screams and
cries, for he had a conviction which nothing would
shake that the correct fare from any one place in London
to any other was a shilling, neither more nor less, and
so there was trouble with the cabman. My great
friend, Sir Philip Burne-Jones, has often described to
me his own boyish memories of Swinburne's epiphany
at his father's house ; how he was sent bundling

downstairs with some more shillings for the indignant
charioteer, and how his mother came down with sooth-
ings and consolations, as for a child that has seen a
naughty bogie. Here it is pleasant to explode the
notion that Swinburne was a heavy drinker and boozed
all day. He drank very little, but he had epileptic
tendencies, which he entirely outgrew in later life,
and on occasion, especially when the excitement and
frenzy of poesy possessed him, a single glass of claret
was sufficient to intoxicate him. Of course he would
have been better without it, but the real cause of these
highly intemperate scenes was not (so Sir Edward
Burne-Jones was sure) heavy drinking, but a sudden
and apparently fortuitous inability to stand any alcohol
at all. He would be completely and absolutely sober
one moment, and the next a couple of sips of some
light wine would fuddle and excite him. This was also
the belief of Edmund Gosse, and they both, who at this
time knew Swinburne better than anybody, were equally
certain that the indications of moral aberration which it
is perfectly easy to find in ' Poems and Ballads ' were
quite foundationless as regards Swinburne's personal
character and conduct. They were the lyrical utterances
of a poet, describing the moods and passions of other
minds, and were as objective as the utterances of Robert
Browning's ' Men and Women.' Swinburne kept up a
lively correspondence with this friend of his, for whom
he had so warm an affection, but his letters, alas ! have
perished : Burne-Jones thought it was prudent to destroy
them, and on one sad morning he burned them all.

Then there dawned that most fateful day when
Destiny in the disguise of the admirable Mr. Theodore
Watts-Dunton (*né* Watts) came knocking at the door of

Swinburne's rooms. A country lawyer by profession, he was a fervent admirer of the pre-Raphaelites, and coming up to London had made the acquaintance of several of the group, including Rossetti, from whom he obtained a letter of introduction to Swinburne, and he went to Swinburne's rooms to present this in person. His tappings at the door met with no response, and he entered to find an empty sitting-room. But from the bedroom (presumably) beyond there were sounds of stirring, and after having again tried to procure permission to penetrate further, he opened the door. He found Swinburne stark naked with his aureole of red hair flying round his head, performing a Dionysiac dance, all by himself in front of a large looking glass. Swinburne perceived the intruder, he rushed at him, and before Mr. Watts-Dunton could offer any explanation or deliver his letter of introduction, he was flying in panic helter-skelter down the stairs, and was driven by the enraged Corybant off the premises.

Such, so Edmund Gosse told me, was the true account of this first meeting, and it cannot be called auspicious. None could have expected that out of it would spring a lifelong and devoted friendship. But Mr. Watts-Dunton was not to be put off by a little mis-understanding of that kind, and he most generously overlooked the incident and the acquaintanceship was formed. Swiftly it ripened into intimacy; Watts-Dunton took Swinburne's financial affairs in hand (for he had as little notion of the symbolical forms of money, like cheques and bank-notes, as Shelley), straightened them out for him, attended to his business letters, which always goaded Swinburne into a frenzy of rage before he had ascertained whether they were pleasant or the reverse, and gradually made himself indispensable. Swinburne still retained what Plato in a different connection called ' inward liberty,' but in 1879 Watts-Dunton took charge of him altogether, and interned him (there is no other word to use) in a villa at Putney for the rest of his life, a period of over thirty years.

This event constitutes a psychological puzzle of the most baffling sort. Doubtless, Watts-Dunton (as he said of himself) was possessed of a dominating quality, which from boyhood had always asserted itself ; doubtless also he had the power of inspiring trust and affection. Moreover, he had a passionate love of literature, and that was a bond between them : he was a critic of some standing on whose judgment Swinburne implicitly relied, and he wrote sonnets and poems and stories which Swinburne admired. But in spite of all this it is hopeless to attempt to understand how Swinburne, arch-rebel as he was against all forms of authority, could have so given up into the hands of his friend all independence, and subjected himself, his choice of associates, his occupation, his diet, his daily round to the ordering of another. There was a strain in him, as in Shelley, of the imperishable child, and Watts-Dunton somehow became to him an omnipotent but kindly nurse who to the child-like mind figures as Fate, and when Nurse said ' Now be a good Algernon, and come along to Putney ' it never occurred to him, either then or afterwards, to question these decrees. At the time he went to Putney he was too ill to resist, but very soon his health began to improve, and under that beneficent regime he became far more robust than he had ever been. But the very desire for liberty seems to have left him, there was no more dancing before mirrors, or screaming at cabmen, but, alas! there was no more poetry. There was verse, plenty of it, huge stories in verse like 'Tristram of Lyonesse'; there was a novel, there was a torrent of prose, appreciations of Charles Dickens, of Charlotte Brontë, and denunciations of Mr. Robert Buchanan and Dr. Furnivall. In all these there was the glow of the coal from the altar, they teem with rage and energy and frenzy, but all this fire was out of place in the furnace of the engine which it now drove.

Swinburne poured the molten stream of lyrical inspiration into a mould which would not hold it without losing its due soberness of colour and its severer lines, and the greater part of this amazing prose, though containing magnificent passages, is bombastic and exaggerated, with pages of unqualified purple. The frenzy without which all lyrical utterances are lukewarm causes prose to boil over, for prose, except when delivered with the passion of the spoken voice, does not admit of frenzy, and critical prose, such as Swinburne was composing, loses all force and dignity if fashioned thus. He loaded it with alliteration gone lunatic, he heaped phrase upon phrase, whether for the eulogy of Dickens or the damnation of Dr. Furnivall, and instead of using his astounding vocabulary to convey his meaning, let his meaning vanish in order to employ his vocabulary. Yet, all the time, we feel that the fire which causes his prose to boil over and become turgid was exactly that which made his lyrics lambent. But he was now a caged bird, voluntarily it is true, because there was nothing to prevent his leaving The Pines, and like the caged bird he could not sing, and his energy found its outlet in seizures of violent pecking, though never at his nurse's hand. Poetry perhaps is a symptom of some divine disease; if so, Putney and the devoted doctorings of Watts-Dunton rendered him tragically immune.

There was no more ' Swinburne,' if by ' Swinburne ' we mean, as we must, that ecstatic Bacchanal who plucked from his lyre ' Atalanta in Calydon ' and ' Poems and Ballads.' He took a walk in the morning, going very briskly and regardless of weather up Putney Hill and across Wimbledon Common. He often made small purchases of books at a stall in Wimbledon, and stowed them in the pockets of his Inverness cape. If he got his feet wet, he took off his socks on his return home, and put them to dry on the fender. A visitor arrived for lunch one morning while they were steaming there : Swinburne shook hands with great cordiality across the table, and kept dodging round it, keeping it always between them, so as to conceal the fact that his feet were bare. After some few moments of this mystic dance, the visitor advanced towards the fireplace and perceived the socks. Perhaps the poet thought he had some design on them, for he exclaimed very earnestly : ' Hold ! They are drying.'

After an excellent plain lunch with a glass of beer, he went up to his bedroom and rested, lying obediently on his bed, and then, refreshed, he read or he wrote. All companionship that was likely to make the old splendours flame up again was denied him, all those who were poets at heart and who thus might be infectious were cut off from him. Burne-Jones and Rossetti were never permitted to penetrate into The Pines, and Edmund Gosse but seldom. And the worst of it was that Swinburne soon got not to miss these brothers of his mind. Edmund Gosse was his intellectual peer, and Burne-Jones the companion of the house of his dreams out of which had come 'Poems and Ballads.' They understood each other completely, knowing that their art for both of them was a visionary faculty that dwelt apart, and that it was in dreams that the one looked on the 'Golden Stairs,' and the other on the slaying of Itylus, and the comprehension that these two, so utterly different in the conduct of life, had of each other was based on the citizenship of the house not made with hands. But now these blood brotherhoods must cease, for all such influences (God help him!) were bad: the 'old familiar glamour' might excite him, and give rise to those cerebral storms which had so nearly wrecked him physically, though out of the foam and fog of them had come the voice of the inimitable singer. 'Much better,' said Mr. Watts-Dunton, 'to have no such songs and no excitement, to have excellent health and unbroken nights with no disturbing dreams, to walk to Wimbledon, to change the socks if wet, to rest afterwards, and then to read Dickens aloud.' Swinburne had the greatest admiration for Dickens, and enjoyed these readings very much: he appears also to have enjoyed hearing his friend reading aloud to him his novel 'Aylwin.' His mind as well as his body was subjected to this health-giving, this wise and deadly guardianship, and it became a ward in Watts-Dunton's Chancery.

Watts-Dunton, for instance, shared Ruskin's and Frith's low opinion about Whistler's art, and perhaps a little personal feeling came in too, for when Watts changed his name to Watts-Dunton Whistler wrote him a memorable note, which ran 'Dear Theodore, What's Dunton?' This seemed to savour of badinage. In any case, What's-Dunton thought Whistler 'a bit of a charlatan,' and though in bygone days Swinburne had

nobly testified in ' Poems and Ballads ' to his admiration
of the painter, his director now persuaded him to write
a bitter and abominable attack on Whistler in the *Fortnightly Review*.   There was no sort of reason for it, except
that Watts-Dunton wanted to get a knife into Whistler,
and so used one that was sharper than his own, and under
this suasion Swinburne produced one of the very worst
pieces of his most violent and monstrous prose.   Whistler
replied to this with a characteristic letter in which he
said he had lost a *confrère*, but gained an acquaintance
' one Algernon Swinburne—outsider, Putney,' but as
the rest of his letter showed, he was very deeply hurt.
The ' outsider, Putney ' rejoined with the following
lines :

To James McNeill Whistler

Fly, little butterfly, back to Japan,
Tempt not a pinch at the hand of a man,
And strive not to sting as you die away ;
So pert and so painted, so proud and so pretty,
To brush the bright down from your wings were a pity.
    Fly away, butterfly, fly away.

It is ludicrous and laughable that two grown men
should behave like this, it is also tragic that friendships
should thus perish.   But it was Watts-Dunton who set
these cantankerous bantams cock-fighting.

It was the same with Walt Whitman : Swinburne
had thought very highly of 'Leaves of Grass,' but Watts-
Dunton could not bear the work of the American poet,
and encouraged Swinburne to write the most savage
of onslaughts on him, a tornado of alliterative abuse.
Swinburne's resentment against personal criticism was as
bitter as Whistler's, and because in a volume of Matthew
Arnold's Letters he found a sentence describing their

meeting and an allusion to himself as a sort of 'pseudo-Shelley' he retorted in his essay on Dickens by describing Matthew Arnold as a man 'whose main achievement was to make himself by painful painstaking into a sort of pseudo-Wordsworth,' and all his old admiration for him went by the board, and thereafter he could see nothing in his poetry except chill pedantry. In all these attacks there still burned the fire that should have been luminous in lyrical work. Instead it spurted and spat and smouldered among damp leaves.

Possibly his days of lyrical utterance were over, but could even Pindar have sung at The Pines? The 'hounds of spring' slept in their baskets by the snug fireside, and instead of his heart thrilling to see how 'blossom by blossom the spring begins,' he looked at the gas-lamps being kindled into flowers of flame up Putney Hill, till Watts-Dunton was ready to continue his reading from 'Aylwin' where he had stopped yesterday evening. It was about gipsies. No one can question that Watts-Dunton was inspired by the worthiest and most moral motives, but all must lament the tragic completeness of his success. Algernon, if care and devotion could compass it, should live to be a healthy old gentleman, but in order to do that he must forget about Fragoletta. And so it was; the wild bird could not sing in that suburban cage, nor yet when Watts-Dunton took it for a holiday to Southwold, and it no longer 'filled the heart of the night with fire.' The most splendid of all the Victorian rebels had long been dead before Swinburne ceased to walk briskly up Putney Hill and across Wimbledon Common, whatever the weather.

CHAPTER XII

MORE VICTORIANS

IN every age and society there are women to whose
houses there gravitate those who are cutting
noticeable figures in the world of letters or art or politics.
Sometimes this movement is due less to their natural
gravitation than to a strong and steady hauling on the
part of the hostess, and her success in the capture of
them is the just reward of her efforts and her infinite
schemings. Such a one must be made of stern and
indefatigable stuff, and she attains the fulfilment of her
innocent desires by the exercise of a ruthless hospitality.

Curious and cunning are her traps for the eminent.
If, for instance, there are two great fish, who are friends
of each other, and who have not yet been gaffed and
landed by her, she will invite them both to dinner on
such and such a day, saying that each will meet the other.
This is a very pleasing device, and it often reaps
the success that its ingenuity deserves, though it is liable
to be detected if the two, before taking the lure, happen
to confer, and are astonished to find that each of them is
engaged to dine with her before he has promised to do
anything of the kind. Or we may figure her as the lion-
hunter who in more crude and primitive fashion goes
out, an Artemis of social ambition, with her cross-bow
and her arrows winged with welcome, and either from

cover or from out in the open proceeds to discharge
these hospitable bolts literally at the throat of her quarry.

When shooting from cover she gets herself asked to
meet her prey at the house of a friend and reminds him
of the non-existent occasion of their previous meeting :
when from the open she merely writes to him and gives
him a plenteous choice of dates for dining.   Sometimes
it takes quiverfuls to disable him, but she goes on till
eventually the great wild creature drags himself for the
sake of peace and quietness to the gate of her Zoo, and
crawls in, a prodigal lion, so to speak, for whom the
fatted calf is always ready.   Probably he enjoys himself
and comes again, and very soon finds that she habitually
alludes to him by his Christian name.   Sometimes she
makes a little mistake over this, and speaks of him as
'Harry,' in order to convey the sense of intimacy,
whereas those who know him best never call him anything but 'Henry.'   This type of lion-hunter, who
appears in fiction as well as life from the early days of
Charles Dickens onwards, is sometimes an object of
derision to the world in general, and in especial to those
who feel themselves to be lions, but have not received
the distinction of being singled out by her for the chase.
They call her a snob and a climber, and very likely she has
a touch of that bright tar.   But it is merely platitudinous
to point out that interesting people are more interesting
than uninteresting people, and like every person with
brains she prefers the former to talk at her table ; if this
is snobbishness, it is a very sensible and intelligent
quality.   She has really little in common with the old
crusted Victorian snob who rated merit by precedence
and preferred the presence of any Duchess however
dreary to that of any Marchioness however amusing.

Lady Jeune, afterwards Lady St. Helier, a very catholic and distinguished hostess of the nineties and the succeeding decade, had nothing whatever in common with these ruthless Dianas, nor with the coronet-hunters so pleasantly portrayed by Du Maurier in *Punch* of the period, nor with that amiable class of hostess, chiefly American in origin, whose self-imposed mission is to introduce eminent English persons to each other. The lions in Lady St. Helier's case eagerly sought her threshold and purred loudly on admittance. Certainly she liked entertaining them, because an interesting dinner party was the result, but she never felt that she had scored by getting them, nor murmured fragments of ' Nunc Dimittis ' between the courses, nor made pot-shots at their Christian names. Still less was she proud of not being proud of seeing them at her table. That sounds a complicated state of mind, but it was perfectly achieved by the late Sir James Knowles, editor of the *Nineteenth Century*, who once in bidding a friend of mine to dinner wrote ' No party, I only expect the Duke of Argyll and Mr. Gladstone ' . . . The great antiques came to her house, Tennyson and Huxley and the like, but her particular *flair* was not so much for those who were already monuments, but for those of whom the world was beginning to talk, and who might be described as monuments in the making. She knew all about her guests, too, however undistinguished, and once whispered to a man whom she was about to present to the woman he was taking down to dinner ' Don't allude to railway accidents : her aunt was cut to ribands on the underground.' Rarely, but very rarely was she not quite up to date, for once she leaned across the table to Mr. Galsworthy who was sitting isolated between two

divergent conversations and said ' We've been talking
about plays, Mr. Galsworthy. Why don't you write
a play? I'm sure you could.' It was quite true
that he could, for the ' Silver Box ' had come out a
week or two before, and we thought that he had already
proved his capacity.

Every species of lion, barbarous or tame, flocked to
her, cabinet ministers and channel-swimmers, poets and
pugilists. Her very maid, she told me, had once sat in
the dentist's chair of Dr. Crippen, the notorious murderer.
He was not a murderer then, but became one soon afterwards : he was a monument in the making. Naturally
I was thrilled by the news, and she gave me leave to
present myself at the back door and ask for first-hand
information about that interesting experience. I much
regret the diffidence that deterred me from doing so.
Indeed it was said (in illustration of her catholicity) that
a certain notable explorer, who had often been a guest
of hers, was once making a journey through the territory
of a cannibal tribe in Africa, and had the misfortune to be
captured by those inhuman folk. They tied him up to
a tree, while a message was sent to the cannibal king
that there was a juicy young English traveller ready for
the royal larder. The king was hungry, and he arrived
with all speed to superintend the preparations for the
banquet. But the moment he set eyes on the captive,
the bright radiance of the gourmet faded out of his face.
' Surely we met at Lady St. Helier's,' he exclaimed in
excellent English, ' I owe you a thousand apologies for
the inconvenience you have suffered. You and I will
dine together on the wretch who tied you up. Kill him
at once. How is her ladyship ? '

Trovato though the story no doubt is, it is very *ben*,

and thus, by means of fiction, conveys fact. She had
a real and living interest in the deeds of all sorts and
conditions of men, and wanted to know all about them,
not from those who could tell her about them, but from
themselves. She did not found a salon (that French
brand of sociality which, like some native wine, cannot
travel and retain its aroma) nor did she attempt to do
anything of the sort, for she knew very well that a salon
is a specialized form of entertainment, which requires
that the circle should consist of homogeneous minds
knit together by common interests ; it requires also that
the hostess should direct and control it. But she preferred a macedoine of many flavours and did not desire
to exercise any control. Keen and tremendously alive,
she had to a most exceptional degree that quality of a
hostess without which all other gifts are nothing worth,
namely that she immensely enjoyed her own parties.
In that, as in all else, she differed from the lion-hunter,
whose feasts while they last are to her matters of the
acutest anxiety, and whose questing eye, like the lantern
of a conscientious policeman on his rounds, is constantly
directed into obscure corners to see that all is well. The
lion-hunter in fact mostly enjoys her achievement afterwards when she licks her chops. Lady St. Helier was
more like a guest in her own house, having a most
delightful evening.

A hostess of less extensive range whose personality
was of a most individual kind was Lady Dorothy Nevill.
She was born in the middle twenties, and though of no
great age in the nineties, retained the most lively memories
of an era that seemed even then unutterably antique and
aristocratic, an age of post-horses and the Grand Tour,
before the crinoline came in, when no lady would go

to the pit of a theatre (which we now call the stalls), or, if young, be allowed in the streets of London without suitable male escort, to protect her against the libertines who were eager to pounce on her. Of these ancient proprieties Lady Dorothy spoke with a demure respect, as if she deplored the laxness of the present day, but all the time she had a little twinkle in her eye, which made her listener wonder whether in her own youth they had appeared quite so sacred to her. Always, up to the time of her death, when she was well over eighty years of age, she preserved an indomitable vitality and the keenest interest in current affairs, and always she had little sharp comments on the age she now lived in and so immensely enjoyed, delivered with a directness that surely pre-dated the Victorian conventions as to how young ladies should express themselves, and with a notable absence of final g's and initial h's which was the fashion in the fifties. 'Look at the girls nowadays,' she would say, 'playin' golf in their thumpin' boots with never a veil or a pair of gloves till their skin's like a bit of mahogany veneer. I should think the young men would as soon think of kissin' a kipper. And to make it worse they are beginnin' to dab themselves with lip-salve and muck. I never saw such a mess.' Her own habit was most consistent with such views, for no one ever looked less like a kipper or a 'mess' than she. She was the daintiest and most exquisite little figure imaginable, never did she stir out of doors without layers of veils to protect her from the kippering effects of sun and wind, and she preserved, untouched by unguents or 'mess,' the complexion of a girl, smooth and soft and unwrinkled. She wore a slightly undulated auburn wig which marvellously became her, and was like some delicious Kate Greenaway

enchantress, who had grown old without ageing. She
dressed in some manner of her own, which it would be
idle to try to identify with that of any epoch : it was very
neat and smart, and somehow coquettish and Quakerish
together, and enriched with innumerable adornments of
amber and amulets and Egyptian beads.

Her Victorianism protested against the restless way
in which so many people left London for the week-end ;
there wasn't time for them to unpack their trunks, she
said, before they were off again goodness knew where.
This protest took the practical form of her giving the
most delightful little lunch parties on Sunday, for those
of her friends who shared her views. She lived for
ever in Charles Street, Berkeley Square, and the house
was full of ornamental relics that vastly predated the
pincushion to which I have before referred. Many of
these were the work of her hands, little boxes encrusted
with shells, little landscapes constructed, with incredible
patience, from snippets and spirals of coloured paper,
peep-shows and kaleidoscopes and examples of that lost
art, skeletonized leaves. 'You pick your leaves,' she
explained, ' vine leaves or what not, and put them to
soak in some chemical muck that eats off the green part,
but it can't tackle the ribs and fibres. Then you wash
them with a bit of fixin' in the water, and dry them and
set them up in bouquets. . . . Very pretty they used to
be reckoned, and keep a girl out of mischief,' she added,
with a little secret smile all to herself. . . . Then there
were ancient sketches and cartoons of a topical nature ;
one of these pictured herself, young and bewitching,
sitting lightly on the curve of a crescent moon. There
was a rope let down to earth from this lunar throne,
and up it were swarming three or four men in peers'

coronets, Disraeli being conspicuous among them and out-distancing the rest. Then came the secret smile again. 'Some saucy young man drew it, and sent it me,' she said; and one wondered which of those coroneted climbers was the artist.

Mixed with this Kate Greenaway daintiness, was a dash of a quality that can only be called ' gamin.' Often it appeared quite unexpectedly and was truly surprising. She told me once how she used to make experiments in food. There were a great many things that made good victuals which were sadly neglected. ' Guinea-pig,' she said, ' there's a tasty dish for you, but it was always a job to make your cook do it. They want bakin' same as the gipsies serve the hedgehogs. I tried eatin' donkey too, but I had to stop that, for it made me stink.' . . . Or, again, I had been lunching with her, and had to drive straight from her house to the station to catch my train to Overstrand, where I was to stay with Lord Battersea : Lady Dorothy was coming to the same house later in the week. ' Give them my love,' she said, ' and say I'll be down by lunch-time on Thursday, and I shall want a good blow-out of Cromer crab.' I gave the message, and when she appeared there was a dressed crab for her and she duly blew herself out with it. In spite of her principles about week-ends, she often did violence to them, and she and I were once guests together in Helen Lady Radnor's riverside house at Cookham. Lady Dorothy spent all Sunday afternoon in our hostess's gondola, plying slowly up and down the reach of the river above Boulter's Lock, deeply interested in the intimate relations rapidly ripening between the couples in punts below the trees of the back water, and occasionally saying to Lady Radnor who was some

twenty years her junior, ' When we get to our age, my
dear, we mustn't be shocked at anything.'   On Monday
morning the carriage was ordered to take her to the
station, but she would have none of it.   ' There'll have
to be a cab as well for my maid and my luggage,' she
explained, ' and I shall have to tip the coachman and then
go searchin' for my maid.   Pop into your cab with your
maid and your luggage, I say, and have done with it ! '

   Though kippered faces and the restless modern
ways of Londoners provoked her scorn, she thoroughly
approved of modern conveniences, and when motors
came in, liked nothing better than a drive in one as fast
as the car could go.   With the arts save those of paper
landscapes and skeletonized leaves she had little sympathy,
and with music none at all.   One evening at that same
house on the Norfolk coast where she had her blow-out
of crab, there came to dine with us that very excellent
violinist Lady Speyer, who had an exotic villa close by,
and she played divinely to us afterwards.   Lady Dorothy
found the noise rather distracting : she could not give
her full attention to her game of Patience while it was
going on, and when Bach's Chaconne or something of
the same monumental sort was over, she said to me in
a discreet aside, ' My dear, I 'ate that scratchin' sound.'
Walpole by birth and Nevill by marriage (and rather
enjoying these distinguished ties), there was not about
her the smallest trait of the Victorian great lady.   But
Puck, with all his charm and something of his mischief,
must surely have been amongst her ancestors, and no
one could have been surprised if, looking out at night
on to a moonlit lawn, he had seen Lady Dorothy
daintily footing a fairy ring to the admiration of the
surrounding fays.

Romance is a bird that will not sing in every bush, and love-affairs, however devoted the sentiments that inspire them, are often so business-like in the prudence with which they are conducted, that romance is reduced to a mere croaking or a disgusted silence. But some of these Victorian ladies could make it sing surprising (though most regrettable) melodies. There were, for instance, in the nineties a man and woman whose history contained some very tuneful passages. He was a prominent public servant of his country, had been abroad on a difficult mission and conducted it with so gay and impudent a success that his chief, on its conclusion, telegraphed to him the message, ' England thanks you.' He came home soon after, and instead of going to his wife's house, went straight by arrangement to that of his lady. The latter had filled her house with a large party to welcome him, but the boat-train was very late, he missed his connection in London, and the party sat down to dinner, where his vacant place, next hers, awaited him. She had given instructions to her butler to tell her and her alone when his carriage was seen approaching, and in the middle of dinner he said something quietly to her, and she got up. Without a word to anyone she radiantly passed out through the door of the dining-room and locked it behind her, so that the butler who attempted to follow and receive the late-comer was, like the rest of the party, confined to the dining-room. So, alone and without the possibility of interruption, she welcomed her lover on the threshold. Then, when the first rapture of their meeting was over, she led him back, unlocked the dining-room door, and entered with him. He had much to tell them all, and the hot summer night was dark before dinner was done.

Long windows opened on to the terrace outside, and now she said that they would all have their coffee there. They seated themselves, and she clapped her hands, and above the lawn in huge letters outlined in rows of electric lights, there flamed out the words ' England thanks you.'

Among the vanished and irrecoverable figures of the Victorian age there were none who more thoroughly enjoyed and contributed to the sunshine of that social pageantry which (momentarily clouded by the South African war) lasted up to its fatal and final collapse in 1914, than Mr. Harry Chaplin, created Viscount Chaplin, and his sister Helen, Countess of Radnor.   He was of a type that has never existed anywhere except in England, and will never exist there again, and he might have sat, body and mind alike, for a national statue of John Bull. His father, rector of a parish near Stamford in Lincoln-shire, died while he was a boy not yet in his teens, and he was brought up at Blankney, the family place, by his uncle, his father's elder brother. The ' old Squire ' died childless, when Harry Chaplin was still at Oxford, and he then inherited a very large property, chiefly of wheat-bearing acres, and the tradition of the English country squire, in whose veins ran the robust yeoman blood.   Many decades of wholesome rural life, of suit-able, substantial marriages and of uncomplicated mental processes had gone to the making of the type, and some of its representatives had grown to be large and very wealthy landowners, exercising in their own territories a benevolent but unquestioned autocracy ; Tom Coke of Norfolk, whose descendants are Earls of Leicester, was, in an earlier generation, of that vanished breed.

Many of them had never crossed the Channel and were quite sure that no foreigner could ever be trusted, and that outside England there was nothing fit to eat. They were the aristocracy of the class which Queen Victoria had so early recognized to be the new ruling class in England. They controlled the local Parliamentary elections, of course in the Tory interest, and their tenants as a matter of course voted according to the squire's views ; the prosperity of their leased farms was their personal concern, farming their business, and their diversions manly and rural. Hunting, horses and hounds, and all that horse-breeding stood for, were their occupations in the winter, when the land was asleep, and in the autumn, when the harvest was gathered, shooting over the high stubbles not yet cropped close by American machinery, where the big coveys of partridges could be walked up. Rural districts were then rural indeed, the railway was still far from Blankney, much of the land fenny and undrained, and Lady Radnor, who, when quite a young girl, kept house for her brother when he came of age and opened Blankney again, has often told me of those days. To the ornithological mind nothing will convey their remoteness better than her story of how, when there was no shooting going on from the Hall, the keeper would come in of a morning to see if there was any particular bird she would like for the Squire's table. She thought perhaps that half a dozen ruffs and reeves would make a pleasant course, for there was abundance of them on the marshy meadows, and the Squire was fond of a fat ruff.

But the young Squire, who, on coming of age, found himself the owner of so fine an inheritance, was not content with the old order under which his forefathers had prospered. He had been the contemporary and friend of the Prince of Wales at Oxford, he had lived there in the best style of Ouida's young guardsmen, so numerous had been the hunters he kept, so benevolent his neutrality towards the authorities of the University, and he had no notion of settling down at Blankney in the manner of the older generation. Besides, he was personally of the type known seventy-five years ago as a ' magnifico.' Young and handsome and rich with an unrivalled appetite for splendid pleasures, and with a host of friends, not country neighbours alone, but the smart young people of Clubland and Mayfair, he sought to combine the rôle of country squire with that of the big landowner on more modern lines. He entertained great parties at Blankney, he had his coach and four, he had his own two packs of hounds, so that he and his friends could hunt six days in the week; he took a house in Lincoln in order to be nearer the centre of the Burton country, and while thus more than maintaining the fox-hunting tradition of the squire, he started a racing stud as well, and by way of making a good beginning he bought a couple of three-year-olds for the sum, absolutely unheard of in those days, of eleven thousand guineas. A deer forest in Scotland was of course a necessity to a magnifico, and though he still often resided at Blankney, it became a modern country house filled, when he was there, with troops of his friends from outside, for whom he provided sport and hunting, but it was empty for long months together while the squire was in London or in Scotland, or at the race meetings he so sedulously attended. He never dreamed of stinting himself of any pleasure which money could procure, and his purse was

equally wide-mouthed for the entertainment of those
with similar tastes.

He had fallen in love at the age of twenty-four with
Lady Florence Paget, known as the ' Pocket Venus,' and
had become engaged to her. The date for the marriage
had been fixed and was imminent, presents had poured in,
Blankney was ready for the reception of the bride. A
few days before the appointed date, Lady Florence went
out one morning to do some shopping. She went into
Marshall and Snelgrove's by a minor entrance, passed
through the shop and came out at the Oxford Street
door, where the Marquis of Hastings was waiting for
her with a cab and a licence, and they were married. She
had come to the conclusion at the very last moment that
she could not face the fulfilment of her promise, and the
experience must have been horribly humiliating for
Mr. Chaplin. The lady made a very poor exchange, for
Lord Hastings did not afford her much happiness, while
Mr. Chaplin made some ten years later one of the happiest
marriages it is possible to conceive with Lady Florence
Leveson-Gower. It was entirely characteristic of him
that not only did he subsequently befriend the woman
who had treated him thus, but also behaved with extraordinary kindness to Lord Hastings himself. The story
concerns one of the most exciting episodes in the history
of the turf.

Mr. Chaplin and Lord Hastings had already been in
rivalry over racing, when this business occurred, and
Lord Hastings now consistently ran horses and betted
against those of Mr. Chaplin's stable. His conduct was
an instance of that well-established piece of psychology
that there is a strong tendency in human nature to hate
those whom we have injured. In 1865 Mr. Chaplin

had bought a colt called Hermit, and had entered him
for the Derby of 1867. It was sufficient for Lord
Hastings that the horse belonged to Mr. Chaplin, and
he bet heavily against him. A fortnight before the race
Hermit, in his training quarters at Newmarket, was
given a ' Derby trial ' (that is to say, a full gallop over
a course of that length), and had a severe haemorrhage
apparently from the lungs. It thus seemed quite impossible that he could run in the Derby at all, but it was
decided not to scratch him. During the next week it
became clear that there was nothing very wrong with
the horse after all : there was no recurrence of the
haemorrhage, and it looked as if it had come merely
from some blood-vessel in the throat. Hermit had a
few fast canters and seemed fit. Accordingly he was
sent down to Epsom and put in some good work there.
The news of his mishap, of course, had become known,
and the betting against him on the day of the race was
66 to 1. Mr. Chaplin believed in the horse and in his
trainer's opinion about him and continued to back him :
Lord Hastings continued to bet against him.

There came a cold spell of weather that year in the last
fortnight of May, and Derby Day was an affair of furs and
thick coats. Hermit had a thick coat too, for he had
not been clipped, and the small interest he excited in the
paddock was chiefly derisive. After the horses had gone
down to the post, a storm of snow and sleet swept across
the course, obscuring any distant view from the stands.
After a long delay they came streaming up the course,
and it was seen that Hermit and Marksman were desperately racing for the first place. Hermit won by a neck,
his owner cleared somewhere about £140,000 and Lord
Hastings had lost £120,000 ; £80,000 of this was due

to Mr. Chaplin, who might of course have insisted on immediate payment. Instead of pressing him he waited for several months and eventually the debt was discharged.

Derby Day 1867 must have been the greatest day of Mr. Chaplin's life ; he had won the Blue Riband at the age of twenty-six : he was young, he was rich, he was popular and he had an absolutely unique power of enjoying himself. He raced, he shot, he hunted, he warmed both hands at the numerous fires of life, and from them both he scattered money as if Pactolus flowed through the park at Blankney, for where was the use of money except to secure a good time for himself and his friends ? He entered Parliament, he made an exceedingly happy marriage, and if the value of agricultural land and the price of home-grown wheat went down, it would surely go up again : something would happen. Something unfortunately did happen, his rents dwindled, his expenditure remained firm and steady, and Blankney already burdened by mortgage passed into other hands.

Never again, it is safe to prophesy, can the conditions in which Mr. Chaplin entered his inheritance at Blankney be revived. In his own instance, he broke it himself, for never before had the Squire of Blankney attempted to play the double rôle of squire and man of the world. If we come to think of it, the two are in their very nature incompatible, for the essence of Squirearchy, as he received it, was rural life (with gaieties no doubt at the county town, hunt balls and what not, and a few weeks in London) and continuous sojourn on the estate, identification of himself with the interests and concerns of his tenants, in all matters of sport and agriculture, and, for reward, a local and ancestral autocracy. The great popular figure that Mr. Chaplin cut in London and at race meetings, even if an unlimited purse had been his, could not have been played by one of the old squires, for it entailed too long absences from his local kingdom, and implied too prolonged immersions in affairs outside it. Wealth and land inherited from a long succession of ancestors are not in themselves enough to constitute it, and though the great nobleman with half a dozen inherited houses and political duties in London for half the year, may be an admirable landlord and a pillar of national stability, he is no more a squire than is the brewer who buys his great places from him and reads the lessons in church of a Sunday morning. In fact Mr. Harry (as he was universally called) had ceased to be Squire of Blankney in the real sense of the word long before Blankney ceased to be his. All over England in the sixties the same thing was going on. The spread of railways provided swifter and cheaper locomotion than posting, dwellers in the country began to move about more, and life generally to be centralized in towns. The break-up of Squirearchy must be considered part of the general break-up of Victorian traditions.

But none of the blows of fate, the elopement of Lady Florence Paget, the death of his wife to whom he was devotedly attached, the loss of money, the loss of Blankney, the acquisition of gout, ever dimmed Mr. Harry's zest for life which made him so remarkable a personage. There were a number of very pleasant things left and vastly he enjoyed them all. His wife had been the sister of the Duke of Sutherland, and now when Blankney was no more, and he a widower, Stafford House and Dunrobin and Lillieshall became home for himself and his children. His sister was now Countess of Radnor, his daughter was soon to marry Lord Castlereagh, and such relations and all his innumerable friends were warm in hospitality to him who had so bounteously dispensed it. Racing, though there were no more Hermits, nor purchasings of colts at six thousand guineas, was every atom as fine a sport as he had found it before, so, too, was hunting, though not with his own packs of hounds, and every day he took the very keenest interest in his dinner, combining, which is rather rare, the capacity of the *gourmand* with the trained appreciation of the *gourmet*.

He placed high among the pleasures of the table, as every true *gourmet* does, victuals of plain perfection. Lady Radnor and he and I were once strolling after lunch on Sunday in her kitchen-garden at Cookham, and he observed a fine row of broad beans. ' My dear,' he said to her, ' those look excellent beans. Do tell your gardener to send some into the house and let us have beans and bacon for dinner. There's nothing in the world so good.' The gardener was off duty, as it was Sunday afternoon, but she said that if he cared to pick them and bring them to the house, he should have his dish. So off came his hat, and we filled it with the bean-pods, and carried it in triumph to the cook, and Mr. Harry said that he would have beans and bacon for dinner, and nothing else whatever ; he could not imagine a more delicious dinner. But then the *gourmet* had a word to say to that, for when dinner-time came, he first refused soup, but then discovered that it had the most attractive aroma, and said he would just have ' a spoonful of soup,' which meant an ordinary helping for a grown man. Some fish was then placed before him, and he ate his fish in an absent-minded manner, almost mournfully in fact, for it was salmon, and it reminded

him of a heavy fish he had lost on the Brora. Then, so
suitably for this hot evening, there was some cold pressed
beef (for he remembered how excellent his sister's pressed
beef always was), and a mouthful of chicken. Then
naturally he must eat the beans and bacon which had
been provided specially for him, and so he had two help-
ings of them and said he had never tasted such excellent
beans and the bacon was very good too. Where did
she get it ? . . . A very pleasant custom of his, if the dish
was remarkable and he made a second attack on it, was
to put a sovereign on the edge of it, to be given, with
his compliments, to the cook. Dinner was a serious
matter demanding his entire attention : his neighbour
in the middle of that function, alluding to the famous
boiseries of the dining-room where they were sitting, once
said to him ' What beautiful carving ! ' And naturally he
replied, ' Yes, the service is always very good in this house.'

Now anyone who thinks that a vivid appreciation of
the exquisite flavours of wine and food implies greed,
is the victim of confused thinking. Taste is one of the
five senses, and the man who tells us with priggish pride
that he does not care what he eats is merely boasting of
his sad deficiency : he might as well be proud of being
deaf or blind, or, owing to a perpetual cold in the head,
of being devoid of the sense of smell. There is no reason
to suppose that taste is in any way a lower sense than the
other four ; a fine palate is as much a gift as an eye that
discerns beauty, or an ear that appreciates and enjoys
subtle harmonies of sound, and we are quite right to
value the pleasures that all our senses give us and
educate their perceptions. The greedy man is he who
habitually eats too much, knowing that he is injuring
his bodily health thereby, and this is a vice to which not

the *gourmet* but the *gourmand* is a slave. But Mr. Harry,
though he undoubtedly was a *gourmand* also, and ate
prodigious quantities of food, could not, so admirable
was his digestion, and so well large masses of solid food
suited him, be called greedy at all. He had a noble and
healthy appetite, *le foie du charbonnier*, and as he once
observed with a very proper satisfaction, ' I should like
to see my stomach disagree with anything I choose to
give it.' Indeed his confidence in that superb organ
was well founded, for never was a man more faithfully
served. He was anxious also that others to the best of
their punier capacities should enjoy like delights : he
observed, for instance, when he and I were both dining
one night at a highly gastronomic table, that I was not
partaking of some particular dish, and held up an ad-
monitory finger to me. ' You oughtn't to pass that,'
he said, ' they do it very well here.'

Over seventy at the outbreak of the European war
and enormously corpulent, he thought that he could
still do a day in the saddle, and wondered whether he
might not be able to manage the duties of a despatch-
bearer at the front. But those days were over for him,
and, as if he knew that the old order was over also, he
accepted a Viscountcy which he might have had if he had
wanted it sixteen years before in 1900. He had sat in
Parliament for close on fifty years and had twice been
in the Cabinet as Minister for Agriculture and as President
of the Local Government Board. These were high
distinctions, but it is not they which make him so
memorable a figure, nor yet that no man ever more
solidly earned his peerage, but because he was so glorious
an example of a type that will never be seen again.

When raised to the peerage he had to choose

supporters for his coat of arms, and instantly he thought
of his racing days, and said that he would have Hermit.
In due time the design came back from the Heralds'
College for his approval, and there was the conventional
heraldic quadruped, something between a dragon and
a dachshund, instead of a striking portrait of his Derby
winner. 'But it's not an atom like the horse,' he
indignantly exclaimed, and routed out an old picture of
Hermit to show them how they had mishandled him.

His sister, Lady Radnor, passed her girlhood in the
same tradition of field-sports and squirearchy, and
covered, with a zest equal to his, a far greater range of
interests. She was really musical in the sense that music
was to her not merely a pleasure but a need; she had
a soprano voice of remarkable beauty and power, which
she preserved, owing to the excellent training which it
had received, till late in life, and it was of a quality, when
it was at its prime, which would undoubtedly have placed
her high in the ranks of professional singers. Her voice
and her real gift for music she put to far wider uses than
Victorian performances at the piano after dinner, and,
breaking through the conventions of the day, she
appeared on such platforms as the St. James's Hall and
the Albert Hall in aid of charities. Then, too, she
organized a string band of girls, daughters chiefly of
friends and relations, to which she added a chorus of
women's voices, and from 1881 for fifteen years, first as
Lady Folkestone and then as Lady Radnor, she gave
annual public concerts in St. James's Hall, training her
band and voices herself, and herself conducting. The
scheme with all the work and organization it implied
was completely her own, and in the early eighties it was,

for a woman in her position, revolutionary of the current
Victorian conventions to a degree which it is now almost
impossible to grasp, and for any woman at any time a
remarkable achievement. The performers were all of
her own class of life, the women appeared in their best
gowns and jewels, and the concerts were of high artistic
merit. For one of the last of the series, when her singers
had grown into a choir of a hundred and twenty voices
and her band numbered over eighty instruments, Sir
Hubert Parry wrote his suite for strings in F major,
the most English and melodious of all his compositions, which confirms his direct musical descent from
Purcell; and he, Arthur Sullivan and Barnby, who from
time to time assisted her, treated her not as an amateur
of the fashionable world with a hobby, but as a serious
musician. She neither possessed nor professed profound technical knowledge, and never attempted music
which she did not thoroughly understand, but she had
immense enthusiasm, a wonderful voice, and, as a conductor, that particular imagination which makes the performers realize the tone and the quality wanted from them.
Musically she was never a pioneer : she did not quickly
grasp new ideas, and she came out, as she told me, from
a concert at the Albert Hall, at which Wagner, on his
visit to England in 1877, conducted his own work, with
the registered conviction that if this was the new music,
the old was better. But in course of time Wagner ceased
to be the new music, and a visit to Baireuth made her
quite suddenly the most fervent of converts. Strauss
she never arrived at, nor yet Debussy ; the one to her
way of thinking dealt in unpleasant crashes of noise, the
other in tinklings. But knowing that she did not
appreciate, she was aware that this might be because she

did not understand, and never in musical matters did she fall into such abysses as some of the most enlightened critics have tripped into. One of these, and he the most authoritative of his time, described in an astonishing article how, wounded and outraged from his first hearing of Strauss's ' Salome,' he hurried home with acute oral indigestion, and, in order to get these monstrous dissonances out of his system, he stretched his hands to the uttermost, and, with the loud pedal of his piano firmly trodden on, played the completest chord of C major that his fingers could compass. It seemed that the great man had failed to notice that the last chord in the dissonant affair, proclaimed by the entire band, was precisely that for which he had hurried home. . . . Lady Radnor never indulged in such ludicrous Jeremiads; instead, with a wiser sincerity, she enjoyed all that was to her mind, said she did not understand the rest, and retained a perfectly frank admiration for the Lost-Chord-music of Victorian taste and for melodies that gave rise to tears.

Horses and sport and material splendour as well as music were in her blood : she was a great rider to hounds, and when her riding days were passing, she had a marvellous pair of high-stepping ponies which Mr. Harry had given her, which she drove herself in London. Behind her was seated the smallest ' tiger ' ever seen, and she always gloried in the fact that her turn-out was just a shade smarter than that of anybody else. So, too, when her husband succeeded, she rejoiced in the magnificence of Longford Castle, its gardens, its chapel, and most of all in its wealth of incomparable pictures, finer, before the American millionaire began to buy, than any collection outside royal or public galleries. Of these she compiled a very noble catalogue, tracing the history

of them, invoking professional aid for the identification
of doubtful ascriptions and from rummaging among
ancient account-books of the estate, finding the prices
that were paid for the purchase of now priceless masterpieces. The unequalled 'Erasmus' by Holbein, for
instance, was bought about the year 1750 for £110, and
the 'Ægidius' by Quentin Matsys for £95. Three of these
pictures were sold to the nation soon after her husband
succeeded to the Earldom, and now are in the National
Gallery: the 'Man' by Morelli, the 'Admiral' by
Velasquez, and the 'Ambassadors' by Holbein. One
of the Ambassadors in this picture, it may be remembered, holds in his hand a small scroll of music. It is
upside down from the observer's point of view, but
before it left Longford Lady Radnor had the picture
turned about and identified the notes with a sixteenth-
century melody. In the centre of the foreground is a
strange slanting object, difficult to recognize, and yet
evidently an important feature in the picture. But if
looked at from below and close to the canvas, the foreshortening makes it clear that it represents a skull.
The inference that it is to be construed into a canting
signature of the painter ('Hohle Beine,' or hollow bone)
has much to recommend it. For these three pictures in
1890 the National Gallery paid £55,000, which was then
reckoned a large price. To-day, in the open market,
not one of these would be purchasable at that figure.

But far more fundamental in Lady Radnor than all these
tastes and decorations was her profound religious sense,
which was truly child-like in its gay, unquestioning simplicity. Among the avenues of approach to the eternal
mysteries of life and death, spiritualism, to her mind, ran
open and broad and straight. One of her greatest friends
was Miss Katie Wingfield, who was certainly possessed of

remarkable mediumistic powers, and with her as medium frequent séances were held at Longford, and very curious manifestations seem to have taken place, levitations, direct voice, correct answers given by the medium in automatic script to questions of which she could have had no normal knowledge. Men like Sir Oliver Lodge, eminent in the world of science and physics, and societies like the Psychical Research, have since then devoted their study to occult phenomena, and much which thirty years ago was believed by spiritualists to be supernatural, and by sensible men (with no nonsense about them) to be the result of trickery on the part of the medium and credulity on the part of the sitters, has been thoroughly tested, and has been brought into the domain of obscure but well ascertained laws : it is no longer possible even for men with no nonsense about them to deride telepathy and all the dim unspoken commerce between the minds of living folk as charlatanry and credulity. But, on the other hand, those who have studied these phenomena believe, and indeed have proved, that most of them are not due to the intervention of discarnate intelligences, but are in accordance with natural laws. Thus the limits of what used to be thought supernatural have been narrowed, and the sphere of natural law extended, though the most thoroughly scientific investigators affirm that phenomena do occur for which no explanation can be found except that of the agency of spirits now no longer on the plane of material things. At the same time they have rightly insisted on a very strict control of the medium before these manifestations can be accepted as genuine. Such tests and such investigations, in order to see whether some at least of these phenomena were not more rightly to be classed among the now known workings of natural though obscure laws, were

not made at these Longford séances : the circle was that
of a party of friends experimenting among themselves,
and all were disposed to accept a supernatural source for
these manifestations, rather than to reject such if a
natural law (such as telepathy) could account for them.
The manifestations, in fact, were not produced under
test conditions, nor were there skilled independent
observers watching. The circle as a whole believed that
supernatural powers, guides and personal protectors
were present, and the phenomena were accepted as proof
of it. But Miss Katie Wingfield was certainly possessed
of those abnormal powers which we call mediumistic,
and doubtless produced phenomena for which no explanations of natural law as then known would account.
Under test conditions these séances might have been of
real scientific value.

These guides in whose active aid in the affairs of
every day Lady Radnor firmly believed, were not by any
means wholly solemn spirits bent on edification, or
superior to the minor trials of human life, nor did the
sitters regard them as other than personal friends, who
lived on a plane of existence different from theirs but
closely connected with it. On one occasion, so she told
me with gusts of laughter, a member of the circle was
suffering from internal bodily aches in the usual region,
and was extremely uncomfortable during the séance.
That night the direct voice of some control was being
heard, and the manner of procedure was that each
member of the circle in turn wrote down (with due pre-
cautions so that none present could see the inquiry) a
question to which, it was hoped, the direct voice of the
control would give an answer : the piece of paper on
which this question was written was folded up and
placed securely under a candlestick in the middle of the

table. When it came to the sufferer's turn, he, full of material woes, and not feeling on at all a high plane, wrote down : ' What shall I do to get rid of my stomach-ache ? ' After a pause the direct voice from a corner of the room (quite away from the medium) answered in deeply impressive tones, ' Put some flannel round your stomach.' This most sensible suggestion on the part of the disembodied spirit caused the circle to laugh itself into dissolution.

This intense, wholly natural and uncritical belief of Lady Radnor's that close round her were intelligences, kind and beneficent, active to protect and eager to bestow, combined with her equally intense enjoyment of the beautiful and jolly things of the world, made up a personality of wonderful quality ; never have I known one so beaming with genial sunshine. Admirable as were to her the pleasures of this life, they were nothing compared to those that were coming, but in the interval it was her business richly to enjoy. Quite deliberately, though in no way from lack of tenderness, she turned away from things painful and distressing, for she knew that powers wise and gracious were looking after her personally, and it was very ungrateful not to respond by being happy. She made it her duty to be happy, and strenuously performed it, banishing from her mind all that stood in its way, her own worries included. She had no great intellectual grip : ethical problems and abstract speculations necessitating close argument set no machinery at work in her mind. She judged genially and broadly, by feeling far more than by logic, and was a Tory of the most convinced school ; in her heart I am sure that she knew that God was a Tory too. She had all the vitality of Mr. Harry, and when on the death of her husband to whom she was utterly devoted, Longford and its spaciousness passed from her, she built up for herself a new life different in scale and scope, with no diminution of her sunlight. She took the *piano nobile* in the Palazzo da Mula in Venice, and spent some six months of the year there. Her past activities, though now less exuberant, blossomed again there like autumn roses, and, just as before she had organized and carried through those concerts at St. James's Hall, so now she took in hand the music of the English Church in Venice : she compiled a hymn-book for use there, she formed a glee-club that met weekly at her house ; just as before her high-stepping ponies were the smartest things in London, so here her gondola was the best turned out on the Grand Canal. She bought a plot of land on the Giudecca, and out of a dust-heap of shards made a Paradise of blossom and fragrance. Her life thus repeated in its diminished scale the old hospitalities and dignities, and to it she brought undimmed the enthusiasms and eagernesses of her earlier days.

Physical infirmities increased : she could no longer manage the journeys to Venice, and the year before the outbreak of the European War, she gave up also her house in London and that on the Thames at Cookham, and settled down for the rest of her life near Ascot. Grandchildren and great-grandchildren multiplied, and though her visits to London and to the houses of relations grew fewer and fewer, she never lost touch with the doings of the world in which she no longer took any part. But though she was still keen and alive to all the interests of her friends, she began herself to live much more in memories, and to those who loved to spend quiet days with her she talked of hunting-fields and royal visits, and séances and her days of song. Many years before, her husband had been the first president of the

Anglo-Israelitish Association, and from that time onwards, and increasingly so as her activities grew more and more limited, she studied the books and pamphlets on the subject of the identification of the Anglo-Saxon races with the Lost Tribes of Israel. She took a busy part in the work, serving on its committees, and writing leaflets and pamphlets for its propagation. Then one day, when I was in London, I received a message from her that she had come up and would like to see me. She was cheerful and quite herself as we talked for a while, and then she said, 'Now my dear, I've got bad news,' and she told me how she had been to see her doctor and that the most terrible of all physical sentences had been passed on her. They did not advise an operation but there was other treatment which she would go through. And then with all her old interest she said : ' That's all : now tell me what you've been doing. And when will you come down to Ascot for a week-end ? '

Movement on her feet which had long been painful and difficult became impossible, and she descended in the lift from her bedroom, and was wheeled to the side of the big armchair in the window of her sitting-room, where she could see the tits swinging in the split coco-nuts hung outside, or sometimes she would be wheeled out on to the stoep overlooking her garden. With her table in front of her, she wrote letters in her beautiful firm hand, she read the paper, she read new books that were recommended to her, and above all she searched her Bible for more evidence on the subject that so occupied her. She loved long quiet talks with friends and relations and laughter and tales of amusing and absurd happenings, and to be with her was to sit in the sun.

CHAPTER XIII

THE MOVEMENT OF THE NINETIES

THERE has lately been a considerable amount of interest exhibited in what is known as 'the literary movement' of the nineties, and it was indeed time that the contemptuous neglect into which it had fallen should be mended. But its chroniclers have found themselves much beset by the temptation to classify, and seem to have swept together into a group certain poets, artists and prose writers who had really very little in common with each other as regards either aims or method. This habit of classification certainly makes for neatness, and is a favourite device of the writer who passes a period in review. He sets up a frame-work or skeleton which he calls 'Underlying Purpose' and proceeds to plaster on to it, in the manner of a sculptor building up his clay model with masses of sinew and muscle, a quantity of contemporary names of literary and artistic folk. But the result is not always happy when he essays to breathe the spirit of life into his image. Its movements lack an internal controlling mind and co-ordinated impulses, and it is really more like a marionette with limbs imperfectly obedient to the strings which the accomplished gentleman behind the scenes is pulling.

This particular 'literary movement' of the nineties is

an example of marionette-making, and the desire to classify and define has proved a snare to the industrious chronicler rather than a guide to his students. He bids us ('Observe, ladies and gentlemen!') notice the symptoms of revolt against Victorian conventions; but under his efforts to make his figures dance, one arm jerks galvanically, the head turns, but the lips remain cataleptic. There is neither unity nor inherent life in his image, for, as a matter of fact, the revolt against Victorian conventions and reticences which is supposed to animate it had already taken place and had long ago been completely successful.

Miss Rhoda Broughton was well aware of that. She told me once that for nearly fifty years she had been busily writing exactly the same sort of novel. When she began writing, her books were deemed to be very risky, she was thought to be of the breed of Zola, and no well brought-up girl was allowed to read them. But now, though her novels were just the same as they had always been, she was considered of the breed of Miss Yonge, and well brought-up girls were strongly urged to read them by their mammas, because they were so thoroughly nice. But the girls thought so too, and could not get far in them. (Upon which, in parenthesis, Howard Sturgis observed 'When she was young she was Zola, and now she's Zola [older] she's Yonge.')

Before the dawn even of the nineties, the old idols had been quite toppled over, and the attempt to demonstrate that there was now marching out of the premises of the Bodley Head under the flying flag of *The Yellow Book* a band of April-eyed young brothers singing revolutionary ditties and bent on iconoclasm is disastrous to any clear conception of what was actually going on.

Aubrey Beardsley, we are told, the greatest of them all, was the artist of the corps of rebels, Oscar Wilde was its dramatist, Arthur Symons, Ernest Dowson, Lionel Johnson, Richard Le Gallienne its poets, Max Beerbohm and Hubert Crackanthorpe its prose-writers. Arthur Symons was also its critic and Aubrey Beardsley was not only its typical and supreme artist, but poet and prose-writer in the same ranks. The banner of *The Yellow Book* went on before.

Now the confusions and misconceptions resulting from such a classified arrangement are numerous and profound. For, to begin with, if these rebels (of a rising already successfully accomplished) were marching under the flag of *The Yellow Book*, they marched under false colours, for *The Yellow Book*, an interesting illustrated quarterly the first number of which appeared in April 1894, so far from being a revolutionary gazette was a respectable, almost high-brow organ, and its contributors (leaving Aubrey Beardsley aside for the moment) were for the most part persons of recognized standing and were no more rebels against Victorian conventions than the Queen herself. In the first four numbers, which, as we shall see, were the only ones which counted, there were pictures by Walter Crane, Wilson Steer, John Sargent, Charles Furse, Joseph Pennell, and above all, Sir Frederic Leighton, President of the Royal Academy, who, incidentally, had the greatest admiration for Beardsley's work. In the letterpress there were two most substantial stories by Henry James, namely ' The Death of the Lion,' which opened the first number, and ' The Coxon Fund,' while Miss Hepworth Dixon, Dr. Richard Garnett, George Saintsbury, John Oliver Hobbes (with George Moore as her collaborator) contributed

stories, articles and dramatic sketches; José Maria de
Heredia (of the French Academy), Edmund Gosse,
William Watson, Theo Marzials, dear to the heart of all
true Victorians by reason of his song 'The Summer
Shower,' were among its bards; but as for Oscar Wilde,
who has been gazetted as the official dramatist of the
group, it is sufficient to state that he never published
a single line of verse or prose in *The Yellow Book* at
all, nor was he in any sense a revolutionary dramatist,
but of the Sheridan school. Apart from a poem by
Arthur Symons called 'Stella Maris' which Mr. Philip
Hamerton found very grievous and profane, it is really
impossible to find in these first four numbers of the
magazine a single piece that could possibly shock the
moral or artistic susceptibilities of that or any other day,
or a single sign that these distinguished contributors
intended to do so. Max Beerbohm, it is true, wrote in
the first number 'A Defence of Cosmetics' which earned
him some startling maledictions, but he explained in the
second number that it was not meant to be taken seriously
and pointed out the joke. Most of these authors had
wit and graceful diction, but there was not one bubble
of revolutionary ferment among them all.

But then there was Aubrey Beardsley, and his work
remains to this day as individual and apart from that of
all subsequent artists as it was then from those of his
period. Instead of being the principal figure in a group
of the like minded, he was unallied to any of the contributors to *The Yellow Book*, and, after four numbers of
it had appeared, the editor and publisher showed how
little they were prepared to risk for the one feature of
the magazine which indeed was startlingly novel. The
editor was Henry Harland, best known as the author of

an excellently written romantic sentimentality called 'The Cardinal's Snuff Box,' and the publisher was John Lane, whose enterprise on behalf of new and startling talent was tempered with sound business instincts : he had no objection, that is to say, against thin ice, provided he felt reasonably sure that it would not let him through. William Watson, one of *The Yellow Book* bards, and of high reputation in the nineties, now sent these two an ultimatum, and told them that his poems should not appear between the same covers as those which carried and contained Beardsley's designs. It was up to them to choose, and after consultation they chose Watson and safety. The fifth number of *The Yellow Book* containing more of Beardsley's work was already in the press, but it was withdrawn and Beardsley's connection with it was severed. Arthur Symons left it also, and in the next year he started a new magazine called *The Savoy* of which eight numbers were issued. He himself, Ernest Dowson, George Moore, and Bernard Shaw were among those who contributed to it, and these are very distinguished names. But as regards *The Savoy* none of them really counted at all, in spite of the excellence of their work. *The Savoy* was admittedly Beardsley's organ.

Admirable stuff appeared in it, for Symons had a very fine critical taste, and *The Savoy* represented a definite point of view which was his, whereas *The Yellow Book* had no point of view at all. But it was only significant because of Beardsley's work and the public subscribed to it (though very meagrely as soon appeared) for that reason. There were published in it not only his drawings, but poems by him and two long and wholly amazing instalments of a story from his pen called 'Under the Hill,' which he also illustrated. Of this it may be said that no prose-writer of that day or perhaps of any other could have written a letterpress to which the drawings were so completely appropriate, and no artist but he could have illustrated the story. Picture and press echo each other like the voices of a fugue, and both reek of that fascinating and evil suggestiveness of which the nineties considered him so skilled an exponent. He wrote further chapters of it, but his health was already far gone in its final decline, and for that reason, as well as perhaps for others, no further instalment of it appeared in the six subsequent issues of *The Savoy*, which from that time was published monthly and then, from want of support, expired. His poems with accompanying illustrations by him were ' The Three Musicians ' (only to be described as ' naughty ') and ' The Ballad of the Barber ' : there was also a masterly translation of Catullus's ode ' Ave atque vale.' Without seeking to depreciate in any degree the value of the rest of the contents of *The Savoy*, of which the last number was entirely written by Arthur Symons and entirely illustrated by Beardsley, there was nothing very distinctive about them. In this last number the editor promised a future revival of the magazine, but nothing further appeared, for Beardsley died, and the sap of it was gone. He had been the *clou* of *The Yellow Book*—for after he ceased to draw for it, it turned grey, as was remarked at the time, in a single night, though it lingered on, feeble and quite respectable, for nine issues more—and *The Savoy* died with him. In a word he had been the life of them both.

These two magazines have since then been taken as having constituted the organs of the ' literary movement ' of the nineties, but for the foregoing reasons I think this is an entirely mistaken view. Moreover, their contents disclose no evidence of the existence of any kind of concerted movement, like that of the pre-Raphaelites, nor were those who are now classed as a school, bound together, as the pre-Raphaelites were, by the common aim of revolt against convention. Those painters, with affiliated members of identical aims in other arts like William Morris and Swinburne, were consciously fighting conventions as definitely stated in their creed, but this literary movement had no such foes to contend against, for Victorianism was already dead and buried, and nobody was concerned to meddle with what was already decaying so nicely. The movement had neither crusading aspirations nor an inspiring aim, and at the time nobody thought of it as a school or even a movement. The interest in the two magazines (and that a very limited one) was due to the fact that Beardsley's drawings appeared in them.

It is, however, perfectly true that in this period there were published a remarkable number of poems which now, after the lapse of more than thirty years, retain the freshness of true classics. There was Lionel Johnson's poem ' A Friend ' which appeared, I think, first in an Oxford undergraduate magazine called *The Spirit Lamp*, there was Ernest Dowson's ' Cynara,' there were sonnets by Lord Alfred Douglas, and the ' Anthology of Nineties Verse,' lately collected by Mr. A. J. A. Symons, proves how remarkable in that decade was the output of poetry which is undated by any mannerisms or artificiality. Lionel Johnson's work in particular might have been that of some Elizabethan singer, for the sheer direct simplicity of it. Lovers of poetry owe a real debt to Mr. Symons for having made accessible once more so surprising a store of lyrical beauty. But what strikes one most about these poets collectively is not their underlying unity but their diversity of aims and technique.

The nineties for the purpose of a short literary survey cannot, of course, be limited to the strict decade. No sharp line of any sort separated them from the later eighties or from the earlier years of the next century, and these sixteen years or thereabouts during which I traversed the period of my own twenties were surely an era of justifiable excitement to one who had been brought up in a very literary home, where books of all sorts were regarded by the thirsty as a perpetual well-spring of pleasure. Not one atom of pedantry was permitted in that household, none of its members wanted to be learned or to improve their minds, they all read omnivorously because it afforded them the greatest pleasure to do so, and they all criticized with untempered frankness ; they were all mad keen to write themselves and most of them were already hard at it. I cannot think of any epoch in the last hundred years and more of English literature in which there was appearing so much diverse and first-rate work which, to judge by its vitality to-day, is as likely to live as anything we know. Sufficient time has elapsed since then to have proved corrosive of the corruptible, and it is astonishing to find how secure so much of the output of those years appears to be. Or, to apply another test, time acts on sound work much as it does on the vintages of the grape, maturing and bringing out, if the juice be noble, the fuller savour of the sunshine in which the berries ripened, while if it is thin by nature, time only reveals its weakness and age its acidity. Though it sounds a paradoxical notion to suggest that a book once written can possibly change, there is a certain truth in it, for a book does change in relation to its age, and what was harsh when it was new, and what was hot and fiery with ideas to which the age was unaccustomed, mellows with time; there comes to it a ripening and a crudeness vanishes.   Much of that vintage of the nineties has thus mellowed, and the harshness which some of the most experienced critics of the day detected then has passed away, leaving a wine which everyone acknowledges to be great.

There was Thomas Hardy, for instance, who during the strict decade was producing some of his finest work; ' Tess of the D'Urbervilles ' came out then and ' Jude the Obscure,' but the reception the press gave to the latter was such that he resolved to write no more novels. True and ardent lovers of literature had been put off by the harshness of Tess when it came out, and failed to appreciate its stoic tenderness.   Henry James, for instance, found it ' vile ' and wondered at ' good little Thomas Hardy.'   But anyone to-day who would refuse to his work the rank of *premier cru* merely shows that he has no palate for literature, for the time comes when an author almost ceases to be subject to the judgment of critics, and his work becomes a criterion of them.   The critic who does not perceive that the Wessex novels are great literature (though they may not be of the type with which he is personally most in sympathy) demonstrates his own deficiency, and his belittling to-day of such a book as ' Tess ' merely belittles his own critical powers. He may not like the book, but that is hardly the point : he has to be able to recognize its qualities.

Though there was no one else quite of the now-accepted stature of Hardy, there were some very tall men. R. L. Stevenson was hard at work up to the day of his death in 1894, and to judge by the estimate of the

thirty-five years that have followed, he must be placed at
least on the threshold of the house of the immortals. But
does he (so we asked ourselves then, and so we ask ourselves still) partake of the ageless quality which is part
of immortality or of that bleak imperviousness to the
vagaries of critical weather? There is, in all that he
wrote, youth and the romance of youth which in life
rendered him the most attractive of human beings and
cast over his friends a glamour which they confess
entirely dazzled them, but when it comes to the solemn
business of canonization, the *advocatus diaboli* must always
be given an impartial hearing, and he suggests that this
sunny and courageous writer has too much of Mark
Tapley in him to join the band of those who, while
realizing the bitter tragedies and sufferings which seem
inseparable from human existence, still turn eyes tender
and unflinching on the grim concert of woe and rapture
and death. He fought his own disabilities and won his
way through them by dint of his determination to dis-
regard them and to continue, while an ounce of strength
remained in that frail body, absorbing himself in the work
he loved. He would have no truck with his tormentors,
he would not do other than despise them, but while
rendering our utmost tribute to that admirable valour,
we feel somehow (says the devil's advocate) that he is
like a boy, who in spite of a severe toothache continues
to bat in some cricket match with unabated vigour and
gaiety. Life to him was a sea sown with Treasure
Islands, and the joy of adventure gilded the blackness of
every driving squall. He had nothing but the breeziest
contempt for his own infirmities, and would not suffer
them to tarnish his brightness, and thus it came about
that he lacks that deep stark tenderness for the sorrows

of the world which, without a touch of sentimentality, runs vibrant through the work of the greatest. That tragic chronicle had nothing to do with him, he turned his back on it, lacking the ultimate courage of admitting and facing it, and blew on his penny whistle. But then (so we answer the devil's advocate) there came out after his death that wonderful unfinished fragment ' Weir of Hermiston,' and those who had seen in Stevenson only a charming essayist of chased and hammered style, and a writer of books of rollicking and brave adventure, wondered whether his death had not robbed the world of a masterpiece of true humanity greater by far than all that the gaiety of his life had given them. He seemed to step within the house of the immortals.

Then there was Rudyard Kipling, with the gorgeous East and the British Empire rattling like loose change in his trouser pockets. He took out a coin and spun it, and with a conjurer's patter he caught it and covered it up with a dishcloth, and when he raised the dishcloth the night of full moon in the jungle among questing beasts spread round us. Nothing the least like it had ever been seen before, and the critics, whose business it was to preserve the public from being taken in by flashing flummery, warned them that this young man from a newspaper office in India was nothing more than a journalist with no sense of style. One serious writer compared him to a potman in shirt sleeves serving out mugs of beer over the counter of a public-house, and Oscar Wilde said that he revealed life by superb flashes of vulgarity. But the public was far too busy swilling the heady stuff and looking at the life he so vulgarly manifested, to care whether they ought to enjoy it or not. The critics speedily came into line, and those who had the dignity of English letters so much at heart perceived that if a writer conveyed with matchless economy precisely the impressions which he desired, there was something to be said for beer. . . . Then there was Conrad, ' full of blown sand and foam,' and Meredith was writing right up to the end of our epoch, and Barrie, and George Moore who attained that unique literary distinction of his not through decorated phrase and jewelled device but through the entire absence of such. Bernard Shaw had begun to send up those rockets of distress to call attention to his own unnoticed talents, and these were the first discharges of that unending pyrotechnical display which dazzles us still, and presently, before the epoch was over, he had come to the rescue of the English stage and taught theatre-goers that plays were not meant to amuse them but to make them think. H. G. Wells to our infinite enjoyment was coining romance out of science ; and Henry James, over whose name I affectionately linger, was applying scientific methods to romance.

Hopefully but sometimes ruefully did this family of young literary aspirants try to follow him into his new manner, for there were no more fervent worshippers than they of his earlier work, ' Roderick Hudson,' ' The Portrait of a Lady ' and such clear gems of story-telling. He had been speaking to my mother about this change. ' All my earlier work was subaqueous, subaqueous,' he said. ' Now I have got my head, such as it is, above the water, such as it was.' One evening when he was staying with us at Addington, he and my father lingered, talking together after tea, while we all drifted away to our various occupations, and though we heard no mention of the contents of that conversation at the time, there came of it an odd and interesting sequel. For, years later, Henry James wrote to my brother, on the eve of the publication of the volume containing ' The Turn of the Screw,' to the effect that the outline of the tale had been told him on that occasion by my father. It is among the grimmest stories of the world, and, as has been noticed by more accomplished critics of his work than I, it has a singular directness and clarity which are not characteristic of Henry James at that period : the development and growing grip of the two spectres which pervade it are singularly simple and uninvolved. Indeed the structure of it apart from the actual style of the writing is not like him, but if the bones and the blood of it were thus given him, the difference is easily accounted for : he followed definite lines. But the odd thing is that to all of us the story was absolutely new, and neither my mother nor my brother nor I had the faintest recollection of any tale of my father's which resembled it. The contents of the family story-box are usually fairly well known to the members of the circle, and it seems very improbable that we should all have forgotten so arresting a tale, if it was ever told us. The whole incident is difficult to unravel, but Henry James was quite definite that my father told him this story though in outline only, as having been one which he had been told in his youth, and he repeats the history of it in the preface he wrote to it, when it was republished in his collected edition. It is possible, of course, that my father merely gave him the barest hint for the story, saying what a shocking tale could be fashioned on the plot of two low and evil intelligences of the dead possessing themselves of the minds of two innocent children. That may have been enough to wind up Henry James's subconscious mind and set it ticking away, so that all but the barest basic idea was his. But in view of the simplicity of the narration, I am inclined to think that the gradual and gruesome approach of Peter Quint, from the time when he was first seen at the top of the tower down to his final assault and the tragic rescue of the boy's soul, was given him also.

I did not know him personally in the pellucid ' subaqueous ' days of his early work, before he got his head above that crystal clearness and (to my mind) emerged into a fog. Enormously admiring, as I do, the beautiful direct simplicity of such a book as 'Roderick Hudson,' it is only natural that I should find his later methods dim and nebulous. But whether or not in the early days his speech had a directness corresponding to his work, I cannot imagine anything more fascinating or more wholly individual than the manner of his talk in the later days, which certainly had much in common with the processes though not the finished product of his later style. Nothing would be further from the truth than to say that he talked like a book, but most emphatically he talked like a book of his own in the making, just as he used to dictate it, with endless erasures of speech, till he got the exact and final form of his sentences. Just so in his talk he tried word after word to express the precise shade he required; he avoided, just as he avoided in his writing, any definite and final statement, if what he meant to say could be conveyed in a picturesque and allusive periphrasis. The most trivial incident thus became something rich and sumptuous with the hints of this cumulative treatment. I remember, as the simplest instance, how he described a call he paid at dusk on some neighbours at Rye, how he rang the bell and nothing happened, how he rang again and again waited, how at the end there came steps in the passage and the door was slowly opened, and there appeared in advance on the threshold, ' something black, something canine.' To have said a black dog, would not have done at all : he eschewed all such bald statements in these entrancing narrations, during which he involved himself in enormous and complicated sentences, all rolling and sonorous to the ear, as if he was composing aloud.

I was staying with him once at Lamb House in Rye in the quite early days of his ownership; a book of his was in progress, so every morning after breakfast he sequestered himself in the garden-room, and till lunch time perambulated between window and fireplace, dictating it to his typist in an intermittent rumble. Hour after hour on those hot June mornings, as one sat in the garden outside, the sound of his voice as he composed, punctuated by the clack of the typewriter, came rolling out through the tassels of wistaria which overhung the open window. Then came a morning when he emerged some half hour before his usual time, and he took me by the arm and walked me up and down the lawn.

' An event has occurred to-day,' he said, exactly as if he was still dictating, 'which no doubt to you, fresh from your loud, your reverberating London, with its mosaic of multifarious movements and intensive interests, might seem justly and reasonably enough to be scarcely perceptible in all that hum and hurry and hubbub, but to me here in little Rye, tranquil and isolated little Rye, a silted-up Cinque-port but now far from the sea and more readily accessible to bicyclists and pedestrians than to sea captains and smugglers; Rye, where, at the present moment, so happily, so blessedly I hold you trapped in my little corner, my *angulus terrae*——'   On and on went the rich interminable sentence, shaped and modelled under his handling and piled with picturesque phrases which I can no longer recapture ; and then I suppose (not having a typist to read it over to him) he despaired of ever struggling free of the python-coils of subordinate clauses and allusive parentheses, for he broke off short and said ' In point of fact, my dear Fred Benson, I have finished my book.'   It took a long time to arrive at that succinct statement, but the progress towards it, though abandoned, was like some adventure in a gorgeous jungle, a tropical forest of interlaced verbiage.   All other talk, when he was of the company, seemed thin and jejune by this elaborate discourse, to which one listened entranced by its humours and its decorations.

I must tell too, not only for the sake of his decorative speech, but on account of the catastrophic sequel in which I was miserably involved, the story of the two nimble and fashionable dames who had a thirst for the capture of celebrities.   Both longed to add Henry James to their collections, and having ascertained that he was at Rye, they travelled down from London, rang the bell at Lamb House, and sent in their cards.   He did not much relish these ruthless methods but, after all, they were in earnest, for they had come far in pursuit, and with much courtesy he showed them his house, refreshed them with tea, and took them for a stroll through the picturesque little town, guiding them to the church and the gun-garden, and the Ypres tower and the Elizabethan inn.   The appearance of these two brilliant strangers in his company naturally aroused a deal of pleasant interest among his friends in Rye, and next day one of them called on him, bursting with laudable curiosity to know who these dazzling creatures were. She made an arch and pointed allusion to the two pretty ladies with whom she had seen him yesterday.

'Yes,' he said, 'I believe, indeed I noticed, that there were some faint traces of bygone beauty on the face of one of the two poor wantons' . . .

At least a couple of years afterwards this story was told me exactly as I have recounted it, without the names of the wantons, and one day, lunching at the house of one of the most enterprising hostesses in London, I recounted this little tale to her, for she was a friend of Henry James's and delighted in his rich speech. I noticed a slightly glazed expression in her eyes, as my artless narrative proceeded, and she was not as much amused as I had hoped ; in fact, as soon as she had a chance, she changed the subject with strange abruptness. After lunch a friend of mine who had been sitting on the other side of her, came up to me and said, 'What on earth possessed you to tell her that ? Don't you know that she was one of them ?' . . .

Only once in my life, so I optimistically believe, have I made a more desperate *gaffe*. On that dismal occasion, my intention, again of the most harmless kind, was to go to a dance to which I had been bidden, at a house in Portman Square. I gave the right direction to my driver (this was in the dark days of hansoms) and in due course drew up at a door from which over the pavement there was spread a red carpet. My hostess, I had been told, was indisposed, and her daughter whom I had never seen, was to take her place, and upstairs I went. Dances used to begin early in those days, and it was about ten o'clock. The door into the rooms on the first floor was open, and by it was standing a young woman (who of course was my hostess) with whom I cordially shook hands and passed within. Close inside was standing Queen Alexandra, then Princess of Wales, but still I felt no qualm, for why should she not be there ? Probably she had dined there. I had just come from Greece, where she had been also, and she asked me a few questions and we had a pleasant little talk. But by degrees this pleasant little talk began to wear the aspect of a nightmare, for looking round the room I perceived that I was the only person in it who was not of Royal birth. There was a galaxy of princes and princesses, but not even an earl or a marquis to bridge the bottomless gulf which lay between them and me. In fact the house to which I had so gaily come was that of the Duchess of Fife who had a big family party. She had asked a few people to come in afterwards, and that was why I was passed upstairs as one of her guests. But she had not asked me. . . . Let us get back to less appalling experiences.

Once in a letter to me Henry James described himself as being ' ferociously literary.' He could not have hit on an apter adverb, and this genial ferocity directed every sentence that came to his tongue, whether it was addressed to his typing secretary for transcription or to the tea-table. In the same letter he urged on me the paramount importance of acquiring a style : ' It is by style we are saved,' he wrote, and to this creed he was fanatically faithful, for (whether we like it or not) his later style is wholly individual. Nobody ever wrote like that before and though certain admirers of his have tried to do so since, the sad hash they have made of it proves how intensely individual it is. Yet, when all is said and done, style must still be regarded as the coach in which the story sits, and the wheels on which it rolls along. Its mission is to convey what the author has to tell us, and though more than shadow it is less than substance. Perhaps his style (that of his later manner) was the best, even as it was for him the only vehicle, that could carry the intricate mental processes of his characters, their subtleties and psychological finesse, their excursions into tortuous labyrinths of thought, which it was his business to record, and these processes perhaps cannot be simply stated, since they are extremely complicated. But where was there ever a richer tapestry than that which he himself in earlier days had woven in his picture of Christina Light? By it he managed to convey great complexities of motive with a triumphant lucidity, and we cannot help wondering whether so fine an artist gained anything by these enigmas and conundrums of his later work. His earlier stories before he found the later manner are conveyed in a style of admirable clarity, but though he was already master of that instrument he sought for a new literary quality in elaboration and allusiveness. Stevenson in a somewhat similar way, who had, as his letters witness, a natural style full of grace and vivid simplicity, forged for himself with infinite pains one that was picturesque but artificial and highly decorated, finding in it the literary quality for which he and Henry James so eagerly sought.

All these masters, young and old, Hardy and Stevenson, Meredith and Kipling, and Wells and James, and the rest, were writing during the years of the nineties, and it is because of them that the epoch is so remarkable. Some were already past-masters of their craft, and had worked on through years of neglect and contempt, others were in the flush of their youthful

vigour, but all were then producing first-rate and individual work, and all seem now to us to have won a
secure seat in the serenity that reigns high above the
gabble of the market-place, where the hawkers daily
proclaim the fresh immortalities, frail as egg-shell and
often addled, which they have detected over-night, and
the money-changers are loud in the courts of the temple.
Books are and have always been subject to the whims of
fashion, like a taste in millinery or ear-rings, but by
degrees from among the mutable forms and popular
fancies there emerges the incorruptible, even as when on
southern beaches the dredged oysters rot away, and
there glimmer the few rare pearls which are the ransom
of a king.

It was in this epoch for which ' the nineties ' are
a convenient expression that the long-retarded spring
burst into fullest summer, and never has there been a
more diverse flowering. Reaction against the old conventions had already done its work, and out of it there
came the new force which reaction generates. It had
its fakes and its hoaxes, ever so many of them, but
spurious reputations are won in every decade and quietly
lost in the next, and time has dealt with them as it will
no doubt deal with those of to-day, whose possessors
now broadcast each other's praises through groves of
loud-speakers. Many volumes of prose and poetry
held by the nineties to be pearls of great price have long
ago crumbled into dust, and certain critics now point
derision at the nineties because they thought that such
were real. Such a method is unsound, for no age has
ever been able to judge of its own output, since fashion
and the whim of the moment invariably selects much that
merely takes its fancy and ascribes to it immortality, but

now we are far enough off from the nineties to be able
to judge with some approach to true perspective, and
those authors, whom I have named, seem to me to be
just as admirable to-day as they did when with the
enthusiasm of youth I hailed each new volume as containing some supreme and ultimate revelation of art.
I confess that I was then tipsy with the joy of life and
the horns of Elfland were continually blowing, but
the ferment still stirs in me and the horns still blow
with undiminished magic when I read ' Tess of the
D'Urbervilles ' or the ' Jungle Book.'

It was not only because in those years I was of an age
ripe but still fresh to enjoy the flowering of fine literature, that I account myself fortunate, but because these
same years saw, glimmering from the darkness of the
unknown, such manifestations of scientific marvels as
no other short period can point to. Motor-cars and
moving pictures, telephones and electric lighting,
X-rays and other ultra-spectrum potencies, flying and
submarines and the beginnings of wireless were all then
in process of discovery and adaption to human uses.
To-day these have passed into the categories of conveniences which we take for granted, but then they were
amazing and scarcely credible. Motoring was an
adventure ; well do I remember staying at a country
house some ten miles from the nearest station, whose
owner had one of those new-fangled spit-fires, a hoarse
tremulous monster of most uncertain gait. Some half-
dozen guests of whom I was one were leaving together
at the end of our stay, and the ritual was as follows. A
cart with our luggage started an hour and a half before
the time of our train. Twenty minutes later the motor

set off with those who were daring enough to trust themselves to it, and, a quarter of an hour after the motor had gone, a brake with a pair of fast horses, so that, if the motor had broken down or become intractable, it would pick up the derelicts and convey them to the station. On this occasion the motor behaved surprisingly well. In spite of its having to stop whenever a horse-drawn vehicle appeared on the road, while the terrified animal was led past it, it came within sight of the luggage-cart half a mile from the station, and arrived there a quarter of an hour before the brake. So those great strong horses had not gained on us at all !

Motors were then built with high wheels and engines much higher from the ground, and a very remarkable incident occurred in a motor-race from London to Brighton. Stoppages for engine-trouble, as well as those due to approaching horse-drawn vehicles (whether from in front or from behind), were of course frequent, and the driver of one of these racers had gone round to the front of his car to tinker it up, for at present it was unable to go any further. He had forgotten to push back the starting lever, and so successful was his tinkering, that his car suddenly moved on again with a jerk, knocked him down and proceeded on its way. He was quite unhurt, for the blow had not been a severe one (more in the nature of a push) and he had passed in safety between the wheels. He picked himself up, spurted after his car, caught it up and sprang in, and so finished his course with joy. I wish that I could add that he was an easy winner, but I am rather afraid that he only came in second.

Then there were very uneasy apprehensions concerning the X-ray, when it was known that it would penetrate

solid substances, and timorous folk greatly feared that
privacy was at an end (so like the general trend of the
age!) if an unscrupulous scientist could direct his baleful
ray on to the walls of your seeming-solid house and discover you in your bathroom. . . . Again, with what
excitement we hurried down to Sandown race-course to
see the French airman Louis Paulhan make, or attempt,
his perilous ascent. Some would not go because they
knew he would not leave the ground, others because
they knew he would be killed. But even those most
sceptical about the possibility of flying, were much impressed by the ease with which his machine mounted,
and described a wide circle above our heads amid the
indignant protests of a rookery. But how they pooh-
poohed the notion that perhaps some day an aeroplane
would cross the English Channel without falling into the
sea! . . . A possible future in store for moving pictures
was faintly adumbrated by the exhibition of the scene
outside St. Paul's Cathedral when Queen Victoria
celebrated her Diamond Jubilee in the year 1897. It was
certainly the west front of St. Paul's that appeared on
the screen, and, sure enough, visible through a blizzard
of flashes and winks and large black dots, there did drive
up an open landau with the Queen, easily recognizable
sitting on the back seat, and the Princess of Wales
opposite her. They had parasols up, so the glimpse was
only momentary. It was all very trying for the eyes,
but it was worth a frontal headache to have beheld such
a marvel.

The Queen was old now, and her anxiety about the
Boer War which broke out two years afterwards swiftly
aged her. She thought from the beginning that neither
her Ministers nor the War Office sufficiently appreciated

the seriousness of it, and she wanted a larger force to be despatched, and the direction of it to be entrusted to other hands. Therein she showed once more that supreme soundness of judgment that had characterized her for the last sixty years. In December 1899 there occurred a very black week, when three disasters to the English arms at Stormberg, Magersfontein and Colenso proved how right she had been. She was very blind now of a morning until she had had her dose of belladonna in her eyes, and early on the day when the news of the third disaster arrived, despatches had been brought up to her before she had her treatment. She dimly deciphered them, but, by some tragic mischance of her infirmity, as she peered at them, she entirely misread their import and thought that here was the tidings of an English victory. Down she went in high spirits and to her daughter who was breakfasting with her she told the good news, and said how rejoiced she was : this would make an excellent impression after the two previous disasters. But by this time the daily papers had come in, and the Princess had to tell her that what she had believed to be a victory was a third disaster far more serious than the others. She received that in silence : then after a moment she said, ' Now perhaps they will take my advice, and send out Lord Roberts and Lord Kitchener, as I urged them to do from the first.' This time her Ministers did take her advice and she lived to see the relief of Ladysmith and Mafeking.

The dawn-bells of the new century had been a muffled peal by reason of the war, but the death of Queen Victoria in January 1901 renewed in an intensified form the general sense of instability. For the war was now practically over and security returning, but the death of the Queen was a thing which no one could at once realize : the pillars of the house were shaken. Only the aged could remember, as children, the days before she had come to the throne; to everybody else she was a cosmic institution, and it was as if an essential wheel from the machine of the Empire, and indeed of the world, had slipped from its spindle. No one could figure the national existence without her. And then it quickly became apparent that the reins, which she had so jealously held, had passed into hands far more capable of masterly coachmanship, and for the first time we had a sovereign who knew Europe, and especially France, not through the reports of ministers alone, or from the visits of foreign monarchs to Windsor, or from short polite conversations with the President of the French Republic in the saloon of the Royal train as it took the Queen to the Riviera or to Florence, but through the King's very sagacious personal observation. In these last years of her reign England was at the very zenith of her unpopularity on the Continent : there was scarcely a European nation which would not have rejoiced to see her in such difficulties as they all hoped might have arisen out of the Boer War, and the Queen's illness and death had been a welcome subject for ribald cartoons in the foreign Press. Though statesmen alluded majestically to England's 'splendid isolation,' the isolation was far more apparent than the splendour. Something had to be done, and largely on the initiative of King Edward and through his skilled handling there came about the grouping of Anglo-Russo-French interests. The King loved his Paris, he had the profoundest distrust of his nephew, the Emperor of Germany, and it seemed as if with these checks on the aggressive

policies of the Central Powers, an era of peace and
prosperity was assured.   Cordialities abounded : there
was a review of the French fleet by the young Czar on
a very rough day off Brest, and the fact that he and the
President of the Republic were exceedingly unwell
together seemed a pledge of mutual sympathy in case of
troubled times.   The resources of Russia were held to
be unlimited, her units of man power beyond the capacity
of any census to compute, and though when she went
forth to chastise Japan she resembled a tipsy moujik
badly stung, hastily retreating from a nest of hornets,
it was supposed without a shred of evidence to support
so satisfactory a theory that she had pulled herself
together and was busy with reforms and effective organization.   She figured in the popular imagination as a
Colossus of the East, in case the Central Empires
attempted to break through the iron ring of battalions
and ships of war which so conveniently enclosed them,
just as in the early days of the European war she figured
as the steam-roller which would presently flatten out a
road to Berlin.   Metaphors failed to express the poten-
tial might of Russia, and England, no longer isolated
but attached by ties of the strongest mutual interests to
her and France, settled down to enjoy for a decade more
a splendour of material prosperity which had never yet
been equalled.   Germany settled down too, to a decade
of ship-building and militarism.

The nine years of King Edward's reign must thus be
reckoned as the epilogue to the chronicles of the Victorian era.   The death of the Queen and the Boer War
had made a certain break between them and the nineties,
but that was soon mended again, and all the movements
of the nineties, the romance of its huge scientific progress,

its literary splendours, its pageantries now glittering more brightly than ever, swept on again with an added momentum. The King was a king indeed, rejoicing in his sovereignty, revelling in the skilful discharge of the work to which he brought an unrivalled cosmopolitan experience, and possessing an enormous personal influence which he used to the utmost. He made his royal visits to foreign courts, and at home his own blazed out again after the widowed quiescence of forty years. No longer was the monarch a craped sequestered presence, with a great prestige which nobody quite grasped, but a power apparent everywhere. The national prosperity was reflected in social brilliance, the fairy tales of science were fast crystallizing into sober facts of commerce and convenience, and throughout his reign no cloud of menace appeared above the glittering horizons of an empire which reached to the ends of the earth. Kings counted in those days, crowns were not being blown about like withered leaves in Vallombrosa, and one niece of his was Empress of All the Russias, another was the Queen of Spain, his daughter was Queen of Norway, his brothers-in-law were Kings of Denmark and of Greece. And his nephew was the German Emperor.

The year after King Edward's death there arose a cloud out of the sea at a place called Agadir, of which most people had never heard. It proved to be on the coast of Morocco. Thunder muttered out of the cloud, and there was a glimpse of the German Emperor clad in shining armour. Responsible level-headed people, ministers and diplomats, were believed to be very much disturbed at the incident, but most of our easy-going countrymen were only amused or irritated

at this royal buffoon ; he was a mere figure of fun, a
preposterous Valentine, a Valkyrie with a fierce mous-
tache.   The Editor of a very well-known comic paper
announced that a rough copy of a telegram had been
brought to him, which had evidently been sent by King
George to the Emperor : the King gave him a breezy
warning that if this sort of thing occurred again he would
jolly well blow all his ships out of the water.   That
reflected the general view : that was the stuff to give
him, and it seemed to be justified, for no more was heard
of this prank of the Emperor's.   Was there any real
danger lurking behind this tomfoolery ?   Certainly not :
it was one of his megalomaniac gestures, an imperial
pirouette, and now he was immersed again in musical
composition.   A hymn to Aegir, wasn't it ?   Aegir
interested him far more than Agadir.   So the whole
affair was forgotten.   It was one of those hoaxes, those
false alarms with which the timorous scare themselves
and of which astute stockbrokers take advantage.

Three years passed in peace and plenty, and I was
spending the month of June 1914 at Capri, that island
of lotus-eating enchantment, on which all thought of
what is going on outside its shores fades into a dream of
things blurred and remote.   Long mornings of swim-
ming through translucent waters interspersed with baskings in the sun, siestas, fresh figs, walks up to the top
of Monte Solaro, home-comings in the growing twilight,
dinner under a vine pergola, games of piquet in the café,
strollings on to the piazza at night to look at the lights
of Naples lying like a string of diamonds along the main
with the sultry glow of Vesuvius behind, filled, to the
exclusion of all exterior interests, the hours of the day.

Sometimes a post brought in letters that must be answered, sometimes the daily paper contained topics from outside that claimed a momentary attention, but these were no more than the faintest jerks and twitches of reminder that one was still attached to the world that lay beyond the sea.

For several years I had been out here for some weeks of the summer, sharing the quarters of a friend of mine resident on the island, but now we had taken between us the lease of the Villa Cercola, and my footing in Capri was on a more permanent basis. The house stood a little above the town, white-walled and cool and covered with morning glory and plumbago. A garden in terraces lay below it with a pergola above the water cisterns, and a great stone pine whispered with the noise of a far-off sea whenever there was the faintest breeze astir.

I had been very busy (for Capri) with furnishings, for the house was much bigger than Brooks's last habitation. I had cupboards and tables and chairs carpentered for me out of chestnut-wood, cushions must be stuffed, rugs laid down, and linen and crockery and cutlery had been arriving from Naples. I purposed, now that our joint occupation of the Villa was accomplished, to spend three or four months of the summer here every year, but during this June I began to think I would go back to England early in July and return again before the end of August, coming out by sea to Naples and bringing with me an assortment of possessions from home. My small house in London was more than replete, this Villa Cercola needed far more furnishing, and I would make this transformation of superfluities into necessities without delay. I wanted more books and bookcases here, more tables and chairs, a complete supply of summer clothes, pictures and a piano, for now Italy was to be my home as well as England, on my journeys to and fro I should be going οἴκοθεν οἴκαδε, and thus at either end I should have that fine luxury of familiar things about me. Besides, what an infinite saving of baggage and bother and registration to start from one home for sojourns of months at the other with no more impediment than a suitcase for the journey. How immensely important it all seemed!

We talked it over, Brooks and I, one morning on the beach between bathes. He urged me not to break into the summer by returning to England now. I could despatch my cases of effects from there when I went back in the autumn. He said I could get along very well for the present with what I had, and he promised to go across to Naples to receive them and bestow them, so that when I arrived again next spring they would all be in place. But there were other considerations as well, for the jerks and twitches which showed that I was in connection with the world outside the island had lately been tugging at me. I wanted to spend a week with my mother, I wanted to see certain people, who, I knew, would be in London during July. I wanted to visit one or two extremely pleasant houses where I had been bidden for week-ends, I wanted to play golf, and most particularly did I want to go to Baireuth for the second cycle of the festival, for which a ticket was waiting for me. It would be something of a rush (but how agreeable a one), and before the end of August I with my packing-cases would be back again for two more months in Capri before the summer was over. . . . But it was time now to take to the sea again, for the tourist boat with trippers for the Blue Grotto had already passed, and that showed, in the absence of watches, that it was round about noon. Just one swim more then, kicking lazily through the tepid water: so clear was it and so steeped with sunshine that the white pebbles at the bottom gleamed like jewels seen through the faintest tinge of blue.

We dressed, and strolled slowly up the stony path between vineyards in the sunspeckled shade of the olives. Lizards basked on the walls, orange trees were in flower and fruit together, the berries of the red grapes were already flushed with colour and growing tight. The yards of the few cottages that we passed were gay with carnations grown in petroleum-tins, and there were friendly greetings for us as we went by. Almost I repented of my resolve to leave here next week (for already June was nearly over, to-day was the 29th), so foolish it seemed to break into the sequence of these summer days in the land which I loved. A couple of the days that I might spend thus would be passed in the baking heat of trains, the nights in a grimy little berth jolting along and shrieking through the midnight stations and at the end I should arrive across a grey and sullen sea in the loud town by the Thames. After that the next six weeks would be mere scurry, though among people I cared for and pursuits that I enjoyed, but why start scurrying when so blissful a quietude was mine now, burned brown from head to foot by baskings in the sun, blessed with so intelligent and sympathetic a house-mate and surrounded by all the loveliness of the enchanted island? But, having talked of all the things I wanted to do, I felt the magnet pulling from the north, and when Brooks asked me finally, was it any use talking or did I really mean to go, I said that I did.

A little jingling victoria, its horse gay with a
pheasant's feather stuck between its ears, was waiting
for us when we emerged from the cobbled path between
the vineyards on to the road, and it set us down at the
piazza. The boat from Naples bringing papers and
letters had already been in some time, and when we went
into the post office the mail was sorted. There were a
few letters and a copy of *The Times* for me, and we went
on to the Villa Cercola on foot, stopping to buy an
Italian paper. Brooks unfolded it as we sat at lunch,
and skimmed the news.

'Hullo,' he said, 'An Archduke was assassinated
yesterday. Franz Ferdinand.'

'What an awful thing!' said I. 'Who is he? And
where did it happen?'

'He's the Emperor of Austria's heir,' he said. 'He
was attending manœuvres at Serajevo.'

'Never heard of it . . . I want to go up Monte
Solaro after tea. Do come. Those tawny lilies should
be in flower.'

'Too hot,' said he. 'Besides, I must water the
garden.'

We separated after lunch for the usual siesta, and I
found him poring over a big atlas when I came yawning
in for an early tea.

'Serajevo is the capital of Bosnia,' he said.

'Serajevo?' I asked. 'Oh, yes, I remember.
Bosnia is it? I'm nearly as ignorant as I was before.'

That was all: we did not allude to it again.

I got back to London during the first week of July.
Apparently some folk, who had seen danger in the affair
at Agadir three years before, had been apprehensive

again as to what this murder of the Archduke might lead to. Austria had tried to prove the complicity of the Serbian Government, and having failed to do that, had made some sort of appeal to Germany. But there the matter had stayed, and London did not much concern itself. Any disturbance of peace that might arise would be localized, and the last few weeks of the season were on. Since boyhood I had been native to that environment, and took it for granted, as part of the eternal order of things, that there should always be round me this sense of stability, of well-ordered and comfortable existence, which took no thought for the morrow except to make pleasant plans. So permanent a consciousness was scarcely analysable, for almost everything I knew was part of it. Work at my own profession, and music, and August in Scotland (or in this particular year at Baireuth), games and winter in the High Alps, and now, for the future, summer in Capri were ingredients in it. Some friends had big houses in the country, others had small flats in London where were to be found frugality and affection and kindred interests. I had my house there, and my mother the home of her widowhood in Sussex, dear and dignified and always welcoming. It was of mellow red brick, seventeenth century, and was encompassed with garden and orchard and fields that sloped down to the stream that burrowed among the copses of the valley. But life was no affair of aimless drifting, there was keenness to work and to enjoy, and behind it all lay this conviction of complete and lifelong security. That conviction was quite outside conscious thought, even as, when sitting in a familiar room, we do not trouble ourselves about the foundations on which the house is built. Of course they can be trusted.

There was trouble in Ireland during that month of
July, and there were threats of serious strikes. But
Ireland was always giving trouble, and there had been
strikes before now. Who cared? There were able
and sensible men who looked after such sporadic fric-
tions, and the duty of the reasonable citizen was to behave
as usual.   So I worked and played with immense enjoyment, and put little adhesive paper stars on the furniture
I should soon take out to Capri, and spent week-ends
in the country, and looked forward to Baireuth.   There
was a choice of routes : *via* Ostend and Cologne was one,
but how about the Paris express to Munich ?

Up till the last week in July which I spent at my
mother's house, this sense of security remained firm.
Then came the first tremors of the solid earth, faint, but
felt in the foundations of the house.   Austria sent Serbia
an ultimatum in which no free State could acquiesce,
demanding her acceptance of it within forty-eight hours.
It was followed by Russian preparations to mobilize and
remonstrances from Berlin.   Backwards and forwards
flew the shuttle, weaving catastrophe, and at every
passage of it the web of war grew on the clashing loom.
Early in August the shirt of fire in which Europe was
to burn for four years, was ready for the wearing, and
the old order of secure prosperity, of which I have been
speaking, smouldered into ash, and England will know
it no more.

INDEX

THE HOGARTH PRESS

This is a paperback list for today's readers – but it holds to a tradition of adventurous and original publishing set by Leonard and Virginia Woolf when they founded The Hogarth Press in 1917 and started their first paperback series in 1924.

Some of the books are light-hearted, some serious, and include Fiction, Lives and Letters, Travel, Critics, Poetry, History and Hogarth Crime and Gaslight Crime.

A list of our books already published, together with some of our forthcoming titles, follows. If you would like more information about Hogarth Press books, write to us for a catalogue:

30 Bedford Square, London WC1B 3RP

Please send a large stamped addressed envelope

HOGARTH FICTION

The Colonel's Daughter by Richard Aldington
New Introduction by Anthony Burgess
Death of a Hero by Richard Aldington
New Introduction by Christopher Ridgway

All in a Lifetime by Walter Allen
New Introduction by Alan Sillitoe

Epitaph of a Small Winner by Machado de Assis
Translated and Introduced by William L. Grossman

Mrs Ames by E.F. Benson
Paying Guests by E.F. Benson
New Introductions by Stephen Pile

A Day in Summer by J.L. Carr
New Introduction by D.J. Taylor

Beat the Devil by Claud Cockburn
New Introduction by Alexander Cockburn

Chance by Joseph Conrad
New Introduction by Jane Miller

Lady Into Fox & A Man in the Zoo by David Garnett
New Introduction by Neil Jordan

Born in Exile by George Gissing
New Introduction by Gillian Tindall
Will Warburton by George Gissing
New Introduction by John Halperin

Saturday Night at the Greyhound by John Hampson
New Introduction by Christopher Hawtree

All Day Saturday by Colin MacInnes
June in Her Spring by Colin MacInnes
New Introductions by Tony Gould

HOGARTH CRITICS

The Condemned Playground by Cyril Connolly
New Introduction by Philip Larkin

Seven Types of Ambiguity by William Empson
The Structure of Complex Words by William Empson

Music Ho! by Constant Lambert
New Introduction by Angus Morrison

The Common Pursuit by F.R. Leavis

By Way of Sainte-Beuve by Marcel Proust
Translated by Sylvia Townsend Warner
New Introduction by Terence Kilmartin

The English Novel from Dickens to Lawrence
by Raymond Williams

The Country and the City by Raymond Williams

The Common Reader 1 by Virginia Woolf
Edited and Introduced by Andrew McNeillie

HOGARTH LIVES AND LETTERS

E. F. Benson
Secret Lives
New Introduction by Stephen Pile

Durham Square seems the height of propriety; only the
rumblings of indigestion, the murmur of gossip and
occasional canine consternation threaten its dignity. But
behind the square's genteel façade hide secret lives.
There is Miss Susan Leg at No. 25, for instance: can a
woman who puts caviare on her scones be altogether
respectable? Riddled with curiosity, mordant pen in
hand, E.F. Benson draws aside the plush velvet drapes –
and reveals in this deliciously ironic novel all the hilarious intrigues and intimacies of life upstairs (and downstairs) in one of the stateliest squares in England.

E.F. Benson
Paying Guests

New Introduction Stephen Pile

Bolton Spa is infamous for its nauseating brine and parsimonious boarding-houses. Exceptional is the Wentworth. Every summer this luxurious establishment is full of paying guests come to sample the waters and happy family atmosphere. But life in the house is far from a rest-cure. Acrimony and arthritis are the order of the day: battles are fought with pedometer, walking stick and paintbrush, at the bridge table, the town concert and afternoon tea. The trials and tribulations of the Wentworth will be relished in drawing-rooms throughout the land for years to come.

E.F. Benson
Mrs Ames

New Introduction by Stephen Pile

Mrs Ames is Queen of Riseborough society. Sceptre firmly grasped in her podgy little hand, she reigns supreme in a world of strawberry teas, high street gossip, and riotous insurrections by misguided pretenders such as Mrs Altham, Miss Brooks and dear cousin Millie. But her rule is threatened when, to the delight of her subjects, her husband's attentions stray from home and Mrs Ames, feeling all of her fifty-seven autumns, goes on the warpath. The series of restorative treatments – Shakespearian, feminist, but mostly out of a jar – with which she sets out to rewoo her gardening major are exquisitely chronicled in this comic masterpiece of provincial life.

E. F. Benson
An Autumn Sowing

New Introduction by John Julius Norwich

Thomas Keeling, pillar of Bracebridge society, dwells at 'The Cedars', a spacious residence decorated with an eye for the gothic, and including in its furnishings such treasures as a small stuffed crocodile rampant holding a copper tray. But Keeling stalks unmoved through this opulence, cherishing instead a secret retreat, his book-lined study – and soon a secret passion. For his forceful young secretary, Norah, surprises him with a solitary glimpse of love. Buried feelings clash with the pompous surface of Benson's uniquely comic world in this poignant and extravagant classic.

E.F. Benson
The Blotting Book
New Introduction by Stephen Knight

Darkness falls in Sussex Square, Brighton, and Mrs Assheton's rosewood table gleams in the lamplight. Around it sit her guests; the port is passed, nuts are cracked – could there be a calmer scene? But all is not as it seems – and this tale of covert violence among the sleepy South Downs develops into a cunning criminal escapade, bristling with intriguing clues and gripping courtroom drama, and investigating the darker shadows of Benson's sparkling leisured world.

Richard Cobb

Still Life

Sketches from a Tunbridge Wells Childhood

Still Life is a classic memoir. In it, Richard Cobb takes us through the streets and houses of his childhood – down Poona Road, along by the Grove Bowling Club, and on past the taxidermist's and 'Love, Fruit and Vegetables' shop – recapturing, with the innocence of a lonely boy, the snobberies and eccentricities of secure middle-class England in the Twenties and Thirties.

'strange and wonderful' – Hilary Spurling, *Observer*

'a rare treasure' – John Carey, *The Sunday Times*